Recommended Country Hotels OF BRITAIN 1996

INCLUDING COUNTRY
HOUSE HOLIDAYS

FHG PUBLICATIONS, Paisley

Highly Commended

Combe Grove Manor

Brassknocker Hill, Monkton Combe, Bath BA2 7HS
Telephone: 01225 834644 Fax: 01225 834961

The magnificent facilities which Combe Grove Manor provides for the leisure interests of their guests perfectly complement the high standards set for bedroom comfort and dining-room quality. If the indoor and outdoor swimming pools, tennis courts, gymnasium, sauna, etc, golf and other on-site activities leave some energy untapped, clay pigeon shooting, hot-air ballooning or horse-riding can be arranged nearby! Back in your deluxe bedroom, with a four poster if you wish, watch the news on satellite TV before you bathe. Then down to the Georgian Restaurant for a formal dinner or a more casual meal in the Manor Vaults Bistro. Combe Grove Manor has various 'Special Breaks' and the use of the sports and leisure facilities is included in all room rates. Why not escape from the busy world into the luxury of this stress-free Hotel with its spectacular surroundings and unrivalled amenities.

Key to Tourist Board Ratings

The Crown Scheme

(England, Scotland & Wales)

Covering hotels, motels, private hotels, guesthouses, inns, bed & breakfast, farmhouses. Every Crown classified place to stay is inspected annually. *The classification:* Listed then 1-5 Crown indicates the range of facilities and services. Higher quality standards are indicated by the terms APPROVED, COMMENDED, HIGHLY COMMENDED and DELUXE.

The Key Scheme

(also operates in Scotland using a Crown symbol)

Covering self-catering in cottages, bungalows, flats, houseboats, houses, chalets, etc. Every Key classified holiday home is inspected annually. *The classification:* 1-5 Key indicates the range of facilities and equipment. Higher quality standards are indicated by the terms APPROVED, COMMENDED, HIGHLY COMMENDED and DELUXE.

The Q Scheme

(England, Scotland & Wales)

Covering holiday, caravan, chalet and camping parks. Every Q rated park is inspected annually for its quality standards. The more ✓ in the Q – up to 5 – the higher the standard of what is provided.

ENGLISH TOURIST BOARD
♛♛♛ HIGHLY COMMENDED

QQQQ

WINNER AA Guest House of the Year Award West of England 1981

WIDEGATES, Nr. LOOE
CORNWALL PL13 1QN
Telephone:
Widegates (01503) 240223

A warm welcome assured by Alexander and Sally Low

A lovely country house surrounded by lawns, meadows, woods and streams with superb views to the sea. Log fires. Delicious home cooking. Candlelit dining. Licensed. All bedrooms are ensuite and have colour TV, radio, tea and coffee-making facilities and direct dial telephone.

In the grounds – many birds, animals and flowers, a swimming pool (heated in summer), a croquet lawn and a stone barn for snooker and table tennis. Nearby – golf, fishing, tennis, horse riding and glorious walks and beaches.
The perfect centre for visiting all parts of Cornwall and Devon.

Bed and Breakfast from £20.00 Four course Dinner from £14.00.
Special Short Break discounts.

Johansens RECOMMENDED

HIGHLY ACCLAIMED

CROSSROADS HOTEL

♛♛♛♛ HIGHLY COMMENDED
Scorrier, Redruth, Cornwall TR16 5BP
Tel: 01209 820551 Fax: 01209 820392

Crossroads Hotel is a purpose-built hotel with modern facilities, situated at the Scorrier exit of the A30, near Redruth. It makes an ideal venue for visiting all parts of Cornwall. We have a fine reputation for our service and food, and endeavour to meet the special requirements of our guests. There are ground floor bedrooms available and a lift. We hope to have the pleasure of welcoming you to Crossorads Hotel. All 36 bedrooms have private bathroom. Parking for 140 cars. B&B from £45 per person.

Link House

Bassenthwaite Lake, Cockermouth, Cumbria CA13 9YD
Telephone: (017687) 76291 Michael & Marilyn Tuppen

A family run traditional Victorian country house at the quieter end of the Lake District and surrounded by lovely scenery, yet providing easy access to all the popular areas. An ideal base for walkers and motorists alike. All 8 bedrooms are ensuite with colour TV, tea/coffee making equipment, central heating, etc. We have single, double, twin and family rooms (one on the ground floor). There is a delightful conservatory to enjoy the evening sun or a pre-dinner drink plus a comfortable lounge with log fire to make the winter evenings even more cosy. Many antique and period pieces of furniture throughout, but more relaxing than formal. The wine list, at moderate prices, is selected to complement imaginative 4 course (plus coffee) freshly prepared dinners served on Wedgwood china. ETB ♛♛♛ AA QQQ

Our beautiful country house is set in five acres of grounds overlooking the lake. Elegant lounges, restaurant and 4-poster bedrooms with jacuzzis, all with lake views. Free local leisure facilities. Special breaks and themed weekends. AA awarded us 'Best in the North'.

Please send for our brochure – you'll see why early reservations are recommended. Iain and Jackie Garside.

Lyth Valley Road, Bowness-on-Windermere LA23 3JP PHONE FREE 0500 432177

♛♛♛ HIGHLY COMMENDED

PHEASANT INN

Bassenthwaite Lake, Cockermouth, Cumbria CA13 9YE

Tel. (01768) 776234 Fax: (01768) 776002 ♛ Highly Commended

A tranquil, traditional, north Lake District inn, adjacent to Bassenthwaite Lake, and surrounded by gardens and woodland providing a wealth of wildlife. Three lounges feature antiques, beams, open fires and fresh flowers. Commended by major guides for high quality English food and service, Pheasant Inn also has twenty individually decorated bedrooms with private facilities. No television or self-service breakfasts. Dogs welcome – kennels available. Parking.

Bed and Breakfast per night: single room from £53-£55; double room from £64-£94. Half Board per person £73-£75 daily, £370-£450 weekly.

LUNCHES AND EVENING MEALS AVAILABLE. ACCESS, VISA.

AA ** RAC **

Brantwood Country House Hotel

STAINTON · PENRITH · CUMBRIA · CA11 0EP

Telephone: (01768) 862748 · Fax: (01768) 890164

Pleasant rural country Hotel in 3½ acres of secluded gardens. Relaxed and friendly atmosphere. Personally run for the last nine years by Susan and John Harvey with their sons Stephen and Mark. Comfortable ensuite rooms with colour television, tea and coffee making facilities, central heating and direct dial telephone. Enjoy a formal dinner in the Restaurant or choose from an extensive Bar menu.

Fully Licensed. Open all year. Open to non-residents.

Large secure car park at rear of Hotel.

Ashley Courtenay Recommended.

"Brantwood" is 1½ miles from junction 40, M6 motorway, off the A66 west and 3 miles from Penrith, 3 miles to beautiful Lake Ullswater.

Welcoming Country House, with 20 luxury ensuite bedrooms, award winning gardens, views across the Axe Valley and near the coast at Lyme Regis.

FAIRWATER HEAD COUNTRY HOUSE HOTEL

Hawkchurch (the village of Roses), Devon, EX13 5TX

Telephone: (01297) 678349

AA ★★★ RAC Awards for Hospitality, Restaurant, Comfort
Egon Ronay, Ashley Courtenay, WCTB ♛♛♛♛ Highly Commended

THE EDGEMOOR HOTEL

Haytor Road, Bovey Tracey TQ13 9LE
Telephone 01626 832466 Fax 01626 834760
♛♛♛♛ HIGHLY COMMENDED
AA RAC ★★★ Les Routiers Johansens

'Loaded with charm' the Edgemoor 'epitomizes a gracious English Retreat' (*Dallas Morning News*). This relaxing Country House Hotel is literally adjacent to Dartmoor National Park, yet is only three miles from the main A38 Exeter/Plymouth dual carriageway. Personally run by resident proprietors. The Edgemoor has twelve delightful bedrooms, including some Four-Posters, lovely gardens, good food (AA Rosette) and helpful caring staff. Wonderful countryside abounds, with numerous places to visit including many National Trust properties. Bargain Breaks available for stays of two days or more. Elegance without pretension.

Moretonhampstead
Devon TQ13 8RE
Tel. 01647 440355
Fax. 01647 440961

AA ★★★★ RAC

Set on the edge of Dartmoor, this magnificent Jacobean style mansion was originally built for Lord Hambleden, the son of W. H. Smith. Now a luxury AA/RAC Four Star Hotel, offering 89 comfortable ensuite bedrooms and elegant, relaxing leisure areas. Set within 270 acres of private estate is our Championship Golf Course, one of England's finest courses. Also available, Tennis, Fishing, Clay Shooting and more.

Leisure Centre with indoor pool – expected completion early 1996.

A PRINCIPAL HOTEL

MILL END HOTEL

♛♛♛♛ HIGHLY COMMENDED

Sandypark, Chagford, Newton Abbot, Devon TQ13 8JN Tel: 01647 432282 Fax: 01647 433106

Converted from a working mill, Mill End has retained all its rural charm. The mill wheel still turns in the courtyard and the Teign, which runs by the door, is one of the ten best sea-trout rivers in the country, with fishing available to guests. The gardens and walks are delightful and the hotel is ideal as a touring centre for the West. *Then again, you could just sleep!* Single, double, twin and triple bedrooms, all with private bathrooms. Parking for 17 cars. B&B per night: single room from £45-£55; double room from £70-£90. Half Board per person: £55-£70 daily. Lunch available 1230-1400 hours by appointment. Evening Meal 1930 hours (last orders 2100 hours).

Cards accepted: Access, Visa, Diners, Amex, Switch/Delta.

String of Horses

Mead End, Sway,
Lymington,
Hampshire SO41 6EH
Telephone / Fax:
01590 682631

Unique secluded, exclusive hotel set in four acres in the heart of the New Forest, with a friendly relaxed atmosphere. Eight luxurious double bedrooms, each with its own fantasy bathroom with spa bath and shower. Every facility is offered including colour television, direct-dial telephone, radio and tea-making facilities. Four-poster rooms are also available, making this an ideal honeymoon setting. Dine in our intimate 'Carriages' restaurant. For relaxation there is a heated outdoor swimming pool. This is superb riding country, and the hotel is close to excellent yachting resorts and several good golf courses.

ETB ♛♛♛♛ Highly Commended AA** Rosette

CHURCH STRETTON
SHROPSHIRE SY6 6AG
TEL: 01694 722244/8 LINES
FAX: 01694 722718

Perched high above the pleasant town of Church Stretton in grounds of ten acres, this fine hotel enjoys sweeping views over the beautiful Welsh border country. A subtle mixture of superb modern and period rooms; luxury suites and bedrooms. Facilities also include an outdoor swimming pool (covered in winter months), 9-hole pitch and putt course, trim gym and also the tonic of a sauna and solarium. Riding, fishing, shooting and gliding may also be arranged nearby. The cuisine is noteworthy for its excellence and variety and there are superb facilities for conferences and other functions. There are also self-catering lodges in the hotel grounds.

A LUXURY GEORGIAN COUNTRY HOUSE HOTEL

The Woodlands Lodge Hotel is a luxury hotel set in 4 acres of grounds opening onto the beautiful New Forest. Although the hotel is totally refurbished with a stunning interior it still offers the peace and tranquillity often only found in buildings of age and establishment. All 18 bedrooms and suites enjoy full ensuite facilities of jacuzzi bath, separate thermastic shower with some bathrooms also having bidets. The sumptuous kingsize pocket sprung beds are possibly the most comfortable beds guests have slept on (this opinion is constantly being expressed by guests). All other amenities are present including 21" fast text television, writing desks, armchairs, hairdryer, trouser press, Teasmaid and telephone. At Woodlands Lodge the hotel service is extremely friendly and informal thus enabling guests to totally relax and feel at home. Our dinner menu is modestly priced at a maximum of £16.95 (inc. à la carte) for three courses and coffee. It offers succulent giant king prawns, garlic mushrooms and many more mouth-watering starters with main courses ranging from fresh local rainbow trout, New Forest venison, poulet sauté Marengo (chicken flamed in brandy and cooked with marsala wine and tomatoes) or plain traditional Scotch sirloin steaks, etc. Modestly priced wine list from £6.95.

Something for absolutely everyone!

Terms: per person per night (inc.VAT).
Luxury doubles from £49.50; De luxe doubles from £59.50; De luxe (with balcony) from £69.50; De luxe suites (with full size sitting room) from £74.50.
All prices are inclusive of Full English Breakfast.

THE WOODLANDS LODGE HOTEL

Bartley Road, Woodlands, New Forest, Hampshire SO40 2GN

AA ★★★ **Reservations: (01703) 292257** ETB ♛♛♛♛ Highly Commended

Stretton Hall Hotel and Restaurant

All Stretton, Church Stretton, Shropshire SY6 6HG
Telephone: 01694 723224 Fax: 01694 724365

Historic Country House idyllically set in own grounds with magnificent views of Shropshire Hills. The House has incorporated in its decor many features of a bygone age and an atmosphere of comfort and gracious living prevail.

Location: Motorway network 15 mins; Rail Station 5 mins; historic towns of Ludlow and Shrewsbury 20 mins, Telford Town Centre 30 mins. **Accommodation:** all rooms ensuite, honeymoon four-poster. **Services:** room service, car parking, laundry. **Bar & Restaurant:** real ale, extensive wine cellar, Egon Ronay recommended, à la carte menu. **Recreation:** golfing, walking, gliding, riding, shooting, sightseeing, cycling. **Local attractions:** The Long Mynd, Ironbridge Gorge Museum, Castles, Severn Valley Railway. Ideally situated for Conferences.

AA ★★★ RAC
ETB ♛♛♛♛
Egon Ronay

BOURTON MANOR

HOTEL : RESTAURANT AND CONFERENCE CENTRE

Bourton Manor Hotel, once an English Country House with 16th century origins, and recently extensively refurbished, is situated in a small, sleepy hamlet nestling at the end of the Corve Dale and close to Wenlock Edge. Situated in its own private landscaped grounds, it is ideal for walking, riding or driving in the beautiful border countryside and is within easy reach of Ironbridge, Telford, Shrewsbury and many other places of historic and cultural interest. The Hotel facilities include a traditional English style diningroom, oak panelled bar and warm, cosy sittingroom, and the grand Queen Anne staircase makes an excellent focal point. Bourton Manor offers luxury bedrooms for single, twin and double occupancy, each with radio, colour TV, and a direct dial telephone.

Non-residents are most welcome in the Hotel Restaurant and Bars.

BOURTON, MUCH WENLOCK
Near Telford,
Shropshire TF13 6QE
Tel: 01746 785531
Fax: 01746 785683

BATCH FARM COUNTRY HOTEL

LYMPSHAM, NR. WESTON-SUPER-MARE
☎ Weston-Super-Mare (01934) 750371
RAC ★★ AA ★★ Egon Ronay Recommended
Ashley Courtenay Recommended

★ Family run Hotel with friendly atmosphere and excellent food ★ Fully licensed Lounge Bar ★ Own grounds with unlimited parking, spacious lawns ★ All bedrooms ensuite with colour TV, tea/coffee making facilities ★ Golfers most welcome; Reduced terms for children. Credit cards accepted ★ Easy access from M5 motorway.

Weston, Burnham, Brean and Worlebury Golf Courses all within 10 minutes' drive
Weston-Super-Mare Hotels and Restaurants Merit Award

Westerclose Country House

Hotel and Restaurant

WITHYPOOL, EXMOOR, SOMERSET TA24 7QR
TELEPHONE: (01643) 831302 FAX: (01643) 831307

AA ★★

RAC ★★

ETB
Highly Commended

AA Red Rosette

Set on beautiful Exmoor, our family-run hotel offers ample opportunity to ride, fish, walk or simply enjoy the spectacular views and relaxed atmosphere. All ten bedrooms have their own bathrooms, are comfortably furnished and have their own individual character. What better way to wind down after a hard day's exploring than to enjoy a drink in the conservatory bar before dining in the excellent restaurant which specialises in traditional English and West Country dishes. To complement your meal there is a wide ranging and interesting selection of wines.

Cleavers Lyng

16th Century Country Hotel

Church Road, Herstmonceux,
East Sussex BN27 1QJ
Tel: (01323) 833131
Fax: (01323) 833617

For excellent home cooking in traditional English style, comfort and informality, this small family-run hotel in the heart of rural East Sussex is well recommended.

Peacefully set in beautiful landscaped gardens extending to 1·5 acres featuring a rockpool with waterfall. Adjacent to Herstmonceux Castle's West Gate, the house dates from 1577 as its oak beams and inglenook fireplace bear witness. This is an ideal retreat for a quiet sojourn away from urban clamour. The castles at Pevensey, Scotney, Bodiam and Hever are all within easy reach as are Battle Abbey, Kipling's House, Batemans, Michelham Priory and the seaside resorts of Eastbourne, Bexhill and Hastings.

Bedrooms are all fully ensuite, and all have central heating and tea/coffee making facilities. On the ground floor there is an oak-beamed restaurant with a fully licensed bar, cosy residents' lounge with television and an outer hall with telephone and cloakrooms. Children and pets welcome.

Peace, tranquillity and a warm welcome await you. Special Attraction: Badger Watch.

Antrobus Arms Hotel

Church Street, Amesbury, Wiltshire SY4 7EY
Tel: 01980 623163 Fax: 01980 622112

APPROVED

Attractive town hotel with a magnificent walled garden at the rear. Situated six miles from Salisbury and half a mile off the A303. All bedrooms have central heating, satellite TV, tea/coffee making facilities, direct-dial telephone, and most are ensuite. Our highly acclaimed Fountain Restaurant serves table d'hôte and à la carte menus; bar meals also available. This is an ideal base for touring many local places of interest including Stonehenge, Woodhenge, Salisbury Cathedral, Wilton House and the New Forest. Fishing, tennis, golf courses, motor racing (Thruxton) close by. Les Routiers.

2 nights table d'hôte dinner, bed and full English breakfast from £70 (including VAT).

AA ★★★★ DELUXE RAC ★★★★

SMALL LUXURY HOTELS OF THE WORLD

1995 Regional Hotel of the Year

Recently awarded the supreme accolade of 4 Red Stars

Balbirnie is a delightful Grade 'A' listed mansion house, the centrepiece of a 400 acre estate, which includes an 18 hole golf course. Located in the heart of Fife, only half an hour between both Edinburgh and St. Andrews, the hotel comprises memorable and delightful public rooms, 30 individually designed bedrooms and suites, private dining rooms, together with a range of traditional or hi-tech special event, banqueting and conference areas. Balbirnie is many things to many people and several things to individuals – feature breaks, corporate gatherings, tailor-made special events, just call for details.

Alan C. Russell, Managing Director and Co-Proprietor.

BALBIRNIE PARK, MARKINCH, GLENROTHES, FIFE KY7 6NE
TELEPHONE: 01592 610066 FAX: 01592 610529

NOTE

All the information in this book is given in good faith in the belief that it is correct. However, the publishers cannot guarantee the facts given in these pages, neither are they responsible for changes in policy, ownership or terms that may take place after the date of going to press. Readers should always satisfy themselves that the facilities they require are available and that the terms, if quoted, still apply.

CROMLIX HOUSE

Cromlix is one of a select handful of Scotland's top rated luxury 'Hotels'. "Enchanting; A Magical Experience; Memorable; Unique; So Hospitable, Incredible Value; Wonderful Atmosphere; Superb Staff" – are a few of the many superlatives written by our Guests – there is no doubt, Cromlix is ***Very*** Special!"

Within its own 3000 acre estate the calm serenity of this 'time capsule' is a different world. Above all Cromlix is for relaxation within surroundings and in a style of times past. 5 minutes off the A9, north of Dunblane; Glasgow 40 minutes; Edinburgh 1 hour; Perth 25 minutes. An enviable location for golf and touring much of Scotland. Built in 1874 as a country mansion, the imposing exterior belies a comfortable and 'homely' interior. Each room is individual in style. The atmosphere is relaxed, welcoming and unpretentious whilst the ambience, antiques, authentic period decor, award-winning cuisine and genuine hospitality recall the luxurious splendour and feeling of a REAL Edwardian home.

TOP AWARDS for QUALITY, HOSPITALITY, CUISINE, AMBIENCE etc

★ 8 Luxury Suites with private sitting rooms ★ 6 further Bedrooms

★ Private House Parties; Dining and Select Meeting Rooms

★ PRIVATE CHAPEL (Christenings/Weddings – max 40)

★ NEW YEAR & CHRISTMAS HOUSE PARTIES ★ SPECIAL BREAKS

RATES – October to May ★ FISHING, TENNIS, WALKS, 3 TROUT LOCHS, etc

KINBUCK, by DUNBLANE, PERTHSHIRE FK15 9JT

Telephone (01786) 822125 Facsimile (01786) 825450 Non UK +44 (1786)

Pool House Hotel

Poolewe, by Achnasheen,
Ross-shire IV22 2LE
Tel: 01445 781272
Fax: 01445 781403

Commended

Ashley Courtenay Les Routiers

With a commanding position at the head of Loch Ewe, Pool House Hotel enjoys beautiful views across the bay to the famous Inverewe Gardens, only half a mile away, the original marital home of Osgood McKenzie, situated on the edge of the sea, and the hills, coastline and islands that typify the grandeur of Wester Ross. Salad bar and hot food servery for meals and a pleasant restaurant overlooking the bay. Vegetarians catered for. Here, visitors will soon feel relaxed and a favourite diversion is watching for salmon, seals and, sometimes, otters. In this area of outstanding natural beauty, one may walk, climb, swim in the lochs or in the indoor pool in the village, play golf and go boating at nearby Gairloch. The hotel is centrally heated and the attractive bedrooms are all equipped with colour television, radio and tea and coffee-making facilities; most have private amenities. Children welcome. Pets by arrangement.

CASTELL CIDWM HOTEL

Betws Garmon, Caernarvon, Gwynedd LL54 7YT
Telephone: 01286 650243

In one of the most beautiful settings in Wales on the west side of Snowdon, this delightfully tranquil lakeside hotel offers magnificent views of mountain, forest and water. Warm friendly hospitality is offered. Eight bedrooms (all en suite), a cosy bar, a lakeside café and an à la carte restaurant with a subtly different cuisine. Children welcome. Car park. Two and three day breaks available.

AVAILABLE FROM THE HOTEL OR NEARBY

★ Private Trout Fishing ★ Boating ★ Water Sports
★ Walking ★ Climbing ★ Pony Trekking

WTB Highly Commended

Recommended COUNTRY HOTELS OF BRITAIN 1996

Publishers' Foreword

'HAVE A GOOD DAY!' Hotels in America are traditionally held up as models of friendly efficiency, in Switzerland and Austria of cleanliness and in France of a certain *'Je ne sais quoi'* which may sometimes be shabby but is generally full of flair and flavour. In Britain, on the other hand, with a few notable exceptions, we have no great reputation for hotel-keeping. Inns and Pubs . . . 'Yes', but Hotels . . . 'No'.

Readers of *RECOMMENDED COUNTRY HOTELS OF BRITAIN* will know that this is unfair and inaccurate. The alleged lack of tradition and the relatively low status of hotels in Britain in international eyes has much to do with the industrial urban environment and the Victorian ethic which shaped many of the 'commercial' hotels in our towns and cities. Ironically it was that same period that produced properties which have joined Elizabethan, Georgian, Regency and more recent counterparts to become the rich resource of small and medium-sized country house hotels which shows the reverse side of the coin. This is the positive, the smiling, face of Britain's hospitality and it is well represented in our selection for 1996 which follows.

In addition to information about location, accommodation, cuisine and cellar, with most entries we also give an indication of price range and of course whatever ratings or awards individual hotels may have achieved. Our hotels are 'recommended' for their reputation, facilities and in many cases, through long association rather than by inspection. As publishers we cannot accept responsibility for any errors or misrepresentations in the descriptions that follow and we are always interested to hear from our readers about their own experiences. Problems are best settled on the spot with the hotel itself but we will record any complaint we receive and follow it up. We regret, however, that we cannot act as intermediaries or arbiters.

In the many years since the first edition of *RECOMMENDED COUNTRY HOTELS* was published, complaints have been few, and rarely serious. You will find straightforward and mainly factual descriptions of a selection of many old favourites and newer entries. As far as we can establish, all details are correct as we go to press, but we suggest that you confirm prices and any other terms when you enquire about bookings.

We would be grateful if you mention *RECOMMENDED COUNTRY HOTELS* when you enquire or book. We will be more than happy to receive your recommendations (in preference, hopefully to problems, as mentioned above!) and in particular of any hotels which you may judge worthy of inclusion.

Peter Stanley Williams
Editorial Consultant

Peter Clark
Publishing Director

Recommended
Country Hotels
OF BRITAIN

CONTENTS

ENGLAND

WALES

SCOTLAND

Other FHG Publications 1996

Recommended Short Break Holidays
Recommended Wayside & Country Inns of Britain
Pets Welcome!
Bed and Breakfast in Britain
The Golf Guide: Where to Play/Where to Stay
Farm Holiday Guide England, Wales, Ireland & Channel Islands
Farm Holiday Guide Scotland
Self-Catering Holidays in Britain
Britain's Best Holidays
Guide to Caravan and Camping Holidays
Children Welcome! Family Holiday & Attractions Guide
Bed and Breakfast Stops
Scotland Welcome

We thank Passford House Hotel of Lymington, Hampshire
for the use of their picture on our Outside Front Cover.

Cover design: Cyan Creative Consultants, Glasgow (0141-638 4860).

1996 Edition
ISBN 1 85055 202 9

Cartography by GEO Projects, Reading
Maps are based on Ordnance Survey maps with the permission of
the Controller of Her Majesty's Stationery Office. Crown copyright reserved.

Typeset by RD Composition Ltd., Glasgow.
Printed and bound in Great Britain by Bemrose Ltd., Derby.
Distribution. **Book Trade:** WLM, Downing Road, West Meadows Ind. Est., Derby DE21 6HA
(Tel: 01332 343332. Fax: 01332 340464).
News Trade: UMD, 16-28 Tabernacle Street, London EC2A 4BN
(Tel: 0171-638 4666. Fax: 0171-638 4665).

Published by FHG Publications Ltd.
Abbey Mill Business Centre, Seedhill, Paisley PA1 1TJ (Tel: 0141-887 0428. Fax: 0141-889 7204).

US ISBN 1-55650-7168
Distributed in the United States by
Hunter Publishing Inc., 300 Raritan Center Parkway, CN94,
Edison, N.J., 08818, USA

Avon

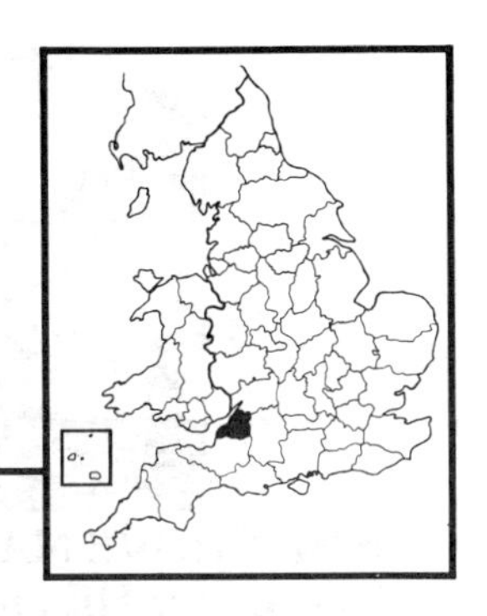

THE BATH TASBURGH HOTEL,
Warminster Road, Bath,
Avon BA2 6SH

Tel: 01225 425096
Fax: 01225 463842

Residential licence; 11 bedrooms, 10 with private bathrooms; Historic interest; Children welcome; City centre one mile; ££.

This family-owned Victorian country house, built for a photographer to the Royal family, is set in two acres of lovely gardens and grounds, with magnificent views across the Avon valley. Extensively refurbished, the house retains many original features, and offers tastefully furnished rooms with all the modern comforts of a good hotel — en suite bath/shower, direct-dial telephone, radio, colour television and tea/coffee facilities in all rooms. Four-poster and ground floor rooms available. There are fine breakfast and sitting rooms and a conservatory for guests. One of the important features is the personal care and attention given by Brian and Audrey Archer, creating a country house atmosphere so near and convenient to Bath city centre. *ETB Highly Commended, AA Selected, RAC Highly Acclaimed, Les Routiers, Johansens Country Houses.*

The **£** symbol when appearing at the end of the italic section of an entry shows the anticipated price, during 1996, for **single full Bed and Breakfast.**

Under £35	**£**	**Over £50 but under £65**	**£££**
Over £35 but under £50	**££**	**Over £65**	**££££**

This is meant as an indication only and does not show prices for Special Breaks, Weekends, etc. Guests are therefore advised to verify all prices on enquiring or booking.

COMBE GROVE MANOR,

Brassknocker Hill, Monkton Combe, Bath, Avon BA2 7HS

Tel: 01225 834644
Fax: 01225 834561

Fully licensed; 41 bedrooms, all with private bathrooms; Historic interest; Children welcome; Leisure facilities; Bristol 11 miles, ££££.

The magnificent facilities which Combe Grove Manor provides for the leisure interests of their guests perfectly complement the high standards set for bedroom comfort and dining-room quality. If the indoor and outdoor swimming-pools, tennis and squash courts, gymnasium, sauna, golf and other on-site activities leave some energy untapped, clay pigeon shooting, hot-air ballooning or horse-riding can be arranged nearby. Back in your de luxe bedroom, with a four-poster bed if you wish, watch the news on satellite TV before you bathe. Then down to the Georgian restaurant for a formal dinner or a more casual meal in the Manor Vaults Bistro. Combe Grove has various 'Special Breaks' and the use of leisure facilities is included in all room rates. Why not escape from the busy world into the luxury of this stress-free Hotel with its spectacular surroundings and unrivalled amenities. 👑👑👑👑👑 *Highly Commended, AA****.* **See also Colour Advertisement on page 2.**

FOR THE MUTUAL GUIDANCE OF GUEST AND HOST

Every year literally thousands of holidays, short-breaks and overnight stops are arranged through our guides, the vast majority without any problems at all. In a handful of cases, however, difficulties do arise about bookings, which often could have been prevented from the outset.

It is important to remember that when accommodation has been booked, both parties — guests and hosts — have entered into a form of contract. We hope that the following points will provide helpful guidance.

GUESTS: When enquiring about accommodation, be as precise as possible. Give exact dates, numbers in your party and the ages of any children. State the number and type of rooms wanted and also what catering you require — bed and breakfast, full board, etc. Make sure that the position about evening meals is clear — and about pets, reductions for children or any other special points.

Read our reviews carefully to ensure that the proprietors you are going to contact can supply what you want. Ask for a letter confirming all arrangements, if possible.

If you have to cancel, do so as soon as possible. Proprietors do have the right to retain deposits and under certain circumstances to charge for cancelled holidays if adequate notice is not given and they cannot re-let the accommodation.

HOSTS: Give details about your facilities and about any special conditions. Explain your deposit system clearly and arrangements for cancellations, charges, etc, and whether or not your terms include VAT.

If for any reason you are unable to fulfil an agreed booking without adequate notice, you may be under an obligation to arrange alternative suitable accommodation or to make some form of compensation.

While every effort is made to ensure accuracy, we regret that FHG Publications cannot accept responsibility for errors, omissions or misrepresentation in our entries or any consequences thereof. Prices in particular should be checked because we go to press early. We will follow up complaints but cannot act as arbiters or agents for either party.

Berkshire

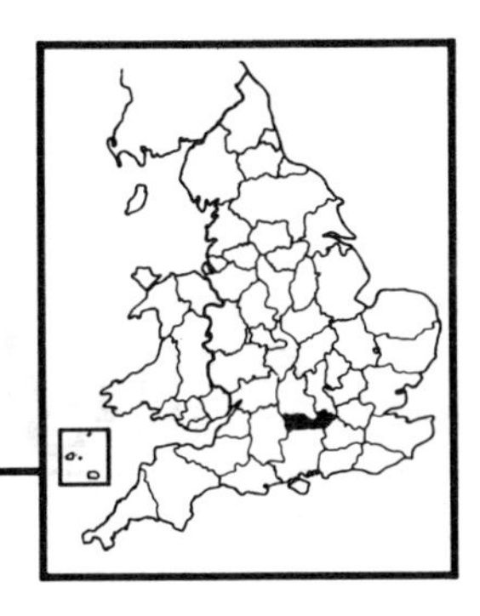

HOLLINGTON HOUSE,
Woolton Hill, Near Newbury,
Berkshire RG15 9XR

Tel: 01635 255100
Fax: 01635 255075

Residential licence; 20 bedrooms, all with private bathrooms; Children welcome; Leisure and conference facilities; Reading 16 miles; ££££.

This fine Edwardian country house, with its stone-mullioned windows, galleried entrance hall and rich wood panelling, was skilfully and sympathetically converted into a warmly welcoming hotel by John and Penny Guy in 1992. Its high-ceilinged rooms and tasteful furnishings give it great character on which the modern appointments that have been introduced do not impinge at all. The luxurious guest rooms are sheer delight: spacious, beautifully appointed and possessed of bathing facilities fit for a Roman Emperor or Empress, many of the huge bathrooms featuring separate showers and whirlpool baths. Lounges also exhibit the ultimate in cossetted comfort and special consideration has been given to guests with disabilities. Traditional English dishes and European specialities of high quality may be enjoyed in an attractive dining room with views over the terrace. The building stands in 25 acres of superbly wooded grounds featuring stately firs, cedars and maples and which house a solar heated swimming pool, tennis court and croquet lawn. The convenient position of this lovely retreat renders it a favoured rendezvous for business meetings and social events. Newbury is only three miles distant and London, Oxford, Bath and Stratford-upon-Avon may be reached in under 90 minutes. Visits to Newbury Racecourse and shooting on private estates may be organised. The amenities provided by this splendid hotel are worthy of the highest recommendation. *AA Three Red Stars and Three Rosettes, Egon Ronay 81%.* **See also Colour Advertisement on page 3.**

Please mention
Recommended COUNTRY HOTELS
when seeking refreshment or
accommodation at a Hotel
mentioned in these pages

Buckinghamshire

BELLHOUSE HOTEL, Oxford Road, Beaconsfield, Buckinghamshire HP9 2XE

Tel: 01753 887211
Fax: 01753 888231

Fully licensed; 136 bedrooms, all with private bathrooms; Children and dogs welcome; Leisure and conference facilities; High Wycombe 5 miles; ££££.

The first sight of this handsome modern hotel brings to mind Moorish architectural splendour. In reality, the outstanding facilities it offers lie in the heart of the Buckinghamshire countryside, just 5 minutes from the M40, 20 minutes from Heathrow Airport and 35 minutes from London. The leisure amenities are second to none; squash courts, swimming pool and gymnasium will attract keep-fit enthusiasts whilst less active diversions may be found playing snooker, relaxing under beauty therapy or just lingering over a delicious meal. The en suite bedrooms are superbly furnished, all having colour television, in-house movies, direct-dial telephone and tea and coffee-makers amongst their fine appointments. *AA/RAC ****.*

THE GROVEFIELD HOTEL, Taplow Common Road, Burnham, Buckinghamshire SL1 8LP

Tel: 01628 603131
Fax: 01628 668078

Fully licensed; 40 bedrooms, all with private bathrooms; Children and pets welcome; Conference facilities; Maidenhead 4 miles; £££.

Built at the turn of the century for a member of the Fuller brewing family, this handsome, well proportioned establishment stands secluded in over seven acres of lawns and woodland — indeed it is hard to believe that it lies only minutes from Heathrow Airport and the motorway network. A variety of en suite bedrooms, all stylishly appointed, offer accommodation to suit all requirements; romantic four-poster rooms and spacious suites provide a very special touch of luxury for a celebration weekend. Elegant decor, fine cuisine and a carefully selected wine list combine to make the John Fuller Restaurant a very popular venue for discerning diners. And to complete the picture, first rate conference and banqueting facilities can cater for all types of functions.

Cambridgeshire

THE NITON, 7 Barton Road, Ely, Cambridgeshire CB7 4HZ

Tel: 01353 662459
Fax: 01353 666619

Fully licensed; 14 bedrooms, all with private bathrooms; Children welcome; Cambridge 14 miles; £.

Just 10 minutes' walk from Ely's beautiful cathedral, this most comfortable and well-appointed hotel stands in 2 acres of attractive grounds and adjoins the 18-hole golf course on which reduced green fees apply to guests. Bedrooms are charmingly furnished and decorated with en suite facilities, central heating, colour television, radio and beverage-makers; some family rooms are available. A pleasant, panelled dining room is the setting for the presentation of excellent English and Continental dishes from both à la carte and table d'hôte menus. Morning coffee and afternoon tea may be enjoyed in the spacious lounge area with its interesting period fireplace and the spruce cocktail bar is a good place for meeting new friends. *EATB* ♛♛♛ *Commended.*

Cheshire

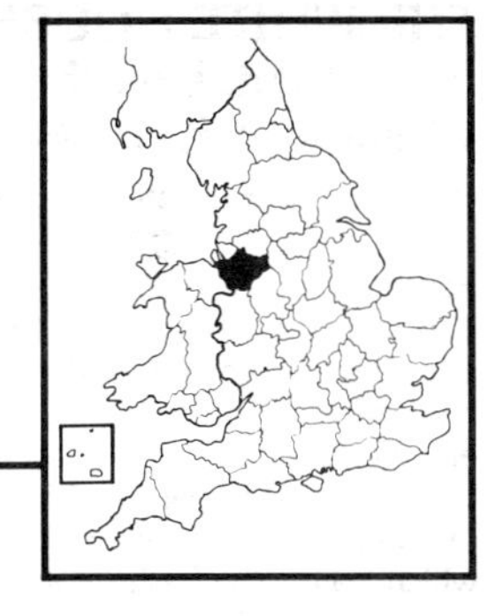

ROWTON HALL HOTEL, Whitchurch Road, Chester, Cheshire CH3 6AD

Tel: 01244 335262
Fax: 01244 335464

Fully licensed; 42 bedrooms, all with private bathrooms; Historic interest; Children and pets welcome; Leisure and conference facilities; Chester 3 miles; ££££.

Over the ages, Chester has delighted and intrigued through its close associations with our nation's history. Built on the site of the Civil War battle of Rowton Moor, the Hall, dating from 1779, is a recommended headquarters for this step back into time. It contains many original features, including an elegant Robert Adam fireplace and superbly carved staircase. All creature comforts are here to cosset and captivate; bedrooms all have en suite facilities and the most up-to-date modern appointments. Seek the bonhomie of the Cavalier Bar before dining memorably in the Langdale Restaurant – and remember to take time out to tone up the system in Hamilton's Leisure Club with its swimming pool, multi-gym, sauna and solarium. *AA/RAC***.*

HOLLY LODGE HOTEL,
70 London Road, Holmes Chapel, Cheshire CW4 7AS

Tel: 01477 537033
Fax: 01477 535823

Fully licensed; 38 bedrooms, all with private bathrooms; Children welcome, pets by arrangement; Conference facilities; Middlewich 4 miles; ££££.

Built in the mid-19th century and recently extensively modernised, Holly Lodge retains the charm and character of its former days whilst presenting the highest modern standards of comfort and cuisine. In the latter context, the delightful Truffles Restaurant has a peerless reputation for its distinctive fixed price and lodge menus at luncheon and dinner. There is an imaginative choice of dishes and prices represent excellent value. Guest rooms have private facilities plus colour television with free satellite channels, telephone, radio and tea and coffee-makers. By reason of its quiet but convenient position within easy reach of the commercial centres of the north-west, the hotel is a popular venue for conferences and business meetings. *ETB ♛♛♛♛ Commended, AA***.*

THE WHITE HOUSE MANOR,
New Road, Prestbury, Cheshire SK10 4HP

Tel: 01625 829376
Fax: 01625 828627

Residential licence; 9 bedrooms, all with private bathrooms; Historic interest; Children welcome; Conference facilities; Macclesfield 2 miles; ££££.

For pressing engagements in Manchester or as a base for exploration of the largely understated rural delights of Cheshire, this 18th century manor house has been imaginatively converted to provide for the modern traveller a standard of accommodation that would be hard to better anywhere, great attention having been given to the exciting decor. Apart from en suite facilities, each guest suite is beautifully furnished and has remote-control colour television, direct-dial telephone, bar, hairdryer and beverage maker. Only a short stroll away, the well regarded White House Restaurant offers interesting à la carte and luncheon menus which feature the freshest of local produce and more than a touch of flair in preparation and presentation. ♛♛♛♛ *Highly Commended, AA 2 Rosettes.*

PLEASE ENCLOSE A STAMPED ADDRESSED ENVELOPE WHEN WRITING TO ENQUIRE ABOUT ACCOMMODATION FEATURED IN THIS GUIDE

Cleveland

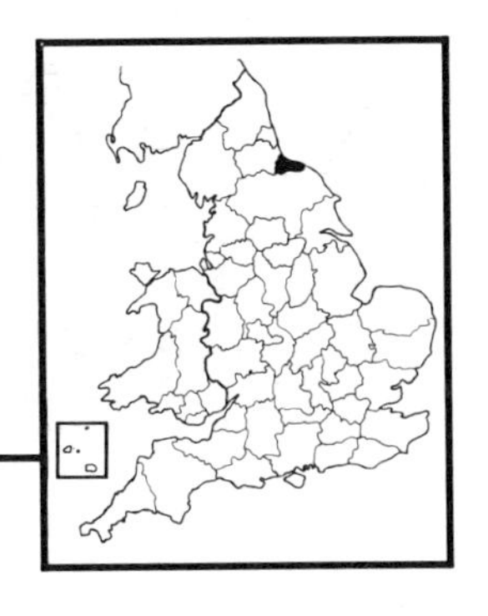

GRINKLE PARK HOTEL,
Easington, Saltburn-by-the-Sea, Cleveland TS13 4UB

Tel: 01287 640515
Fax: 01287 641278

Fully licensed; 20 bedrooms, all with private bathrooms; Children welcome, no dogs in public areas; Leisure and conference facilities; Redcar 4 miles; ££££.

Between the rolling Cleveland Hills and the coast at Robin Hood's Bay, this late Victorian mansion is impressive in appearance and imposing in its standards of comfort and service. 35 acres of parkland surround the house and guests may stroll through the gardens, enjoy a game or two on the superb tennis court or play croquet on the lawn. Snooker may be played indoors. Beautifully decorated, the spacious bedrooms, named after local flora and place-names, all have a private bath or shower, colour television, direct-dial telephone, trouser press and tea-making facilities. Dining by candlelight is a supreme pleasure and there is always a welcome for the casual diner. ♛♛♛♛ *Highly Commended.*

Cornwall

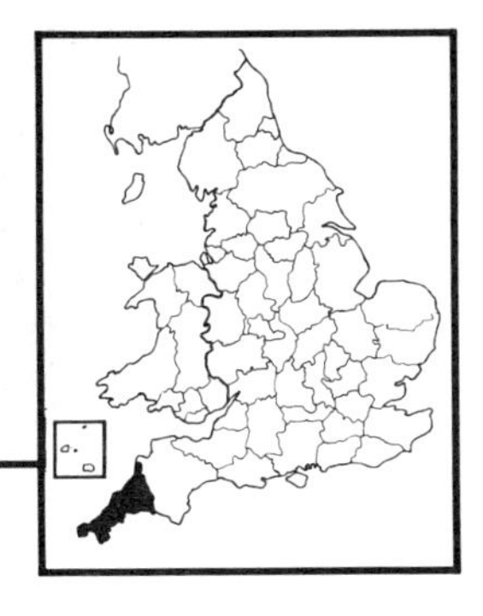

TREDETHY COUNTRY HOTEL,
Helland Bridge, Bodmin, Cornwall PL30 4QS

Tel: 01208 841262
Fax: 01208 841707

Residential and restaurant licence; 11 bedrooms, all with private bathrooms; Historic interest; Children welcome; Leisure facilities; Bodmin 3 miles; ££.

Equidistant from Cornwall's north and south coasts, this delightful retreat basks in 9 acres of glorious grounds, a haven of peace and contentment. Through the lush valley in which Tredethy stands, the River Camel meanders its way to Padstow and the sea. In these idyllic surroundings, there are opportunities for riding, walking, sailing, golf and both river and sea fishing; in the grounds there is a fine, sheltered, heated swimming pool. The accommodation is spacious and of a high standard, guest rooms of various sizes all having en suite facilities, colour television and telephone. Also, in the grounds, there are several self-catering cottages. All arrangements are under the personal supervision of proprietors, Beryl and Richard Graham. *WCTB* ♛♛♛.

WILLAPARK MANOR HOTEL, Bossiney, Near Tintagel, Cornwall PL34 0BA

Tel: 01840 770782

Restaurant and residential licence; 14 bedrooms, all with private bathrooms; Children and pets welcome; Camelford 4 miles; £.

ONE OF THE MOST BEAUTIFULLY SITUATED HOTELS IN ENGLAND. Beautiful character house, perched on the cliffs amidst 14 acres of landscaped gardens and secluded woodland overlooking the Bay. Direct access to coast path and beach with wonderful walks in every direction. 14 bedrooms, all en suite, with colour television and tea makers. Excellent cuisine, well stocked cocktail bar and a unique friendly and informal atmosphere. *ETB* ♛♛♛ *Commended.*

THE OLD MILL COUNTRY HOUSE, Little Petherick, Near Padstow, Cornwall PL27 7QT

Tel: 01841 540388*

Residential licence; 7 bedrooms, most with private bathrooms; Historic interest; Pets welcome except in bedrooms; Car park (10); Wadebridge 4 miles; £.

The Old Mill Country House is a sixteenth century Grade II Listed corn mill complete with waterwheel. Set in its own streamside garden at the head of Little Petherick Creek, just two miles from Padstow and in a designated Area of Outstanding Natural Beauty. The Old Mill is furnished throughout with antiques and collections of genuine artefacts to complement the exposed beams, original fireplaces and slate floors. This ensures that the Old Mill's original character and charm is retained. A varied supper menu is served. We regret minimum age is 14 years. *ETB* ♛♛♛ *Commended, RAC Acclaimed, AA QQQ, Ashley Courtenay.*

MOLESWORTH MANOR,
Little Petherick, Padstow,
Cornwall PL27 7QT

Tel: 01841 540292*

Fully licensed; 10 bedrooms, all with private bathrooms; Historic interest; Children welcome in family suites; Wadebridge 4 miles; £.

This lovely old country house graces some of the most beautiful estuary and coastal scenery in the country. Dating from the early 17th century and enlarged and "improved" in late Victorian times, this warm and welcoming retreat stands in attractive gardens, just two miles from the delectable little fishing port of Padstow and in an area renowned for its outstanding natural beauty and wildlife. Comfort and utter contentment are the rewards of a holiday spent here, attributes ensured by unobtrusive modern amenities. The views are splendid and so is the friendly service. Terms are most reasonable and our recommendation emphatic.

COOMBE FARM,
Widegates, Near Looe,
Cornwall PL13 1QN

Tel: 01503 240223

Licensed; All bedrooms with private bathrooms; Leisure facilities; Looe 3 miles; £.

This lovely country house is surrounded by lawns, meadows, woods and streams, with superb views to the sea. Delicious home cooking is served in the candlelit dining room. All bedrooms are en suite and have colour television, radio, tea and coffee making facilities and direct-dial telephone. In the grounds there are many animals and flowers, a swimming pool (heated in summer), croquet lawn and a stone barn for snooker and table tennis. Nearby are golf, fishing, tennis, horse riding and glorious walks and beaches. This is a perfect centre for visiting all parts of Cornwall and Devon. Special Short Break terms, details on request. A warm welcome is assured by Alexander and Sally Low. *ETB ♛♛♛ Highly Commended, AA QQQQ and Winner Guest House of the Year (West of England) 1981, RAC Highly Acclaimed, Johansens.*
See also Colour Advertisement on page 4.

TRELAWNE HOTEL,
Mawnan Smith, Falmouth,
Cornwall TR11 5HS

Tel: 01326 250226*
Fax: 01326 250909

Licensed; 16 bedrooms, 14 with private bathrooms; Children and pets welcome; Leisure facilities; Truro 13 miles, Falmouth 5; ££.

Nestling on the coastline between the Helford and Fal rivers in a beautiful and tranquil corner of Cornwall, this fine country house hotel enjoys a magnificent outlook across Falmouth Bay to the Roseland Peninsula. Maenporth beach is but a short distance away and there are numerous idyllic coves nearby. The tastefully furnished and centrally heated bedrooms have en suite facilities, as well as colour television, radio, telephone and tea and coffee makers. There is a charming cocktail bar where new friends are easily made, and for recreation there is an indoor pool and games room. The cuisine comes high on the list of attractions at this well-run hotel, dishes being attractively prepared by award-winning chefs and backed by an extensive wine list. *ETB ♛♛♛♛, AA ***.*

STEEP HOUSE,
Portmellon Cove, Mevagissey,
Cornwall PL26 2PH

Tel: 01726 843732

Residential licence; 7 bedrooms, 2 with private bathrooms; Children over 10 years welcome; Leisure facilities; Newquay 20 miles, St Austell 6.

Steep House stands in an acre of ground by the sea, in a natural cove with a safe sandy beach twenty yards from the large garden. Comfortable, centrally heated double bedrooms with washbasins and sea or beach views, colour television and tea/coffee makers; two are en suite. Generous English breakfast and dinners are served in the diningroom overlooking Portmellon Cove. Covered summertime swimming pool. Guests welcome all year. Modest prices, special weekly and winter break rates. Residential drinks licence. Private parking. Fire Certificate. Colour brochure. *ETB* ♛♛.

CROSSROADS HOTEL,
Scorrier, Redruth,
Cornwall TR16 5BP

Tel: 01209 820551
Fax: 01209 820392

Licensed; 36 bedrooms, all with private bathrooms; Car park (140); Redruth 2 miles; ££.

Crossroads Hotel is a purpose-built hotel with modern facilities, situated at the Scorrier exit of the A30, near Redruth. It makes an ideal base for visiting all parts of Cornwall. We have a fine reputation for our service and food, and endeavour to meet the special requirements of our guests. There are ground floor bedrooms available and a lift. We hope to have the pleasure of welcoming you to Crossroads Hotel. ♛♛♛♛ *Highly Commended.* **See also Colour Advertisement on page 4.**

Available from most bookshops, the 1996 edition of THE GOLF GUIDE covers details of every UK golf course – well over 2000 entries – for holiday or business golf. Hundreds of hotel entries offer convenient accommodation, accompanying details of the courses – the 'pro', par score, length etc.

Endorsed by The Professional Golfers' Association (PGA) and including Holiday Golf in Ireland, France, Portugal, Spain and the USA.

£8.99 from bookshops or £9.80 including postage (UK only) from FHG Publications, Abbey Mill Business Centre, Paisley PA1 1TJ.

BOSSINEY HOUSE HOTEL, Tintagel, Cornwall PL34 0AX

Freephone: 0800 454581*

Residential and restaurant licence; 20 bedrooms, all en-suite; Children and dogs welcome; Leisure facilities; Bodmin 20 miles, Bude 19, Camelford 6; £.

At one time Bossiney had its own mayor and corporation, and in the 16th century Sir Francis Drake was one of its two MPs. Today a cluster of houses nestle close to a sandy cove with interesting rock formations, ideal for bathing, surfing or just unwinding. With wonderful cliff walks on either side this is the glorious situation of the beautifully furnished Bossiney House Hotel, standing in grounds of two and a half acres. Guests may relax in the gardens, the indoor heated swimming pool, the sauna or solarium; take in the sweeping sea views; or try their skills on the putting green. Inside, one is immediately impressed by the spacious cleanliness of the public and private rooms, and in particular by the imaginative and pleasing colour schemes. This is a really happy place in which to stay, and the proprietors and staff work hard to achieve this end. Pleasant lounges, one with a bar, are convivial meeting places in which to enjoy refreshment; the well-appointed bedrooms make the most of sea and country views. In the catering department, fine English cooking is a feature of the menus which offer excellent choice and variety. Quaint Tintagel is near at hand, and the surrounding King Arthur's country provides an almost bewildering choice of beauty spots, historic locations and sporting activities. 👑👑👑 *Approved, AA and RAC **.*

Key to Tourist Board Ratings

The Crown Scheme

(England, Scotland & Wales)

Covering hotels, motels, private hotels, guesthouses, inns, bed & breakfast, farmhouses. Every Crown classified place to stay is inspected annually. *The classification:* Listed then 1-5 Crown indicates the range of facilities and services. Higher quality standards are indicated by the terms APPROVED, COMMENDED, HIGHLY COMMENDED and DELUXE.

The Key Scheme

(also operates in Scotland using a Crown symbol)

Covering self-catering in cottages, bungalows, flats, houseboats, houses, chalets, etc. Every Key classified holiday home is inspected annually. *The classification:* 1-5 Key indicates the range of facilities and equipment. Higher quality standards are indicated by the terms APPROVED, COMMENDED, HIGHLY COMMENDED and DELUXE.

The Q Scheme

(England, Scotland & Wales)

Covering holiday, caravan, chalet and camping parks. Every Q rated park is inspected annually for its quality standards. The more ✓ in the Q – up to 5 – the higher the standard of what is provided.

Cumbria

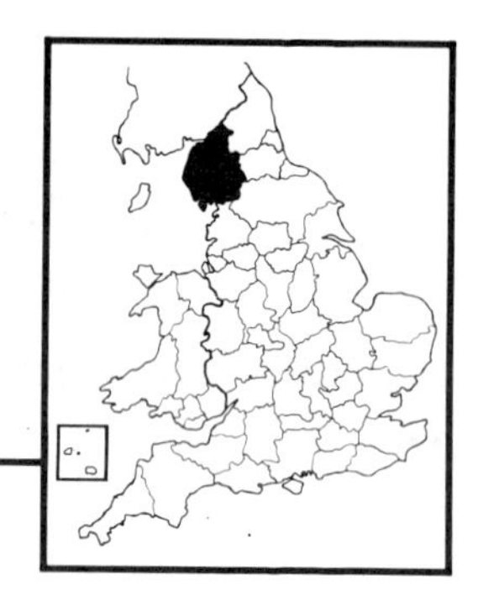

CROW HOW HOTEL,
Rydal Road, Ambleside,
Cumbria LA22 9PN

Tel: 015394 32193*

Restaurant licence; 9 bedrooms, all with private bathrooms; Children and pets welcome; Windermere 4 miles; £.

In a quiet situation, overlooking Loughrigg Fell and the River Rothay, yet within walking distance of Ambleside and Rydal Water, this comfortable country house has recently been extensively refurbished. Good home cooking and a warm and convivial atmosphere will soon encourage relaxation and the excellent accommodation comprises individually furnished guest rooms, all of which have private facilities, colour television, tea-makers and controllable heating. The hotel has lovely 2 acre gardens with ample gated parking, and guests are invited to use, free of charge, the hotel's permit to fish in local tarns and rivers. Also available, a three bedroomed self-catering holiday cottage, situated in the hotel grounds for weekly lets. Dogs welcome. *ETB & CTB* ♛♛♛ *Commended. AA**.*

---

* The appearance of an asterisk after the telephone number indicates that the hotel in question is closed for a period during the winter months. Exact dates should be ascertained from the hotel itself.

HIGHFIELD HOUSE COUNTRY HOTEL,

Hawkshead Hill, Ambleside, Cumbria LA22 0PN

Tel: 015394 36344
Fax: 015394 36793

Restaurant and residential licence; 11 bedrooms, all with private bathrooms; Children welcome, pets by arrangement; Windermere 9 miles; £.

Built in traditional Lakeland stone in late-Victorian times, Highfield House has been impressively converted into a country hotel of some standing — and stand it does, amidst a lovely garden bedecked with colourful shrubs and with far-reaching views across the undulating countryside from its large windows. Brightly decorated and furnished with style and taste, the house offers peace and quiet, superb food and charming accommodation, each room having en suite facilities, remote-control colour television, easy chairs, hair dryer, clock/radio, electric blanket and tea and coffee tray; fine amenities to add to its individual character. This is good walking terrain and in the spacious lounge a selection of maps, guides and books will facilitate planning one's excursions, returning with happy anticipation at the end of the day assured of a tempting choice of dishes from an inspired menu that changes every day. Vegetarians and those on special diets are well catered for, as are children. Brisk exercise is certainly recommended here for the magnificent food, including traditional breakfasts and puddings, will pay no heed to waistlines. A small but well-stocked bar serves excellent local bitter and there is an interesting range of reasonably-priced wines. The hotel is just three-quarters of a mile from Hawkshead village on the road to Tarn Hows (1½ miles) and Coniston (3½ miles) whilst a bus service operates to Ambleside (5 miles) and Windermere (9 miles). *CTB ♛♛♛ Highly Commended, RAC ** Merit, AA **, Ashley Courtenay.*

APPLEBY MANOR COUNTRY HOUSE HOTEL, Roman Road, Appleby-in-Westmorland, Cumbria CA16 6JB

Tel: 017683 51571

Fully licensed; 30 bedrooms, all with private bathrooms; Historic interest; Children and pets welcome; Leisure facilities; Penrith 13 miles, Brough 8; £££.

Set in wooded grounds overlooking Appleby's fine castle, with panoramic views of the Pennines and Eden Valley, Appleby Manor is a hotel in which you will feel immediately at home. Where nicer to return to after a great day out in the Lakes or Yorkshire Dales than this relaxing and friendly country house with its log fires, beautiful public rooms and high quality, fully equipped bedrooms. Take a refreshing dip in the heated indoor pool in the leisure club before enjoying a superb meal in the award-winning restaurant, and then retiring to one of the comfy chairs in the lounge with a malt whisky selected from a choice of over 70. ♛♛♛♛ *Highly Commended, AA and RAC ***.*

ABBEY HOUSE HOTEL, Abbey Road, Barrow-in-Furness, Cumbria LA13 0PA

Tel: 01229 838282
Fax: 01229 820403

Fully licensed; 28 bedrooms, all with private bathrooms; Historic interest; Children and pets welcome; Lancaster 18 miles; ££.

Taking its name from the neighbouring ruins of one of the greatest Cistercian foundations in the country, this fine sandstone mansion was designed in the grand manner by Sir Edwin Lutyens. Itself a building of profound presence, the Abbey can fairly claim to be one of our most distinguished country hotels. Elegantly appointed and standing in woodland and well-tended gardens, the hotel is surrounded by open farmland, a tranquil setting from which to explore the verdant Furness Peninsula and the Lake District. The standard of refreshment is high indeed; accent being on classical French cuisine although the choice of dishes is wide and uniformly tempting. Guest rooms are luxurious and there are excellent facilities for business and social functions. *ETB* ♛♛♛♛, *RAC****.*

FAYRER GARDEN HOUSE HOTEL, Lyth Valley Road, Bowness-on-Windermere, Cumbria LA23 3JP

Tel: 015394 88195
Fax: 015394 45986

Licensed; 14 bedrooms, all with private facilities; Children and pets welcome; Kendal 10 miles, Ambleside 5; £/££.

Our beautiful country house is set in five acres of grounds overlooking the Lake. Guests can relax in the elegant lounges and enjoy excellent cuisine in the restaurant. The comfortable bedrooms include four-poster rooms with jacuzzis. Free use of local leisure facilities. FREEPHONE 0500 432177 for a brochure and you will see why early reservations are recommended. ♛♛♛ *Highly Commended.* **See also Colour Advertisement on page 5.**

SCAFELL HOTEL,
Rosthwaite, Borrowdale, Near Keswick, Cumbria CA12 5XB

Tel: 017687 77208*
Fax: 017687 77280

Fully licensed; 24 bedrooms, all with private bathrooms; Historic interest; Children and dogs welcome; Derwent Water 3 miles; ££.

Former coaching inn set in the heart of impressive Borrowdale, 24 en-suite bedrooms, with lounges warmed by log fires in winter, and a restaurant renowned for fine food and wines. Run by a staff providing a warm and friendly service.

TARN END HOUSE HOTEL,
Talkin Tarn, Brampton, Carlisle, Cumbria CA8 1LS

Tel: 016977 2340
Fax: 016977 2089

Licensed; All bedrooms with private bathrooms; Children and pets welcome; Brampton 3 miles; £.

Tarn End House Hotel is situated in its own grounds running down to the shores of the Tarn, and is only 500 yards from Brampton Golf Club. The bar, restaurant and residents' lounge all overlook the Lake, as do most of the bedrooms, all of which have colour television and tea/coffee facilities. Other relaxations include fishing, birdwatching, sailing and walking. Hadrian's Wall, Lanercost Abbey and the Roman Army Museum are all close at hand, as is the renowned Settle to Carlisle railway line. Resident proprietors, David and Vivienne Ball, invite you to relax and wind down at this traditional hotel in its own delightful secluded setting. All food in the restaurant and bar is home-made and freshly cooked to order. Telephone for colour brochure and tariff. 👑👑, *Egon Ronay.*

PICKETT HOWE,
Buttermere Valley,
Cumbria CA13 9UY

Tel: 01900 85444
Fax: 01900 85209

Residential licence; 4 bedrooms, all with private bathrooms; Historic interest; Children over 10 years welcome; Cockermouth 6 miles; ££.

A National Winner of the English Tourist Board's "England for Excellence" Award, which acknowledges tourism ventures leading the way in quality and innovation, this Listed 17th century longhouse offers the unique combination of the amenities of top country house hotels — whirlpool baths, antique bedsteads, direct-dial bedroom telephones — within the welcoming, relaxing ambience of a cosy, oak-beamed, slate-floored farmhouse. The cuisine is outstanding, with imaginative dinners and a choice of breakfast rarely found. Set in a totally peaceful area of the Lake District, Pickett Howe sits away from the road with direct walking access to the lakes and fells. Pickett Howe is worth experiencing — but book well in advance . . . it's small, special and often full. *ETB ♛♛♛ De Luxe, AA Premier Selected; recommended by all major independent guides.*

OVERWATER HALL,
Ireby, Carlisle,
Cumbria CA5 1HH

Tel. and Fax: 0176-87 76566

Restaurant and residential licence; 13 bedrooms, all with private bathrooms; Historic interest; Children and pets welcome; Wigton 6 miles; £.

Lying peacefully in 18 acres of secluded woodland and gardens, this delightful house has great character and a good deal of architectural and historic interest. Skiddaw (3100 ft.) looms in the middle distance and it is but two miles from Bassenthwaite Lake. A recommended centre from which to explore the beauties of the Lake District, the hotel has well-planned accommodation that is considerably above average, guest rooms having en suite facilities, colour television, radio, telephone and excellent views. Dining here is an experience not to be missed, the day starting with a hearty Cumbrian breakfast with a superb 5-course dinner to look forward to later. Relaxation may be sought in the drawing room, on the sun terrace or in the unique Piano Bar where the bar is the grand piano itself! *AA**, AA 2 Red Rosettes.*

LINK HOUSE,
Bassenthwaite Lake, Cockermouth, Cumbria CA13 9YD

Tel: 017687 76291*
Fax: 017687 76670

Residential licence; 8 bedrooms, all with private bathrooms; Historic interest; Children over 7 years welcome; Keswick 6 miles; £.

A family-run traditional Victorian country house at the quieter end of the Lake District and surrounded by lovely scenery, yet providing easy access to all the popular areas. An ideal base for walkers and motorists alike. All eight bedrooms are en suite with colour television, tea/coffee making equipment, central heating, etc. We have single, double, twin and family rooms (one on the ground floor). There is a delightful conservatory to enjoy the evening sun or a pre-dinner drink, plus a comfortable lounge with log fires to make winter evenings even more cosy. Many antique and period pieces of furniture throughout, but more relaxing than formal. The wine list, at modest prices, is selected to complement imaginative four-course freshly prepared dinners (plus coffee), served on Wedgwood china. Credit cards accepted. *ETB* ♛♛♛, *AA QQQ.* **See also Colour Advertisement on page 4.**

PHEASANT INN,
Bassenthwaite Lake, Near Cockermouth, Cumbria CA13 9YE

Tel: 017687 76234
Fax: 017687 76002

Licensed; 20 bedrooms, all with private bathrooms; Children welcome, kennels available for dogs; Cockermouth 6 miles; £££.

This tranquil, traditional North Lake District inn lies adjacent to Bassenthwaite Lake, surrounded by gardens and woodland which are home to a wealth of wildlife. Three lounges feature antiques, beams, open fires and fresh flowers; two have cosy open fires. The inn is centrally heated to ensure comfort and the individually decorated bedrooms have electric blankets and private facilities. No television or self-service breakfasts. A high standard of traditional English food and friendly service is maintained. *BTA Commended.* **See also Colour Advertisement on page 5.**

GRAYTHWAITE MANOR HOTEL,
Fernhill Road, Grange-over-Sands, Cumbria LA11 7JE

Tel: 015395 32001/33755
Fax: 015395 35549

Fully licensed; 22 bedrooms, all with private bathrooms; Children welcome; Leisure and conference facilities; Morecambe 9 miles; ££.

A gracious and grand establishment set in its own glorious gardens which extend to eight acres, Graythwaite Manor is well-known for the excellence of its cuisine, with home produce figuring prominently on the menus. Many of the beautifully decorated bedrooms afford views over the gardens to the distant Pennines, and all have a private bathroom and a full range of modern amenities. Guests may take their ease in the drawing room, billiards room or bar, or perhaps enjoy a stroll through the gardens or a leisurely game of tennis or putting. Those wishing to venture farther afield to explore this most delightful part of the English landscape can be provided with substantial picnic lunches on request. ♛♛♛♛ *Highly Commended, RAC Restaurant Award.*

---

* The appearance of an asterisk after the telephone number indicates that the hotel in question is closed for a period during the winter months. Exact dates should be ascertained from the hotel itself.

SWINSIDE LODGE HOTEL,
Newlands, Keswick,
Cumbria CA12 5UE

Tel: 017687 72948*

Unlicensed; 9 bedrooms, all with private bathrooms; Children over 12 years welcome; Penrith 16 miles; ££.

Stroll along the placid shores of Derwentwater, taking in the breathtaking scenery of one of the most idyllic spots in Lakeland, and direct your feet towards this lovely Victorian house. It is lucky you booked in earlier, for Swinside Lodge is fast gaining a reputation for its well-appointed accommodation, and, in particular, for its award-winning cuisine. A hearty Cumbrian breakfast sets the standard and after a day's sightseeing, one has the assurance of a delicious five-course dinner prepared by Cordon Bleu chefs and served in the candlelit dining room. The hotel operates a no smoking policy and is unlicensed, but guests are welcome to bring in their own favourite wines and there is no corkage charge. *De Luxe, AA Red Star and Two Rosettes for Food.*

BRANTWOOD COUNTRY HOUSE HOTEL,
Stainton, Penrith,
Cumbria CA11 0EP

Tel: 01768 862748
Fax: 01768 890164

Fully licensed; 11 bedrooms, all with private bathrooms; Historic interest; Children welcome; Penrith 3 miles; ££.

Standing in secluded gardens in the picturesque village of Stainton, this attractive country residence retains its olde worlde charm with oak beams and open log fires. It is situated two and a half miles west of Penrith, three miles from Lake Ullswater, and just two minutes from the M6 and A66. All bedrooms have private shower room and WC, colour television, direct-dial telephone, tea making facilities and full central heating. Guests can enjoy a formal dinner in the restaurant or choose from an extensive bar menu. This relaxed and friendly hotel has been personally run for the last nine years by Susan and John Harvey and family. *Commended, AA and RAC **.* **See also Colour Advertisement on page 6.**

WHEYRIGG HALL HOTEL,
Wigton,
Cumbria CA7 0DH

Tel: 016973 61242
Fax: 016973 61020

Fully licensed; 13 bedrooms, all with private bathrooms; Children welcome; Conference facilities; Carlisle 11 miles; £.

Converted from an old farmhouse, the Hall has been skilfully extended and modernised into a first-class family hotel and restaurant noted for its good food. Its rural situation, four miles from Wigton and only seven from the sea, is quite delightful either for an evening out in the country or as a peaceful holiday venue. Dining room, lounge and bar are spacious but there is a homely cottage atmosphere enhanced by an interesting collection of hunting paraphernalia and other antiques. Accommodation is provided in en suite bedrooms of varying sizes with some family suites available; all have colour television, telephone and beverage-makers. Several separate function rooms prove popular and special golfing breaks are organised. *RAC/AA**.*

MOUNTAIN ASH HOTEL,
Ambleside Road, Windermere,
Cumbria LA23 1AT

Tel: 015394 43715

Fully licensed; 19 bedrooms, all with private bathrooms; Historic interest; Children and pets welcome; Kendal 7 miles; £.

Windermere has many hotels, in our experience some good, some very good and some exceptional. Just out of town and surrounded by lovely woodland walks, this fine hotel we consider to fall into the last category. The reception lounge with its welcoming log fire and "malty" cocktail bar sets one off in the right spirit, and first acquaintance with one's en suite room with colour television etc. will induce a purr of satisfaction. This, indeed, could be a squeal of rapture should occasion warrant the selection of a suite with a four-poster water bed and corner spa bath. A full range of leisure facilities is available to guests at the nearby Parklands Private Leisure Club. ♛♛♛♛, *ABTA Recommended.*

BELMONT MANOR HOTEL,
Ambleside Road, Windermere,
Cumbria LA23 1LN

Tel: 0153-94 33316/7

Fully licensed; 13 bedrooms, all with private bathrooms; Children welcome; Conference facilities; Lakeside near Newby 10 miles; ££.

One approaches this spruce little hotel via a delightful drive which cuts through 7 acres of beautiful grounds. On the A591, midway between Windermere and Ambleside, this is a particularly well-appointed venue for a Lakeland holiday. Imaginatively decorated, the colour co-ordinated bedrooms have bathrooms with shower, whirlpool bath, television, radio and tea and coffee-making facilities. Also available is a four-poster Honeymoon Suite with circular bath. The elegant restaurant seats 100 guests. Food of the highest quality is freshly cooked and each night a 5-course dinner, plus coffee, is served, home-grown produce featuring prominently. Full luncheons and bar snacks are also obtainable. Social functions are expertly catered for. *RAC***.*

HAWKSMOOR,
Lake Road, Windermere,
Cumbria LA23 2EQ

Tel: 015394 42110

Licensed; All bedrooms with private bath/shower; Children welcome; Kendal 7 miles; £.

Hawksmoor is a friendly, family-run guest house offering peace and quiet for a relaxing holiday. It is also very well placed to enjoy all the local attractions and amenities: Lake Windermere is only minutes away and the town, with shops, information centre and railway station, is just as easy to reach. Twin, double and family bedrooms all have en suite bath or shower, individual heating, shaver points and colour TV; tea and coffee making facilities are also provided. Full English breakfast is served each morning, and delicious evening meals are available if required. Afterwards guests can relax with a drink in the cosy lounge. The Lake District is a perfect area to visit at any time of year, and special terms are available for off-season breaks. *ETB ♛♛♛ Highly Commended, AA Selected, RAC Highly Acclaimed.*

BEECH HILL HOTEL,
Windermere,
Cumbria LA23 3LR

Tel: 0153-94 42137
Fax: 0153-94 43745

Fully licensed; 50 bedrooms, all with private bathrooms; Children and pets welcome; Leisure and conference facilities; Lakeside near Newby 10 miles; ££.

The views of Lake Windermere and distant fells from the lounge bar, restaurant and the majority of the hotel's superb rooms are breathtaking, emphasising its lovely position. Beautiful terraced gardens reach down to the lake shore with its 60ft jetty and where sailing instruction may be arranged. Although visually beguiled, guests are unlikely to transfer attention from the cuisine for too long for the restaurant has a legendary reputation for its tempting choice of dishes. The hotel has a fine indoor heated pool and a sauna and solarium will aid relaxation. Sweet repose is assured at this hospitable place by attractive guest rooms replete with private bathroom and shower, television, telephone, radio and tea and coffee-making facilities. *CTB ♛♛♛♛ Commended, AA and RAC ***.*

Derbyshire

DONINGTON MANOR HOTEL,
High Street, Castle Donington,
Derby, Derbyshire DE7 2PP

Tel: 01332 810253
Fax: 01332 850330

Fully licensed; 36 bedrooms, all with private bathrooms; Children welcome; Conference facilities; Derby 8 miles, Nottingham 12 miles, M1 2 miles; ££.

Built as a posting house and coaching inn in 1794 and subsequently extended, this delightful place, now a country hotel of great distinction, retains its air of Regency elegance. The bowed, curved glass windows and decorative plasterwork ceiling in the Adam dining room remain to charm every aesthetic sense yet, in the guest rooms, the appointments represent practical sophistication including bathrooms en suite, colour television, radio, direct-dial telephone, baby alarm, tea and coffee making facilities, and central heating. The nine four-poster suites have exceptional appointments. The restaurant, open to non-residents, fosters a reputation for excellent cuisine, the à la carte menu featuring over 30 specialities. Conferences and social occasions are expertly catered for. *ETB ♛♛♛♛, RAC***.*

MAKENEY HALL COUNTRY HOUSE HOTEL,
Makeney, Milford,
Derbyshire DE56 0RS

Tel: 01332 842999
Fax: 01332 842777

Residential and restaurant licence; 45 bedrooms, all with private bathrooms; Conference facilities; Derby 6 miles; £££/££££.

Set in a restful location on the River Derwent, Makeney Hall is surrounded by over 6 acres of beautifully landscaped gardens just 10 minutes' drive from Derby. This quiet, capacious hotel, with its mid-Victorian features, offers guests a warm distinctive welcome and the carefully chosen decor imparts an air of bygone comfort. Bedrooms in the main house are spacious and individually appointed and many overlook the gardens; a splendid covered courtyard gives access to a further eighteen new rooms. Guests may dine in Lavinia's AA Rosette restaurant, where expert cooking and fresh local produce create cuisine of the highest standard. The fare is British in flavour and a selection of fine wines is available. Places of interest locally include the Derwent Valley — an Area of Outstanding Natural Beauty — the Peak District, the stately homes of Chatsworth and Haddon Hall, and Alton Towers.

Devon

DOWNREW HOUSE HOTEL, Bishops Tawton, Barnstaple, Devon EX32 0DY

Tel: 01271 42497/46673*
Fax: 01271 23947

Restaurant and residential licence; 12 bedrooms, all with private bathrooms; Historic interest; Children and pets welcome; Leisure and conference facilities; Barnstaple 2 miles; ££.

Escape to the rolling green countryside of rural North Devon for peace, utter relaxation and the holiday of a lifetime at this lovely old country house. Only four miles from Barnstaple and ideally placed for Exmoor, Dartmoor and the thousand-and-one unsophisticated pleasures of countryside and coast, elegant Downrew House was built in 1640 and extended during the reign of Queen Anne. More recent extensions have provided delightfully decorated guest rooms in the main house and coach house annexe, all of which have en suite facilities, colour television, radio, direct-dial telephone and coffee-makers. The views towards Dartmoor from the cosy drawing room and restaurant are breathtaking but not enough to divert attention for long from the excellent cuisine. One could spend a complete and rewarding holiday without venturing beyond the confines of the picturesque grounds of 12 acres. Stroll in the gardens, take a dip in a superb heated swimming pool sheltered by lush greenery, burnish up that tan in the solarium, challenge expertise (or otherwise!) on the approach and putt golf course and return to the house for a game on the full-sized billiard table. Diversions away from the hotel include coastal walks, golf, horse riding, pony trekking and coarse and fly fishing quite apart from a variety of local sights to see. Fun-packed hours but do leave time to return to eat — it is well worth it! *WCTB* 👑👑👑👑 *Commended, RAC**, Ashley Courtenay.*

BLAGDON MANOR COUNTRY HOTEL,

Ashwater, Beaworthy,
Devon EX21 5DF

Tel: 01409 211224
Fax: 01409 211634

Restaurant and residential licence; 7 bedrooms, all with private bathrooms; Historic interest; Leisure facilities; Holsworthy 6 miles; ££.

As one approaches, this mid-17th century manor is a joy to behold. Built on the site of a Saxon edifice, the beautifully restored, Grade II listed building nestles amidst a tapestry of rolling green fields and noble trees. There are 8 acres of pleasant grounds in which to stroll, practise golf or play croquet whilst within the Hotel's walls, all is unpretentious elegance and supreme comfort, especially emphasised in the en suite bedrooms. Guests dine together in house party style as they appreciate the finest English cooking. Quiet evening diversion is provided by a library, snooker table and bar. *WCTB ♛♛♛ Highly Commended.*

HALMPSTONE MANOR COUNTRY HOUSE,

Bishop's Tawton, Barnstaple,
Devon EX32 0EA

Tel: 01271 830321*
Fax: 01271 830826

Fully licensed; 5 bedrooms, all with private bathrooms; Historic interest; Pets welcome; Conference facilities; Instow 3 miles; ££££.

A mellow country house in the finest English tradition, Halmpstone is an idyllic retreat with a history as rich as the verdant North Devon countryside that surrounds it. First mention of the manor appeared in 1166 and of the house itself in 1630 when it was owned by one John Mulys. His detailed will gives a fascinating insight of how the mansion was furnished and decorated in the 17th century. Today, intimate, tranquil and utterly charming, the house has magnificently appointed accommodation for the discriminating — romantic four-poster, brass and coronet beds, sumptuous bathrooms, harmonious furnishings and comforts to cosset and captivate. And to complete the tantalising picture, the imaginative, award-winning cuisine which only one word describes — inspired!

THE PINES AT EASTLEIGH, Eastleigh, Near Bideford, Devon EX39 4PA

Tel: 01271 860561

Restaurant and residential licence; 6 bedrooms, 5 en suite; Historic interest; Children and pets welcome; Bideford 2 miles; £.

A Georgian house set in seven acres with glorious views from the grounds towards Bideford and the sea at Hartland Point and Lundy Island. All rooms have colour television, direct-dial telephone and tea/coffee making facilities. The beach, Exmoor and Torridge Valley are minutes away. Enjoy fine farmhouse-style food, a quiet drink in the residents' bar, and browse our collection of maps and books. The hotel has full central heating. We are well placed for golfing, riding, watersports and cycle hire. Short breaks available. ♛♛, *AA QQQ, RAC Acclaimed.*

BEACONSIDE COUNTRY HOUSE HOTEL, Landcross, Near Bideford, Devon EX39 5JL

Tel: 01237 477205

Licensed; 9 bedrooms, 5 with private bathrooms; Children welcome, pets by arrangement; Leisure and conference facilities; Bideford 2 miles; £.

Nestling in lush countryside only a few miles from where the Taw and Torridge flow into Bideford Bay, this lovely Victorian house is set in 25 acres of grounds, a feature of which is the woodland trail and water garden, a delightful hour's walk. Guests may also find active diversion in the swimming pool and playing tennis. In this peaceful setting relaxation comes easily and pleasant moments may be spent watching a variety of wildlife from the windows. Comfort and contentment is the order of the day. Each bedroom is centrally heated and has colour television and bathroom or shower en suite. The cuisine is the final ingredient in a memorable holiday mix with a traditional English breakfast that will sustain for hours. *AA***.*

THE EDGEMOOR, Haytor Road, Bovey Tracey, Devon TQ13 9LE

Tel: 01626 832466
Fax: 01626 834760

Residential and restaurant licence; 12 bedrooms, all with private bathrooms; Historic interest; Children and pets welcome; Conference facilities; Exeter 12 miles, Newton Abbot 8; ££.

Set in two acres of delightful gardens, minutes from the A38 Exeter to Plymouth road and on the edge of Dartmoor, The Edgemoor is ideally located for enjoying the beauty of the surrounding countryside. The delightfully decorated bedrooms are all en suite, with direct-dial telephone, television, tea-making facilities, hairdryer, trouser press and other thoughtful details. The hotel bar and lounge offer comfortable surroundings, and the candlelit restaurant has a wide selection of French and English dishes, accompanied by a carefully chosen wine list. There are many interesting and beautiful riverside and moorland walks nearby; fishing, shooting and golf are available locally. ♛♛♛♛ *Highly Commended, AA*** and Rosette, RAC ***, Johansens, Les Routiers.* **See also Colour Advertisement on page 7.**

BRACKEN HOUSE,
Bratton Fleming, Barnstaple,
Devon EX31 4TG

Tel: 01598 710320*

Residential and restaurant licence; 8 bedrooms, all with private bathrooms; Children over 8 years and pets welcome; Barnstaple 6 miles; £.

Situated on the western edge of Exmoor, this attractive hotel was formerly a wealthy, college-endowed rectory. It is set in eight peaceful acres of garden, pasture, pond and woodland with extensive views across a rural landscape to Bideford Bay and Hartland Point in the far distance. The eight en suite bedrooms include two on the ground floor. Interesting Devon food is cooked with care in an Aga. Service is both friendly and efficient. Dogs are welcome to bring well-trained owners. It is convenient for Arlington, Marwood, Rosemoor and the spectacular Exmoor coastline. Self catering cottage for two also available. ♛♛♛ *Highly Commended, AA QQQQ Selected.*

GIPSY HILL HOTEL,
Gipsy Hill Lane, Pinhoe, Exeter,
Devon EX1 3RN

Tel: 01392 465252
Fax: 01392 464302

Fully licensed; 38 bedrooms, all with private bathrooms; Children welcome, pets by arrangement; Conference facilities; Moretonhampstead 12 miles; £££.

We have seen this fine hotel prosper over the years, keeping abreast of modern expectations and honing its standards of accommodation, cuisine and service. It lies in 3 acres of attractive gardens and many of its handsomely appointed rooms have splendid views over the countryside to the coast. All have en suite facilities, remote-control colour television, radio, courtesy tray, trouser press and hair dryer; two are delightful four-poster rooms. The light and spacious restaurant sports interesting table d'hôte and à la carte menus and is open to non-residents. Conveniently placed for business or excursions to Dartmoor and the coast, the hotel is less than a mile from Junction 30 of the M5 and only a few hundred yards from the A30. *WCTB* ♛♛♛♛ *Commended, AA/RAC ***.*

FAIRWATER HEAD COUNTRY HOUSE HOTEL,
Hawkchurch,
Devon EX13 5TX

Tel: 01297 678349*

Licensed; 20 bedrooms, all with private bathrooms; Children and dogs welcome; Lyme Regis 5 miles, Axminster 3; ££££.

A peaceful country house with magnificent views across the Exe Valley and set in one of Ashley Courtenay's "ten best hotel gardens in Britain". No conferences or wedding receptions or taped background music. Award-winning restaurant and highest rated AA*** hotel in the area. Family hospitality. Golf at reduced green fees at Lyme Regis, and endless places of interest nearby. *ETB* ♛♛♛♛. **See also Colour Advertisement on page 6.**

FOSFELLE COUNTRY HOUSE HOTEL,
Hartland, Bideford,
Devon EX39 6EF

Tel: 01237 441273

Fully licensed; 7 bedrooms, 4 with private bathrooms; Historic interest; Children and pets welcome; Clovelly 4 miles; £.

This 17th century manor house is set in six acres of grounds in peaceful surroundings with large ornamental gardens and lawns. Fosfelle offers a friendly atmosphere with excellent food, a licensed bar, and a television lounge with log fires on chilly evenings; central heating throughout. There is a games room for children. The comfortable bedrooms, some en suite, all have washbasins and tea making facilities; family rooms and cots are available. Within easy reach of local beaches and ideal for touring Devon and Cornwall. Trout and coarse fishing, clay shooting available at the hotel; riding and golf nearby. Open all year. Reductions for children. *AA Listed.*

THE BEL ALP HOUSE,
Haytor, Near Bovey Tracey,
Devon TQ13 9XX

Tel: 01364 661217*

Residential and restaurant licence; 9 bedrooms, all with private bathrooms; Children and pets welcome; Plymouth 33 miles, Exeter 14; ££££.

This happily-placed and elegant Edwardian country mansion is, in essence, a magnificently furnished family house that has opened its doors for the delectation of guests. Lovingly cared for by the Curnock family, the house holds many architectural delights characterised by sweeping arches, an impressive oak staircase and high-ceilinged and spacious rooms to which the warm decor, rich furnishings and antiques act as the perfect complement. Nestling in beautiful grounds on the hillside, 900 feet up on the fringe of Dartmoor, the house enjoys breathtaking views. Here the highest standards of comfort, hospitality and good food obtain — all the ingredients for a perfect holiday in a perfect setting. With all three "Merit Awards" at Three Stars from both the AA and RAC, and "Highly Commended" grading and Four Crowns from the Tourist Board.

THE BELFRY COUNTRY HOTEL, Yarcombe, Honiton, Devon EX14 9BD

Tel: 01404 861234
Fax: 01404 861579

Residential and restaurant licence; 6 bedrooms, all with private bathrooms; Children over 12 years and pets welcome; Honiton 7 miles, Chard 5; £.

The skilfully converted Victorian village school has been tastefully refurbished to offer the comforts and luxuries of a country house hotel. Each en suite room is comprehensively equipped and has beautiful views over the Yarty valley. It is ideally placed for touring the West Country and visiting the many National Trust properties, sporting activities, places of scenic beauty and coastal resorts nearby. Free entry to 10 classic gardens of South Somerset and East Devon. Jackie and Tony Rees, the resident proprietors, offer a warm welcome to their guests. Jackie's home cooking has been awarded an AA Rosette for high quality; the table d'hôte menu changes daily and there is a small but superb à la carte menu. The cosy restaurant with its corner bar and log fire, comfortable lounge and pretty, terraced garden make this a peaceful, relaxing and friendly hotel of high quality. *Commended, AA** 74%.*

DEER PARK HOTEL, Buckerell Village, Honiton, Devon EX14 0PG

Tel: 01404 41266
Fax: 01404 46598

Residential licence; 28 bedrooms, all with private bathrooms; Historic interest; Children welcome, pets in mews only; Honiton 3 miles; ££/£££.

A Georgian squire's mansion set in 30 acres of parkland, the impressive Deer Park Hotel retains the lofty hauteur of the period, its all-round elegance enhanced by the excellent modern amenities that have been introduced. The cuisine represents country house cooking at its very best. Guests soon respond to the convivial atmosphere and the holiday options of the area are manifold: the East Devon seaside resorts are easily reached as are the rugged expanses of Exmoor and Dartmoor. Five miles of fishing rights on the River Otter, a heated open-air swimming pool, sauna and solarium plus other sporting activities are available. *AA and RAC***.*

LIFTON HALL COUNTRY HOUSE HOTEL, Lifton, Devon PL16 0DR

Tel: 01566 784863/784263
Fax: 01566 784770

Fully licensed; 11 bedrooms, all with private bathrooms; Historic interest; Children welcome, kennels for dogs; Leisure and conference facilities; Launceston 4 miles; £££.

Recently the subject of complete renovation and refurbishment, this delightful, 400-year-old country house deep in the leafy fastness of West Devon, exhibits flair and imagination in its determination to please. Credit for this apparent personification must go to Owners, Mary and Gary Dodds who have supervised every detail of this revelation. The restaurant menu makes fascinating reading, an exercise calculated to stimulate the salivary ducts: such variety and at such reasonable prices, too! We were particularly impressed by the way the superb guest rooms have been appointed with thoughtful and much appreciated extras as thick towelling bath robes, hand-wrapped soaps and snug duvets provided. Riding, pony trekking, shooting and fishing may be arranged locally. So much to enjoy inside and out! *, AA Two Red Rosettes.*

MANOR HOUSE HOTEL & GOLF COURSE, Moretonhampstead, Devon TQ13 8RE

Tel: 01647 440355
Fax: 01647 440961

Licensed; 89 bedrooms, all with private bathrooms; Children and pets welcome; Leisure facilities; Exeter 17 miles; ££££.

Set on the edge of beautiful Dartmoor, a luxury 4 star Hotel, with ornate public rooms and comfortable en suite bedrooms, some featuring superb views of the North Bovey Valley. Our new Chef, Tim Marchant, invites you to enjoy superb cuisine, using only the finest local produce in our Hambleden Restaurant. Play golf on one of England's finest inland Championship courses and relax in 270 acres of glorious private estate, offering Tennis, Fishing, Shooting, Squash and more. *AA **** RAC.* **See also Colour Advertisement on page 7.**

LYDFORD HOUSE HOTEL,
Lydford, Okehampton,
Devon EX20 4AU

Tel: 01822 820347
Fax: 01822 820442

Licensed; 13 bedrooms, all with private bathrooms; Children over 5 welcome; Exeter 33 miles, Plymouth 25; ££.

On the fringe of Dartmoor, this splendid early Victorian house is one of the finest country hotels in the area. Centrally heated throughout, the delightful guest rooms all have colour television, direct-dial telephones, radio, tea/coffee making facilities, and private bathrooms and WCs. Food here is a high priority, starting with a full English breakfast and concluding with a superb dinner, with a wide choice at each course. There is a comfortable lounge, with a log fire in winter, and a cosy cocktail bar with lounge adjoining. Fishing and golfing enthusiasts are well catered for nearby. Free use of local keep-fit and leisure pool facilities for residents. The hotel has its own stables in the grounds, serving riders of all ages and abilities. Inclusive riding holidays or riding by the hour is offered for the entire family at reasonable rates. *ETB* ♛♛♛♛.

WHITE HART HOTEL,
The Square, Moretonhampstead,
Devon TQ13 8NF

Tel: 01647 440406
Fax: 01647 440565

Fully licensed; 20 bedrooms, all with private bathrooms; Historic interest; Children over 10 years welcome; Exeter 11 miles; £££.

Moretonhampstead is the "gateway" to the 365 square miles that make up the Dartmoor National Park, ideal for walking and relaxing. The White Hart, an historic coaching inn, has stood in the town square for over 350 years. It has 20 de-luxe en suite bedrooms, with colour television, courtesy trays, hairdryers and telephones; bathrooms have power showers, big fluffy towels and complimentary toiletries. The restaurant is famous for good food (and plenty of it!), using local meat, fresh fish, vegetables, and cream from Devon farms. Bar snacks are served in our cosy lounge and in the oak-beamed bar which has a selection of real ales. "The most famous coaching inn on Dartmoor." Recommended by leading food and travel guides of the world. ♛♛♛♛ *Highly Commended, AA and RAC **, Egon Ronay, Logis.*

MILL END HOTEL,
Sandypark, Chagford, Newton Abbot, Devon TQ13 8JN

Tel: 01647 432282
Fax: 01647 433106

Residential and restaurant licence; 16 bedrooms, all with private bathrooms; Historic interest; Children and pets welcome; Moretonhampstead 4 miles; ££.

Converted from a working mill, Mill End has retained all its rural charm. The mill wheel still turns in the courtyard and the Teign which runs by the door is one of the ten best sea-trout rivers in the country, with fishing available to guests. The gardens and walks are delightful and the hotel is ideal as a touring centre for the West. Then again, you could just sleep! Single, double, twin and triple bedrooms are available, all with private bathrooms. ♛♛♛♛ *Highly Commended, AA and RAC***, Good Hotel Guide.* **See also Colour Advertisement on page 7.**

FLUXTON FARM HOTEL,
Ottery St Mary, Devon EX11 1RJ

Tel: 01404 812818

Restaurant and residential licence; 12 bedrooms, 10 with private bathrooms; Historic interest; Children and dogs welcome; Exeter 11 miles; £.

This lovely sixteenth century farmhouse is situated in the beautiful Otter Valley, with two acre gardens including a stream, trout pond, garden railway and putting green. Superb home cooking, prepared from fresh local produce, is served in the beamed, candlelit dining room, and there are two comfortable lounges, one non-smoking. All double bedrooms have central heating, en suite facilities and Teasmaids. Peace and quiet, all mod cons. Pets are welcome free of charge. This is a cat lovers' paradise. This beautiful part of Devon is convenient for touring, and the beach at Sidmouth is only four miles away. *ETB ♛♛♛, AA Listed.*

BROWNLANDS COUNTRY HOUSE HOTEL,
Brownlands Road, Sidmouth, Devon EX10 9AG

Tel: 01395 513053*

Fully licensed; 14 bedrooms, all with private bathrooms; Historic interest; Leisure facilities; Exeter 13 miles; ££/£££.

Sidmouth's only Country House Hotel, nestling on the wooded slopes of Salcombe Hill, in the heart of the countryside, yet within a mile of Sidmouth and the seafront. Relax in the garden room and enjoy the beautiful views across Sidmouth and Lyme Bay — a perfect escape to peace and quiet. For the energetic there is an all-weather tennis court or enjoy a gentle game on the putting green. *RAC** and HRC Awards, AA** 76% and One Red Rosette.*

ELFORDLEIGH HOTEL AND COUNTRY CLUB,

Colebrook, Plympton, Devon PL7 5EB

Tel: 01752 336428
Fax: 01752 344581

Fully licensed; 18 bedrooms, all with private bathrooms; Historic interest; Children welcome; Leisure and conference facilities; Plymouth 4 miles; £££.

Within easy reach of the fine modern city of Plymouth, which rose like a Phoenix from its wartime ashes, this ultra-luxurious hotel and country club stands imposingly in its own, lovely 65-acre grounds, surrounded by its own golf course (Par 68) and with Dartmoor and the coast added nearby attractions. Sports enthusiasts may not be tempted to venture far, however, for the leisure facilities at this super holiday haven (heaven!) are breathtaking. One may work out in a well-equipped gym, splash or swim in either the indoor or outdoor pool, play tennis on the all-weather courts, jog on a special track and play snooker, pool and table tennis. And for the younger set, there is a play area with a variety of entertainments. Jacuzzi, sauna, steam room and sunbeds aid relaxation and there is even a beauty therapist. Magnificently furnished, the accommodation is of the very highest order and the à la carte and table d'hôte cuisine available in two charming restaurants is memorable. There are several cheerful bars and a coffee lounge where light snacks are served. Aided by friendly personal service, this is a complete holiday resort in its own right, outstanding in every respect. Superb facilities for conferences and functions also exist. 👑👑👑👑, *AA and RAC ***.*

MARSH HALL COUNTRY HOUSE HOTEL,

South Molton,
Devon EX36 3HQ

Tel: 01769 572666*
Fax: 01769 574230

Restaurant and residential licence; 7 bedrooms, all with private bathrooms; Conference facilities; Barnstaple 11 miles; ££.

On the gentle slopes of the Exmoor National Park in delightful grounds of 3 acres, Marsh Hall dates, in part, from the 17th century. Rooms are spacious and elegantly appointed with modern conveniences mixing happily with its period features, the latter including a magnificent stained glass window that dominates the sweeping staircase. The well-proportioned bedrooms are furnished to a high standard of comfort, amenities including controllable central heating, colour television, clock/radio alarm, direct-dial telephone and tea and coffee-making facilities. The impressive Squire's Room has a large four-poster bed and curved bathroom. The cuisine is of the highest calibre with vegetarian meals and special diets catered for by prior request. *WCTB* ♛♛♛♛ *Highly Commended, AA Rosette for Food.*

PRINCE HALL HOTEL,

Two Bridges, Yelverton,
Devon PL20 6SA

Tel: 01822 890403*
Fax: 01822 890676

Residential licence; 8 bedrooms, all with private bathrooms; Historic interest; Dogs welcome; Tavistock 8 miles, Yelverton 7; £££ (DB&B).

The Prince Hall Hotel is a small, friendly and relaxed country house hotel, in a peaceful and secluded setting, commanding glorious views over open moorland. All bedrooms are en suite; some have four-poster beds. The hotel offers gourmet cooking by the French owner-chef, walks from the hotel, fishing, riding and golf all close by. *ETB* ♛♛♛ *Commended, AA and RAC **, Ashley Courtenay and Johansens Recommended.*

WOOLACOMBE BAY HOTEL, Woolacombe, Devon EX34 7BN

Tel: 01271 870388*

Licensed; 59 bedrooms, all with private bathrooms; Children welcome; Leisure facilities; Lynton 21 miles, Ilfracombe 6; ££/£££.

An elegant, gracious *** hotel set in six acres of grounds running down to Woolacombe's three miles of golden sands and Blue Flag beach. Built in the days of gracious living, the hotel exudes a feeling of luxury and traditional style, coupled with a lively sporting complex with unlimited use of tennis, indoor and outdoor pools, steam room, spa bath, sauna, solarium, billiards, children's club, our NEW fitness centre and much more. All rooms with bath, toilet, shower, hairdryer, TV, radio, satellite TV, direct-dial telephone, tea-making facilities and baby listening. Relaxation is easy, but for the person with boundless energy the Woolacombe Bay Hotel has a sportsman's choice of amenities and a variety of indoor pursuits available. Traditional Christmas Breaks — a Winter Wonderland of gracious living. Write for brochure to Mr C.H. Holiday. *ETB ♛♛♛♛♛ Highly Commended, AA and RAC ***. An elegant hotel on Devon's golden coast.*

Dorset

BRIDGE HOUSE HOTEL, 3 Prout Bridge, Beaminster, Dorset DT8 3AY

Tel: 01308 862200
Fax: 01308 863700

Restaurant and residential licence; 14 bedrooms, all with private bathrooms; Historic interest; Children and pets welcome; Conference facilities; Bridport 5 miles; £££.

Delightful little Beaminster is one of our favourite Hardy Country haunts. Fitting well into the scene, Bridge House is a typical clergy house dating back to the 13th century. Open fires, oak beams and candlelit dining room create a wonderfully laid-back atmosphere yet unobtrusive modern appointments await to serve the needs of today. Rooms are charmingly furnished and full of character, each guest room having en suite facilities, colour television and tea and coffee-makers; most have a direct-dial telephone and some are on the ground floor. As for cuisine, this hospitable little hotel has an award-winning restaurant making superb use of fresh local produce, well supported by an intriguing wine list. *AA***, 2 Rosettes.*

ANVIL HOTEL,
Salisbury Road, Pimperne, Blandford, Dorset DT11 8UQ

Tel: 01258 453431/480182

Fully licensed free house; 10 bedrooms, all with private bathrooms; Historic interest; Children and pets welcome; London 107 miles, Salisbury 24, Bournemouth 26, Poole 16; ££££ (double room).

A long, low, thatched building set in a tiny village deep in the Dorset countryside — what could be more English? And that is what visitors to the Anvil will find — a typical old English hostelry offering good, old-fashioned English hospitality. A mouthwatering full à la carte menu with delicious desserts is available in the charming beamed and flagged restaurant, and a wide selection of bar meals in the attractive, fully licensed bar. All bedrooms have private facilities. Ample parking. Clay pigeon shooting and tuition for individuals. ♛♛♛ *Commended, AA**, Good Food Pub Guide, Les Routiers.*

ROUNDHAM HOUSE HOTEL,
Roundham Gardens, West Bay Road, Bridport, Dorset DT6 4BD

Tel: 01308 422753*
Fax: 01308 421145

Restaurant and residential licence; 8 bedrooms, all with private bathrooms; Children welcome; Dorchester 14 miles; £.

This splendid small hotel offers kind personal attention, homely comforts and superlative food which has regularly attracted the Red Rosette Award from the AA. Fresh, mainly 'cooked to order' meals are offered from a well-balanced table d'hôte menu which is changed daily. Conveniently situated in an elevated position between Bridport and West Bay, the house stands in a lovely garden which supplies much of the produce used. Sustenance of a liquid variety is dispensed in an attractive lounge bar. The decor and furnishings throughout are a joy to behold and the comfortable and spacious bedrooms each have a private bathroom/shower and toilet. ♛♛♛ *Commended.*

EYPE'S MOUTH COUNTRY HOTEL,
Eype, Bridport, Dorset DT6 6AL

Tel: 01308 423300
Fax: 01308 420033

Fully licensed; 18 bedrooms, all with private bathrooms; Children and pets welcome; Conference facilities; Dorchester 14 miles; £.

We first discovered this quiet and comfortable retreat some while ago and our opinion of it has grown with the years. A country lane off the A35, a mile or so to the west of Bridport, leads down to the hotel and the sea, a delectable and tranquil spot. There is everything here for a relaxing and memorable holiday; a fine old-world cellar bar with garden patio overlooking the sea, an attractive restaurant presenting gourmet-acclaimed à la carte and table d'hôte fare with an extensive wine list and accommodation in the multi-starred class. All rooms have en suite facilities, colour television, telephone and tea and coffee-makers as well as superb views. A peaceful holiday haven in scenic West Dorset. *AA/RAC**.*

BROADVIEW,
East Street, Crewkerne, Near Yeovil
(Dorset Border), Somerset TA18 7AG

Tel: 01460 73424

Unlicensed; 3 bedrooms, all with private bathrooms; Children welcome, pets by arrangement; Yeovil 8 miles; £.

Friendly, informal atmosphere — extremely comfortable and relaxing in an unusual colonial ambience. Carefully furnished en suite rooms have easy chairs, colour television, tea/coffee making facilities and central heating. Set in "National Garden Scheme" feature gardens with many unusual plants. Enjoy award-winning traditional English home cooking; stay a while and explore varied and contrasting places, National Trust gardens, houses, moors, quaint old villages, Dorset coast and Hardy country (a list is provided of 50 places). This is a no smoking house. Open all year. *ETB* ♛♛♛ *De Luxe, AA QQQQQ Premier Selected (both top quality awards).*

MILLMEAD COUNTRY HOUSE HOTEL,
Goose Hill, Portesham,
Dorset DT3 4HE

Tel: 01305 871432
Fax: 01305 871884

Residential and restaurant licence; 6 bedrooms, all with private bathrooms; Pets welcome; Weymouth 6 miles; ££.

Steeped in history and immortalised by Thomas Hardy, the countryside around the village of Portesham, West Dorset, is designated an Area of Outstanding Natural Beauty. West Dorset offers an abundance of stately homes, ancient monuments, museums, craft workshops, and tourist attractions for both young and old. Close to Abbotsbury with its world famous Swannery, sub-tropical gardens and Abbey, and Chesil Beach. All rooms are en suite, with colour television, radio alarm clock, hairdryer, and complimentary tea, coffee and hot chocolate; some rooms are on the ground floor. After exploring the surrounding countryside, return to the comfort of the hotel and relax and recoup while enjoying a finely prepared evening meal, where local and home grown produce is regularly used. ♛♛♛ *Commended, AA and RAC **, Logis, Minotels.*

The £ symbol when appearing at the end of the italic section of an entry shows the anticipated price, during 1996, for **single full Bed and Breakfast.**

Under £35	**£**	**Over £50 but under £65**	**£££**
Over £35 but under £50	**££**	**Over £65**	**££££**

This is meant as an indication only and does not show prices for Special Breaks, Weekends, etc. Guests are therefore advised to verify all prices on enquiring or booking.

THE DOWER HOUSE HOTEL, Rousdon, Near Lyme Regis, Dorset DT7 3RB

Tel: 01297 21047
Fax: 01297 24748

Fully licensed; 9 bedrooms, all with private bathrooms; Children and pets welcome; Leisure facilities; Lyme Regis 3 miles; ££.

This beautiful, family-run country house hotel stands in its own lawned and wooded grounds, which ensures safe and convenient parking. All rooms are en suite, with central heating, colour television, radio, telephone, beverage tray and hairdryer. Guests can enjoy open fires, fine cuisine and old-fashioned courteous service; amenities include an indoor heated swimming pool and sauna. There are many lovely walks in the area, as well as the bracing coastal footpath, and golf can be played nearby. Special Winter and Spring Breaks. Colour brochure, sample menu and tariff on request. 👑👑👑👑 *Highly Commended, RAC ***, Ashley Courtenay Recommended.*

KNOLL HOUSE HOTEL, Studland, Near Swanage, Dorset BH19 3AZ

Tel: 01929 450450*

Restaurant and residential licence; 80 bedrooms, 56 with private bathrooms, including 30 family suites; Children and dogs welcome; Leisure facilities; Corfe Castle 6 miles, Sandbanks Ferry 3; Full Board £££/££££.

On the Dorset Heritage coast this delightful hotel is surrounded by National Trust land and some of the prettiest scenery in the West Country. Knoll House is an independent country house hotel under the personal management of its owners. It overlooks three miles of beach from an attractive setting in pine trees and pleasant gardens, and offers facilities for sport and relaxation that must be counted amongst the finest in the country — two hard tennis courts, a pitch and putt course and a swimming pool. The Health Spa offers a sauna, steam room, jacuzzi and other leisure pursuits. Young children are catered for in their own dining room. **See advertisement Inside Back Cover.**

PLUMBER MANOR,
Sturminster Newton,
Dorset DT10 2AF

Tel: 01258 472507*
Fax: 01258 473370

Fully licensed; 16 bedrooms, all with private bathrooms; Historic interest; Children and pets welcome; Leisure and conference facilities; Blandford 8 miles; ££££.

Set in tranquil and lovely grounds and surrounded by all the delights of Hardy's Dorset countryside, this is very much a family home being owned by the Prideaux-Brunes dynasty since the early 17th century. A real 'away-from-it-all' gem, it prefers to be styled as a restaurant with bedrooms, the emphasis, naturally enough, being on the excellent dinners served here. However, the standard of accommodation is just as high, guest rooms in the main house, converted barn and courtyard being charmingly appointed. There is a hard tennis court and croquet lawn in the grounds and there are numerous opportunities for country sports in the vicinity. Free stabling is available on a do-it-yourself basis with a full livery service nearby. *SETB* ♛♛♛.

Durham

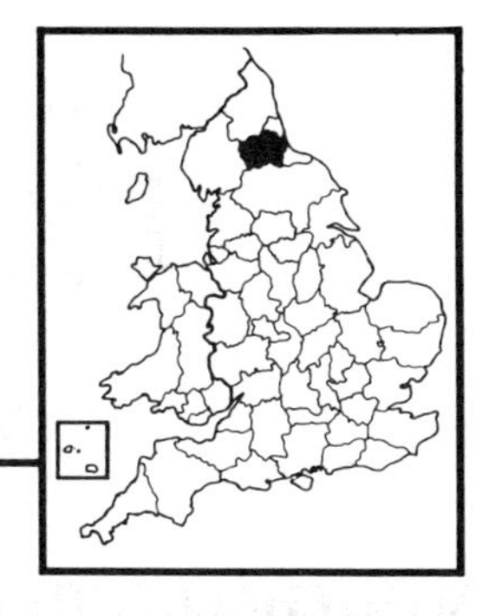

BOWBURN HALL HOTEL,
Bowburn,
Co. Durham DH6 5NH

Tel: 0191 3770311
Fax: 0191 3773459

Fully licensed; 19 bedrooms, all with private bathrooms; Children and pets welcome; Conference facilities; Durham 4 miles; ££.

The light and spacious rooms of this fine hotel on the outskirts of Durham City are tastefully decorated and impeccably furnished in contemporary style. All the en suite guest rooms have colour television, radio and telephone; premier rooms have king-size beds, hair dryers and trouser presses. Standing in 5 acres of garden and woodland, the hotel is known for its excellent traditional English cuisine, meals being served in a charmingly refurbished restaurant and new conservatory extension which attracts the maximum amount of sunlight as befitting such a cheerful and informal venue. A visit to the lounge and bar area for a drink and/or tasty snack will establish the happy atmosphere. *ETB* ♛♛♛♛.

RAVEN COUNTRY HOTEL,
Broomhill, Ebchester,
Co. Durham DH8 6RY

Tel: 01207 560367
Fax: 01207 560262

Licensed; 28 bedrooms, all with private bathrooms; Children welcome; Conference facilities; Consett 3 miles; £££.

In a quiet rural setting but within easy reach of Newcastle, Gateshead Metro Centre and Durham, this spruce, relaxing hotel combines stylish comfort with a flair for tasteful colour schemes. Its main components are arranged in contiguous single-storey fashion yet a very English ambience shines through for which the friendly and efficient staff deserves much credit. Each en suite bedroom enjoys fine views and incorporates facilities in the best contemporary mode with a choice of twin, double or family rooms. The attractive lounge bar is a popular meeting place and an interesting selection of bar meals is on offer. For more formal dining, the Conservatory Restaurant is well known for its excellent standard of luncheon and dinner dishes. ♛♛♛♛, *AA*** and Rosette for Cuisine.*

Essex

WHITEHALL HOTEL,
Broxted,
Essex CM6 2BZ

Tel: 01279 850603
Fax: 01279 850385

Restaurant licence; 25 bedrooms, all with private bathrooms; Historic interest; Children welcome; Leisure and conference facilities; Thaxted 3 miles; ££££.

This lovely old Elizabethan manor house sits on a hillside overlooking a peaceful and undulating countryside. Founded by the Keane family in 1985 its comfort and cuisine are of the highest order, the latter known internationally for its excellence. Suites and guest rooms are luxuriously appointed and feature many thoughtful extras. Its ease of access renders the hotel a popular rendezvous for businessmen — Stansted Airport and the M11 are only ten minutes' drive away and there are helicopter landing facilities in the grounds. Those who fancy the sporting life are well catered for with a swimming pool and hard tennis court in the grounds; Newmarket races are a nearby attraction and clay pigeon shooting, trout fishing and golf may be arranged locally. ♛♛♛♛.

PONTLANDS PARK COUNTRY HOTEL,
West Hanningfield Road, Great Baddow, Near Chelmsford, Essex CM2 8HR

Tel: 01245 476444
Fax: 01245 478393

Licensed; 17 bedrooms, all with private bathrooms; Children welcome; Leisure and conference facilities; London 30 miles; ££££.

A grand Victorian mansion built on the site of a mid-16th century building, Pontlands Park was tastefully converted into a country hotel in 1981, since when it has become acknowledged as a holiday complex with additions and improvements constantly being made. Today, it attracts discriminating guests by reason of its luxurious hotel facilities and superb Trimmers Leisure Centre in the grounds. Here, the indoor and outdoor swimming pools, jacuzzis and sauna may be enjoyed free of charge by residents. Available within the hotel at extra cost and by appointment are hairdressing and beauty treatments, figure toning and dance classes. The conference and function amenities that can be arranged are some of the best in the country. Guest rooms are spacious and individually appointed to a very high standard and incorporate bathrooms en suite, colour television, radio, direct-dial telephone and such thoughtful extras as trouser presses, hair dryers, fresh fruit and even bath robes on request. The outstanding cuisine deserves special mention; the restaurant offers a wide variety of menus throughout and is open from Tuesday to Friday for lunch and from Monday to Saturday for dinner. Special events are held regularly throughout the year in the silk-lined marquee at very reasonable prices. *ETB ♛♛♛♛♛ Highly Commended, AA****.*

KINGSFORD PARK HOTEL,
Layer Road, Colchester, Essex CO2 0HS

Tel: 01206 734301
Fax: 01206 734512

Licensed; 10 bedrooms, all with private bathrooms; Children and pets welcome; Elmstead Market 4 miles; £££.

An elegant 18th century house transformed into a superb country hotel in the swinging 60's, Kingsford Park has been in the hands of the Mussi family for over 25 years. That their tenure has been an unqualified success is almost an understatement for, backed by understanding and attentive service, an unmatched reputation has been built up for supremely comfortable accommodation and remarkable cuisine. Bedrooms, blessed with uninterrupted country views, are luxuriously appointed, each having a bathroom en suite, an emperor-size bed and a plethora of modern conveniences, including colour television, radio, direct-dial telephone, mini-bar and tea and coffee-making facilities. Special mention must be made of the romantic Honeymoon Suite with its antique posted bed — every bride's dream! Opening out on to lawns and parkland, extending to 20 acres, La Terrazza Ristorante is a charming place in which to dine, its superb cuisine presenting a varied and tempting choice of Italian dishes. Quiet moments may be spent in a cosy cocktail bar warmed by a cheerful log fire in chilly weather and morning coffee and afternoon tea is served here. Well organised in every respect, the hotel is a popular venue for social events of all types, being only two miles from Colchester Town Centre and five minutes from the A12. *EATB ♛♛♛ Commended.*

THE BELL INN AND HILL HOUSE, High Road, Horndon-on-the-Hill, Essex SS17 8LD

Tel: 01375 673154/642463
Fax: 01375 361611

Fully licensed; 14 bedrooms, all with private bathrooms; Historic interest; Children welcome; Conference facilities; Basildon 5 miles; ££/£££ (double).

At first sight an attractive private house, closer inspection reveals this 17th century building to have been discreetly transformed into a charming little country hotel in a gem of a village setting. The facilities, too, would shame many a multi-starred establishment although the atmosphere here is far more friendly and relaxed. Guest rooms, all of individual character, have bathrooms en suite (some with spa baths), teletext television and direct-dial telephone, whilst, in the courtyard, a stable block has been converted into a self-contained unit with a spiral staircase leading to a bedroom that was originally a hayloft. A delightful restaurant with a huge fireplace offers enjoyment of an interesting and imaginative cuisine, popular with non-residents as well. Good news spreads fast.

Gloucestershire

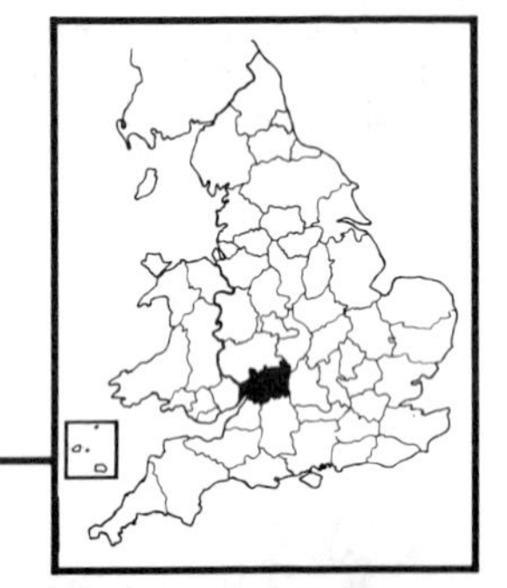

CHARLTON KINGS HOTEL, Cheltenham, Gloucestershire GL52 6UU

Tel: 01242 231061
Fax: 01242 241900

Restaurant and residential licence; 14 bedrooms, all with private bathrooms; Children and dogs welcome; Bourton-on-the-Water 12 miles, Tewkesbury 10, Winchcombe 8; £££.

The ideal venue for Cheltenham and the Cotswolds situated in an acre of garden in an area of outstanding natural beauty on the edge of town. Newly opened in 1991 after extensive refurbishment. All rooms (some reserved for non-smokers) have views of the Cotswold Hills, which are easily reached on foot — there is a footpath right alongside the hotel leading onto the famous Cotswold Way. There is plenty to do and see (our room information folder lists over 200 sights/activities), or simply watch the world go by from the conservatory. During your stay you will be tempted to try our cosy restaurant offering an imaginative and varied menu. Above all, we offer a standard of service only a small hotel can provide. *ETB* 👑👑👑👑 *Highly Commended, Johansens Recommended.*

PRESTBURY HOUSE HOTEL,

The Burgage, Prestbury, Cheltenham, Gloucestershire GL52 3DN

Tel: 01242 529533
Fax: 01242 227076

Fully licensed; 17 bedrooms, all with private bathrooms; Historic interest; Children welcome; Leisure and conference facilities; Gloucester 8 miles; £££.

A Cotswold gem in a beautiful setting, this 300-year-old, Georgian manor house with its Elizabethan coach house has beguiled succeeding flocks of visitors (ourselves included) with its historic ambience and the graceful style that permeates the richly panelled Oak and Polo Rooms. Log fires crackle a welcome in the cosy cocktail lounge, a relaxing accompaniment to an intriguing selection of malt whiskies, vintage ports and brandies. Thence, perhaps, to the 'pièce de resistance', a candlelit dinner, a display of the Head Chef's skill and expertise. The house stands in 4 acres of lovely grounds and the sporting opportunities of the area are numerous. Accommodation is of the highest standard and the hotel is hard to better as a touring base. *Commended, AA and RAC***.*

SEVERN BANK,

Minsterworth, Near Gloucester, Gloucestershire GL2 8JH

Tel and Fax: 01452 750357

Unlicensed; 6 bedrooms, 4 with private bathrooms; Gloucester 4 miles; £.

Severn Bank is a fine country house standing in six acres of grounds on the banks of the Severn, four miles west of Gloucester. It is ideally situated for touring the Cotswolds, the Forest of Dean and the Wye Valley, and is the recommended viewpoint for the Severn Bore tidal wave. It has a friendly atmosphere and comfortable rooms with superb views and full central heating. The en suite, non-smoking bedrooms have tea and coffee making facilities and colour television. Ample parking. *Commended.*

NOTE

All the information in this book is given in good faith in the belief that it is correct. However, the publishers cannot guarantee the facts given in these pages, neither are they responsible for changes in policy, ownership or terms that may take place after the date of going to press. Readers should always satisfy themselves that the facilities they require are available and that the terms, if quoted, still apply.

OLD COURT HOTEL,
Church Street, Newent,
Gloucestershire GL18 1AB

Tel: 01531 820522

Restaurant licence; 6 bedrooms, 4 with private bathrooms; Historic interest; Children and pets welcome; Conference facilities; Gloucester 8 miles; ££.

Surrounded by an acre of walled gardens, this magnificent 17th century country house is an oasis of peace and seclusion. Old Court has a fascinating history and still retains an atmosphere of unhurried elegance and comfort. All bedrooms are individually styled to the highest standards with colour television, radio, tea/coffee and direct-dial telephone. Our four-poster bedroom is particularly spacious and perfect for that special occasion. Before dinner guests can relax with a drink in the Green Drawing Room with its fluted pillars and intricate ceiling plasterwork. Dining is a must, with a menu and wine list carefully developed by the resident owners. *ETB 👑👑👑, RAC ***.

STONEHOUSE COURT HOTEL,
Bristol Road, Stonehouse,
Gloucestershire GL10 3RA

Tel: 01453 825155

Fully licensed; 36 bedrooms, all with private bathrooms; Historic interest; Children welcome; Stroud 3 miles; ££££.

On the edge of the Cotswolds and standing in 6 acres of secluded gardens, complete with gazebo, this handsome 17th century manor house is ideally positioned for visiting the world famous Slimbridge Wildfowl Trust created by Sir Peter Scott. The mellow wood panelling of the lounges is echoed in the delightful restaurant and cocktail bar. The cuisine is of a high standard and this is a popular dining-out venue. No less noteworthy is the accommodation, all guest rooms having en suite bath and shower, colour television, tea and coffee making facilities, trouser press and hairdryer. Guests have the opportunity to try a breathtaking trip in a hot-air balloon or engage in the graceful art of gliding, and terms inclusive of these activities are very reasonable. Clipper Hotels. *AA and RAC ****.

The **£** symbol when appearing at the end of the italic section of an entry shows the anticipated price, during 1996, for **single full Bed and Breakfast.**

Under £35	**£**	**Over £50 but under £65**	**£££**
Over £35 but under £50	**££**	**Over £65**	**££££**

This is meant as an indication only and does not show prices for Special Breaks, Weekends, etc. Guests are therefore advised to verify all prices on enquiring or booking.

BURLEIGH COURT HOTEL,
Burleigh, Minchinhampton, Near Stroud, Gloucestershire GL5 2PF

Tel: 01453 883804
Fax: 01453 886870

Fully licensed; 17 bedrooms, all with private bathrooms; Historic interest; Children welcome, pets by arrangement; Leisure and conference facilities; Stroud 3 miles; £££.

At this warm and welcoming 18th century manor house, all the talk was about the superb cuisine. Inspired chatter as it turned out and, almost inevitably, inspired skills exhibited by an enthusiastic cadre of chefs beavering away to produce culinary gems and with vegetarian and special diets also well catered for. However, there are other notable facets to attract visitors to the charming house which is set in 6 acres of lovely grounds. As a centre from which to explore the delights of the Cotswolds, Burleigh Court provides a plethora of reasons to recommend it. Each guest room has its own character and many thoughtful touches complement the fine appointments which include a private bathroom, direct-dial telephone, colour television and radio. *AA****.

AMBERLEY INN,
Amberley, Near Stroud, Gloucestershire GL5 5AF

Tel: 01453 872565
Fax: 01453 872738

Licensed; 14 bedrooms, all with private bathrooms; Historic interest; Children and pets welcome; Conference facilities; Nailsworth 1 mile; £££/££££.

Still retaining the ambience of a traditional English village inn, this charming retreat has progressed to hotel status by reason of its excellent facilities. Still a country hostelry at heart, the Amberley Inn is a homely and attractive place to visit and, indeed, stay. Delightfully equipped bedrooms all have close-carpeted bathrooms, colour television, radio, telephone and tea and coffee-makers. Mellow antique furniture, shining brass and colourful hanging baskets create visual pleasure and a relaxing atmosphere. The restaurant's fixed price menu offers a good choice of interesting dishes whilst the chef's specialities always command attention. The inn occupies a lovely hillside position close to all the scenic joys of the Cotswolds. **.

Hampshire

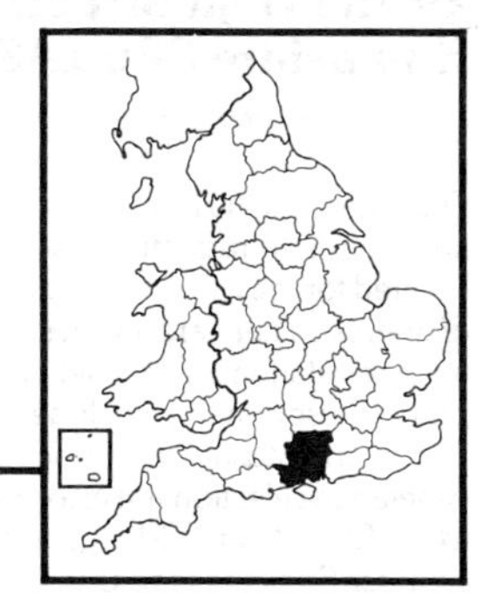

WOODLANDS LODGE HOTEL,
Bartley Road, Ashurst, Woodlands, Hampshire SO4 2GN

Tel: 01703 292257
Fax: 01703 293090

Licensed; 16 luxury bedrooms and suites, all with private bathrooms; Historic interest; Dogs and horses welcome by arrangement; Totton 3 miles; ££££.

This beautiful Georgian building, originally a Royal hunting lodge, has been extensively renovated and refurbished to offer the highest standards of luxury and comfort, while retaining the welcoming, informal atmosphere the hotel has always enjoyed. All of the individually designed bedrooms are en suite (all with whirlpool baths), and have remote-control colour television, direct-dial telephone, trouser press etc; the spacious suites have the additional luxury of a fully furnished sitting room. Set in its own grounds in the heart of the New Forest, Woodlands Lodge is ideal for walking or riding, and stabling is available for those who wish to bring their own horses. **See also Colour Advertisement on page 9.**

THE MASTER BUILDER'S HOUSE HOTEL,
**Buckler's Hard, Beaulieu,
Hampshire SO42 7XB**

Tel: 01590 616253
Fax: 01590 616297

Licensed; 23 bedrooms, all with private bathrooms; Historic interest; Children and pets welcome; Beaulieu 2 miles; £.

The hotel occupies a superb location overlooking the Beaulieu River, in the 18th century shipbuilding village of Buckler's Hard, which has been owned by Lord Montagu's family since 1538. There are six rooms in the original 18th century building (three with four-poster beds) and 17 others in a comfortable new wing; all have private bathroom and shower, hairdryer, trouser press, colour television, and tea and coffee making facilities. The Restaurant, with views of the Beaulieu River, offers excellent table d'hôte and à la carte menus of traditional English fare, with fresh local produce and game in season. The Residents' Lounge with welcoming log fire provides a place of quiet retreat; the Yachtsman's Bar and Yachtsman's Galley, with adjacent beer garden, offer real ale and traditional pub fare. Children under 10 years free in parents' room. *ETB* ♛♛♛♛, *AA*** and Rosette for Food, RAC***, Egon Ronay Recommended.*

LIONS COURT RESTAURANT AND HOTEL,
**29 The High Street, Fordingbridge,
Hampshire SP6 1AS**

Tel: 01425 652006
Fax: 01425 657946

Licensed; 6 bedrooms, all with private bathrooms; Historic interest; Children welcome; Bournemouth 18 miles, Salisbury 11, Ringwood 5; £/££.

This charming 17th century family hotel is set on the edge of the New Forest, with all its amenities and rural pursuits. The delightful, sleepy, small town of Fordingbridge is centrally situated for the cathedral city of Salisbury, Bournemouth, Stonehenge and many other places of interest. There are six en suite bedrooms, one with a four-poster. The à la carte restaurant has a reputation for excellent cuisine in a relaxed, intimate atmosphere. Favouring fresh local produce, specialities include Salad of Smoked Venison and Grilled Calves' Liver with a Bacon and Mushroom Concasse flavoured with Basil; unusual fish dishes and an extensive vegetarian selection are also available. This is a classic English setting with gardens extending to the River Avon. Fishing, golf, horse riding available locally. New Proprietors, Michael and Jennifer Eastick; Chef, Danny Wilson. ♛♛♛ *Commended, AA, Les Routiers, Logis.*

NEWTOWN HOUSE HOTEL,
**Manor Road, Hayling Island,
Hampshire PO11 0QR**

Tel: 01705 466131/2/3
Fax: 01705 461366

Fully licensed; 28 bedrooms, all with private bathrooms; Historic interest; Children and pets welcome; Leisure facilities; Chichester 14 miles; ££.

18th century converted farmhouse, set in own delightful grounds with indoor leisure complex and tennis court. Each of the 28 fully en-suite centrally heated bedrooms is tastefully furnished and features every modern facility, including colour television, tea/coffee facilities, hairdryer, radio and direct-dial telephone. Indoor leisure complex features a heated swimming pool, jacuzzi, sauna, steam room and gymnasium. The restaurant is open seven days a week and is ideal for special occasions. We also serve tempting bar meals in the cosy atmosphere of the Oak Bar with its olde worlde ship beams and log fires in winter. Children are accommodated free when sharing with adults and pay only for meals.

PASSFORD HOUSE HOTEL,
Mount Pleasant Lane, Near Lymington, Hampshire SO41 8LS

Tel: 01590 682398
Fax: 01590 683494

Fully licensed; 53 bedrooms, all with private bathrooms; Children welcome, pets by arrangement; Leisure and conference facilities; Bournemouth 15 miles; £££.

All that one could wish for in a country house hotel, Passford House stands in 10 acres of well-tended grounds, its long Georgian facade overlooking peaceful lawns. The informal charm of the panelled lounge, cocktail bar and antique furniture is matched by the de luxe bedrooms, all with private bathroom, television, telephone, radio, baby listening, trouser press, hairdryer and tea/coffee making facilities. The restaurant and the catering are, of course, of the highest standard. For indoor and leisure facilities, the Dolphin Centre offers a heated swimming pool, sauna, solarium, gym and games room, while outdoors, guests can enjoy nine-hole putting, croquet, heated swimming pool (in season) in the idyllic setting of a sunken garden, alongside a first-class modern hard tennis court. There is a choice of at least eleven golf courses within easy driving distance, horse-riding stables within half a mile, and the glorious New Forest on the very doorstep. *ETB ♛♛♛♛ Highly Commended, AA***, RAC*** and Merit Award, Ashley Courtenay, Johansen, Egon Ronay.*

FIFEHEAD MANOR,
Middle Wallop, Stockbridge, Salisbury, Hampshire SO20 8EG

Tel: 01264 781565
Fax: 01264 781400

Fully licensed; 15 bedrooms, all with private bathrooms; Historic interest; Children and pets welcome; Conference facilities; Andover 7 miles; ££.

This gracious country manor, parts of which date from the 11th century, has seen a varied history, and was at one time a nunnery. It now serves equally well as a haven for those who appreciate high standards of food, wine and accommodation, as well as courteous and friendly service. Various sizes of guest rooms cater for all requirements and are charmingly decorated and well equipped; each has its own private bathroom. The dining room, in which the remains of a minstrels' gallery may be seen, is warmly welcoming, especially by candlelight. The manor stands in several acres of lovely gardens, and is most conveniently situated for visiting Winchester, Salisbury and Stonehenge. *♛♛♛♛ Commended, AA** and Two Rosettes, RAC*** and Merit Award, Egon Ronay, Good Food Guide.*

STRING OF HORSES,
Mead End, Sway, Lymington, Hampshire SO41 6EH

Tel and Fax: 01590 682631

Residential and restaurant licence; 8 bedrooms, all with private facilities; Bournemouth 15 miles, Southampton 15; ££/£££.

Unique, secluded, exclusive hotel set in four acres in the heart of the New Forest, with a friendly, relaxed atmosphere. Eight luxurious double bedrooms, each with its own fantasy bathroom with spa bath and shower. Every facility is offered, including colour television, direct-dial telephone, radio and tea-making facilities. Four-poster rooms are also available, making this an ideal honeymoon setting. Dine in our intimate candlelit "Carriages" restaurant. For relaxation there is a heated outdoor swimming pool. This is superb riding country, and the hotel is close to excellent yachting resorts and several good golf courses. *ETB* ♛♛♛♛ *Highly Commended, AA** Rosette.* **See also Colour Advertisement on page 8.**

NEW FOREST HEATHLANDS HOTEL,
Romsey Road, Ower, Near Romsey, Hampshire SO51 6JZ

Tel: 01703 814333
Fax: 01703 812123

Fully licensed; 52 bedrooms, all with private bathrooms; Historic interest; Children and pets welcome; Leisure and conference facilities; Cadnam 3 miles; £££.

We discovered this delightful holiday concept in picturesque gardens on the northern edge of the New Forest, just a few miles off the M3. Developed out of the 16th century Vine Inn which still plies its traditional trade as a free house under its original beams, Heathlands has acquired a reputation for superb food and accommodation of the highest standard. Charmingly furnished bedrooms all have en suite facilities plus colour television with satellite channels, radio and hospitality tray. Some executive rooms are available with whirlpool bath and mini-fridge/bar. A further attractive feature is the Health Suite with multi-gym, sauna and solarium, just the place to assuage one's over-indulged conscience! ♛♛♛♛, *AA/RAC****.

BUSKETTS LAWN HOTEL,
Woodlands Road, Woodlands, New Forest, Near Southampton, Hampshire SO40 7GL

Tel: 01703 292272
Fax: 01703 292487

Restaurant and residential licence; 14 bedrooms, all with private bathrooms; Children and pets welcome; Totton 3 miles; ££.

Busketts Lawn is a delightful Victorian country house hotel in quiet New Forest surroundings, ideal for visiting Beaulieu and Broadlands. It is set in large gardens with a swimming pool (heated in season), putting, croquet and mini football pitch. The hotel offers excellent food, service and comfort, all rooms being en suite, with colour television, direct-dial telephone, tea making facilities, hair dryers and trouser press. Dinner dances some weekends. Established 1968. Colour brochure on request. *ETB* ♛♛♛♛ *Commended, AA and RAC* **.

Herefordshire

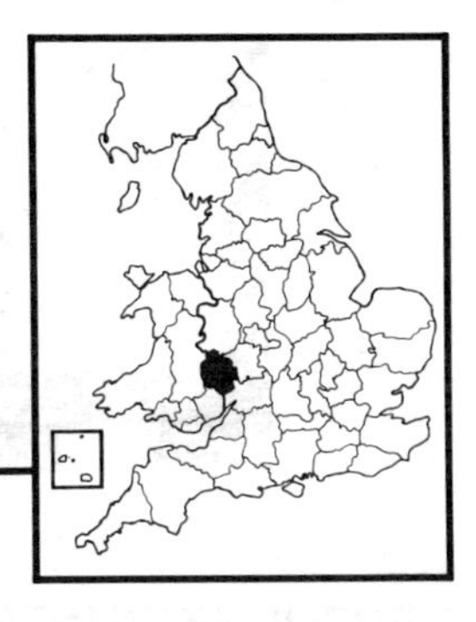

THE BOWENS COUNTRY HOUSE,
Fownhope,
Herefordshire HR1 4PS

Tel and Fax: 01432 860430

Fully licensed; 12 bedrooms, 7 fully en suite and 5 with shower; Historic interest; Children welcome, pets by arrangement; Hereford 6 miles; £.

Growing gracefully from a 17th century farmhouse, this little gem of a place has a magic and unhurried air about it, thanks perhaps, to its rural setting in a mature garden with noble trees, a putting green and play lawn. The house nestles on the fringe of a black and white Wye Valley village with surroundings including such thought-provoking names as Haugh Wood, Cherry Hill and Capler Wood. Sounds like a place for a 'Famous Five' adventure! The magic certainly exists in the splendid old house despite recent additions and extensions. The oak-beamed dining room, cosy sitting room warmed by a log fire in winter and the skilfully adapted guest rooms are all delightfully appointed. A romantic place to escape to. ♛♛♛ *Commended, AA QQQ Recommended.*

VERZONS COUNTRY HOUSE HOTEL,
Trumpet, Near Ledbury,
Herefordshire HR8 2PZ

Tel: 01531 670381

Fully licensed; 9 bedrooms, all with private bathrooms; Historic interest; Children and pets welcome; Conference facilities; Ledbury 4 miles; ££.

A stately yet somewhat rambling late Georgian building, Verzons exudes character. Many original features have been retained to which modern conveniences have been unobtrusively added. The en suite bedrooms, including a four-poster Bridal Suite, are most attractively decorated and have colour television and tea and coffee-makers. Some large family rooms are available. Overlooking 4 acres of grounds, the Garden Room Restaurant offers an appetising choice of table d'hôte and à la carte dishes and children have their own menu. Less formal is the Farmhouse Bar and Restaurant; the extensive selection here includes several fish and vegetarian specialities. This delightful rural retreat is within easy reach of many beauty spots and historic cities. ♛♛♛ *Commended, AA**.*

ORLES BARN HOTEL,
Wilton, Ross-on-Wye,
Herefordshire HR9 6AE

Tel: 01989 562155*
Fax: 01989 768470

Restaurant and residential licence; 9 bedrooms, all with private bathrooms; Children and pets welcome; Leisure facilities; Monmouth 9 miles; ££.

In neatly-tended gardens of 1½ acres, the wide facade of this 17th century country house bids welcome to those seeking a relaxing holiday by the incomparable River Wye. There is the promise of excellent food and comfort for which enlightened Proprietors, Julio and Marion Conteras are jointly responsible. The restaurant is already renowned for its excellent English and Continental fare and reasonable prices. Vegetarian dishes and special diets are catered for on request. The attractively furnished guest rooms have bathrooms en suite, colour television and tea and coffee-making facilities. Ground-floor and family rooms are available. The heated swimming pool in the garden is a pleasant diversion. *Heart of England TB* ♛♛♛ *Commended, AA and RAC **.*

PETERSTOW COUNTRY HOUSE,
Peterstow, Ross-on-Wye,
Herefordshire HR9 6LB

Tel: 01989 562826
Fax: 01989 567264

Fully licensed; 9 bedrooms, all with private bathrooms; Historic interest; Children over 7 years welcome; Leisure and conference facilities; Ross-on-Wye 2 miles; £/££.

This lovely house, as it stands today, is the realisation of a dream for Jeanne and Mike Denne who fell in love with the dilapidated rectory in 1987. With determination and dedication they set about restoring the house and, by the end of 1989, were able to share its enhanced appeal with guests who, themselves, became enchanted. Today, it is a stylish and charmingly decorated country house hotel of character and distinction. Private and public rooms are exquisitely furnished, the en suite guest rooms offering either half-tester canopied beds or double or twin-bedded rooms. To complete the happy picture, the English and French cuisine is of wondrous quality, imaginative and beautifully presented. A dream to share! ♛♛♛♛ *Highly Commended, AA Two Rosettes, Courtesy & Care Award.*

THE STEPPES COUNTRY HOUSE HOTEL,
Ullingswick, Near Hereford,
Herefordshire HR1 3JG

Tel: 01432 820424
Fax: 01432 820042

Residential licence; 6 bedrooms, all with private bathrooms; Historic interest; Children over 12 years and dogs welcome; Hereford 8 miles; DB&B £££.

Sometimes the traveller has to wander off the beaten track to find something truly original, and "The Steppes", peacefully resting in the tiny Wye Valley hamlet of Ullingswick, will more than repay those who visit it. This charming creeper-clad country hotel is furnished and decorated entirely in keeping with its seventeenth-century character. Beamed en suite bedrooms are located in a restored courtyard barn and stable, and are complete with television, clock/radio, tea/coffee making facilities and mini-bar. The cordon bleu cuisine is personally prepared by Mrs Tricia Howland, for whom each dinner served is a special occasion, appealing particularly to those with more adventurous tastes, and deserving of the best locally grown vegetables. And what better, after an ample breakfast, than to tour the area's ancient villages, walk in the Black Mountains and Malvern Hills, visit the porcelain works in Worcester or a local cider mill. See also our advertisement on the Outside Back Cover. ♛♛♛♛ *Highly Commended. AA**, Two Food Rosettes.*

Hertfordshire

EDGWAREBURY HOTEL,
Barnet Lane, Elstree,
Hertfordshire WD6 3RE

Tel: 0181-953 8227
Fax: 0181-207 3668

Fully licensed; 47 bedrooms, all with private bathrooms; Historic interest; Children welcome, pets by arrangement; Leisure and conference facilities; Watford 5 miles; ££££.

Placed to the best advantage for a really relaxing holiday with the options of unexacting excursions to London, Windsor Castle, Hatfield House, etc., this handsome hotel supplies all the ingredients. Set in 10 acres of natural woodland, it has the character and appearance of a Tudor manor house with huge stone fireplaces, carvings and oak beams. Richly furnished, it exudes the warmest of welcomes. Guest rooms all have a bathroom en suite, colour television with satellite channels, direct-dial telephone and numerous little extras. Superb de-luxe suites and four-poster rooms are available. The oak-panelled bar is a favourite meeting place, perhaps prior to dining sumptuously in the delightful Cavendish Restaurant. Tennis provides a sporting diversion. ♛♛♛♛ *Highly Commended, AA Two Rosettes, RAC Restaurant Award.*

The **£** symbol when appearing at the end of the italic section of an entry shows the anticipated price, during 1996, for **single full Bed and Breakfast.**

Under £35	**£**	**Over £50 but under £65**	**£££**
Over £35 but under £50	**££**	**Over £65**	**££££**

This is meant as an indication only and does not show prices for Special Breaks, Weekends, etc. Guests are therefore advised to verify all prices on enquiring or booking.

DOWN HALL COUNTRY HOUSE HOTEL,

Hatfield Heath, Near Bishop's Stortford, Hertfordshire CM22 7AS

Tel: 01279 731441
Fax: 01279 730416

Fully licensed; 103 bedrooms, all with private bathrooms; Historic interest; Children welcome, pets by arrangement; Leisure and conference facilities; Bishop's Stortford 5 miles; ££££.

This elegant and imposing Italianate mansion is a perfect example of the quality craftsmanship of the Victorian age. Set in over 100 acres of beautiful woodland, park and landscaped gardens, this grand building is rich in history and has recently undergone many innovative changes to provide the ultimate in modern facilities for vacationing guests and formal functions. Popular the hotel may rightly be, but it still retains an aura of dignified tranquillity. The focal point is the main lounge with its Italian stone fireplace and magnificent chandeliers, and it is here that morning coffee and afternoon tea are served. The impeccable guest rooms are well-proportioned and tastefully furnished with much apparent attention to detail, whilst the Downham and Lambourne Restaurants offer a superlative range of international and traditional English dishes, all prepared by imaginative Cordon Bleu chefs. If wining, dining and dallying awhile here is an unforgettable experience, then so too is the peerless range of indoor and outdoor leisure amenities — heated pool, whirlpool, sauna, croquet and putting lawns, giant chess, tennis and fitness trail amongst them. For private dinners or conferences for up to 250 people, the same excellent standards apply in the hands of experienced banqueting and party catering support teams. ♛♛♛♛♛ *Highly Commended.*

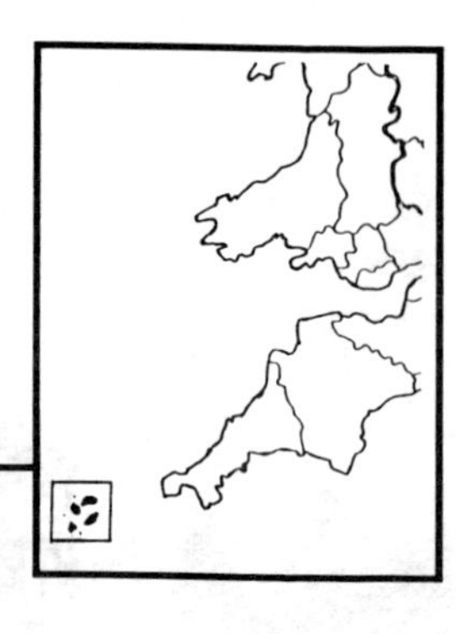

Isles of Scilly

ST MARTIN'S HOTEL, St Martin's, Isles of Scilly TR25 0QW

Tel: 01720 422092*
Fax: 01720 422298

Fully licensed; 24 bedrooms, all with private bathrooms; Children and pets welcome; Leisure and conference facilities; Land's End 28 miles; £££.

The third largest island of the Scillies, this is most people's idea of paradise on earth — the ultimate escape: long white beaches, clear blue water, sheltered coves ideal for snorkelling or sailing, a profusion of fascinating flora and fauna, and, best of all, peace and quiet. The hotel complex has been imaginatively designed as a cluster of cottages nestling into the hillside, and the harmonious blend of colour and style in the decor and furnishings enhances one's appreciation of the magnificently appointed rooms and suites. The cuisine presented in the newly refurbished Tean Restaurant is superb, and naturally features locally caught seafood. Just 28 miles from Land's End, the Scillies are remarkably easy to reach by air and sea. ♛♛♛♛ *Highly Commended, AA*** and Two Rosettes.*

Isle of Wight

LAKE HOTEL, Shore Road, Lower Bonchurch, Isle of Wight PO38 1RF

Tel and Fax: 01983 852613*

Residential licence; 21 bedrooms, all with private bathrooms; Historic interest; Children over 3 years and pets welcome; Shanklin 3 miles, Ventnor half-mile; £.

"Truly unbeatable value for money". This lovely country house hotel is set in a beautiful quiet two-acre garden on the seaward side of the olde worlde village of Bonchurch. Run by the same family for over 30 years, the hotel offers first class food and service, all in a relaxed and friendly atmosphere. All rooms are en suite with complimentary tea/coffee facilities and TV, and are decorated in the "Laura Ashley" style. We can offer an Isle of Wight car ferry inclusive price of just £115.00 for four nights' half board during March/April/May and October, and we really do believe that you will not find better value on our beautiful island. ♛♛♛ *Commended, AA QQQQ Selected, RAC Highly Acclaimed.*

Kent

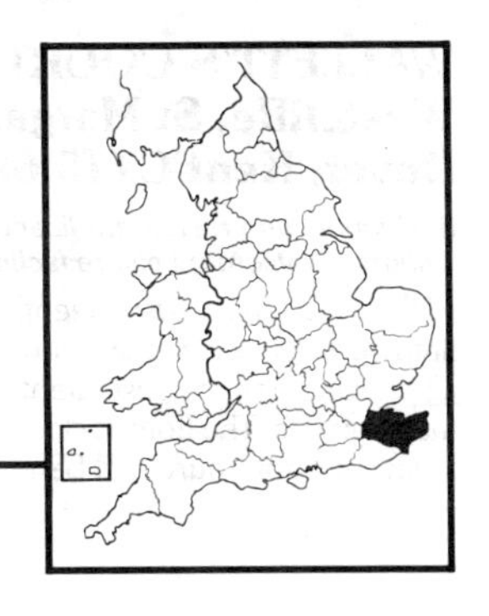

BOXLEY HOUSE HOTEL,
Boxley, Maidstone,
Kent ME14 3DZ

Tel: 01622 692269
Fax: 01622 683536

Fully licensed; 18 bedrooms, all with private bathrooms; Historic interest; Children welcome, pets by prior arrangement; Leisure and conference facilities; Maidstone 2 miles; ££.

A feature of an idyllic village nestling at the foot of the North Downs, this lovely 17th century house is splendidly set in 20 acres of parkland graced by many fine trees. Skilfully modernised, the house retains its period character to the full. Dining is a delight, the splendid restaurant with its minstrels' gallery catering for occasions as diverse as a superb intimate dinner or a full-scale reception. Bedrooms all have a bath or shower en suite, colour television, radio, telephone and tea and coffee-makers. Outside, a south-facing patio leads to a sheltered solar heated swimming pool. This rural gem is renowned for its accommodation, refreshment and service yet, unbelievably, Maidstone is only two miles away. ♛♛♛♛, *AA and RAC**.*

ST. MARGARET'S HOTEL AND COUNTRY CLUB,
Reach Road, St Margaret-at-Cliffe,
Dover, Kent CT15 6AE

Tel: 01304 853262
Fax: 01304 853434

Licensed; 24 bedrooms, all with private bathrooms; Children welcome, guide dogs only; Leisure facilities: Dover 4 miles; £.

A fine modern complex including a country club and fitness centre, this is an inspired holiday venue with the requirements of every member of the family borne in mind all year round. Modern double and twin-bedded rooms offer the very latest in comfort, with bathrooms en suite, television, telephone and tea-making facilities, whilst the restaurant has a reputation for superb home cooking. The day starts with the option of a full English breakfast or the lighter Continental variety, and lunchtime (and evening) snacks are served in either of two bars. The atmosphere is informal and there are countless activities to enjoy: heated indoor swimming pools, a large family pool and a superb exercise pool for the serious swimmer, a fully equipped gymnasium, sauna, solarium, tennis courts and much more. Never a dull moment! For children there is a special activity play area and opportunities for instruction in swimming, scuba diving or canoeing. And for the body conscious, osteopathy, massage and beauty therapies are available. High on the cliffs above the bay, St. Margaret's lies between the historic ports of Dover and Deal and is surrounded by National Trust land. There are many outdoor pursuits to be enjoyed in the area as well as numerous places of historic interest. *SEETB* ♛♛♛.

WALLETT'S COURT HOTEL,
Westcliffe, St Margarets-at-Cliffe, Dover, Kent CT15 6EW

Tel: 01304 852424*
Fax: 01304 853430

Residential and restaurant licence; 10 bedrooms, all with private bathrooms; Historic interest; Children welcome; Leisure facilities; Canterbury 15 miles, Eurotunnel 11, Dover Docks 3; £/££.

Wallett's Court is a seventeenth century manor house with wood carvings, beams and ornate fireplaces. It is set in rolling countryside above the White Cliffs of Dover. The ten bedrooms are all en suite and the restaurant, presided over by Chef/Proprietor Chris Oakley, is noted in major guides. The hotel is close to Dover Harbour, championship golf courses and the historic towns of Canterbury and Sandwich. *SEETB* ♛♛♛♛ *Highly Commended.*

HEMPSTEAD HOUSE,
London Road, Bapchild, Sittingbourne, Kent ME9 9PP

Tel and Fax: 01795 428020

Residential and restaurant licence; 7 bedrooms, all with private bathrooms; Historic interest; Children and well behaved pets welcome; Leisure and conference facilities; Sittingbourne 2 miles; £££.

Exclusive private Victorian country house hotel situated on the main A2 between Sittingbourne and Canterbury, surrounded by beautiful Kentish countryside and protected from traffic noise by three acres of beautifully landscaped gardens. Guests are welcomed as friends by Proprietors, Mandy and Henry Holdstock, who encourage full enjoyment of the spacious and elegant reception rooms and grounds in which there is a fine heated swimming pool. Dining is an informal and eagerly anticipated occasion, the fine cuisine being freshly prepared using home-grown and local produce. Special diets are catered for. The bedrooms are all luxuriously appointed with en suite, colour television and tea and coffee makers, toiletries and bath robes. ♛♛♛ *Highly Commended, AA QQQQQ Premier Selected, Logis Three Fireplaces, RAC Highly Acclaimed.*

COLLINA HOUSE HOTEL,
East Hill, Tenterden, Kent TN30 6RL

Tel: 01580 764852/764004

Fully licensed; 17 bedrooms, all with private bathrooms; Children welcome, pets by arrangement only; Ashford 10 miles; £.

This charming hotel is quietly situated in the country town of Tenterden, yet is only a few minutes' walk from the Leisure Centre. There are many National Trust properties and places of interest in the area, including Sissinghurst Castle, Leeds Castle, Scotney Castle Gardens and the Kent and East Sussex steam engines. Personal attention is assured by the Swiss-trained owners of this comfortable hotel, who provide home cooking of the highest standard, enhanced by the use of home-grown produce. All the well-appointed bedrooms, including five family rooms, have private bathrooms, central heating and colour television. Further details on request. ♛♛♛.

LITTLE SILVER COUNTRY HOTEL,
Ashford Road, St. Michaels, Tenterden, Kent TN30 6SP

Tel: 01233 850321
Fax: 01233 850647

Fully licensed; 10 bedrooms, all with private bathrooms; Children welcome; Conference facilities; Ashford 10 miles; £££.

Imaginatively furnished, Little Silver is not just an hotel but an expression of the artistry exhibited by Proprietors, Rosemary Frith and Dorothy Lawson and guests are enchanted by the sumptuous comfort and attention to detail. In the lovely 'Garden of England', the house reposes in beautiful gardens. Luxury en suite bedrooms are equipped with colour television, radio, direct-dial telephone and tea-makers and, for that special occasion, there is a four-poster bedroom with jacuzzi bath. An elegant, 40ft oak-beamed sitting room is a feature and excellent meals are served in an intimate and delightfully appointed dining room. This is an established function venue with peerless facilities and up to 130 people can be seated in the remarkable, octagonal Kent Hall. *SEETB ♛♛♛♛ Highly Commended.*

Lancashire

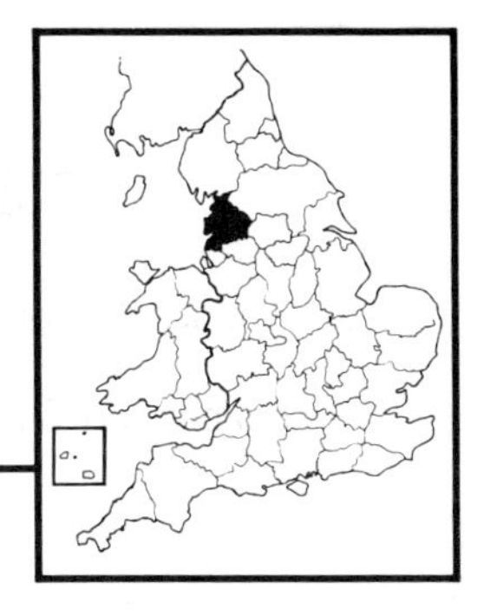

NORTHCOTE MANOR,
Northcote Road, Langho, Blackburn, Lancashire BB6 8BE

Tel: 01254 240555
Fax: 01254 246568

Restaurant licence; 14 bedrooms, all with private bathrooms; Children welcome; Conference facilities; Blackburn 4 miles; ££££.

Hidden away in glorious countryside between the beautiful Trough of Bowland and the Ribble Valley, this Victorian manor house is well known for its imaginative kitchen. Under the guidance of joint owner Nigel Haworth, Egon Ronay Chef of the Year, dining is an experience to be cherished. No less worthy of the highest praise is the delightful accommodation. Reached by means of the original oak staircase, guest rooms are sumptuously appointed. Another new extension has recently been added and the handsome decor is complemented by en suite facilities, colour television with satellite channels, direct-dial telephone, trouser press and tea and coffee-makers. Sporting arrangements may be made for game and clay pigeon shooting, horse riding, cycling, fishing and golf. *WWTB ♛♛♛♛ Highly Commended.*

HAMPSON HOUSE HOTEL & RESTAURANT, Hampson Lane, Hampson Green, Near Lancaster, Lancashire LA2 0JB

Tel: 01524 751158
Fax: 01524 751779

Fully licensed; 14 bedrooms, all with private bathrooms; Historic interest; Pets welcome; Manchester 40 miles, Morecambe 8, Lancaster 4; ££/£££.

This family-run, fully licensed hotel has 14 bedrooms, all with private facilities, radio, telephone, television, and welcome tray. Set in two acres of mature gardens, the original house was built in 1600 and was the home of the Welsh family from 1666 until 1973, when it was sold and converted into a hotel. Situated in the area known as the "Gateway to the Lakes", it is an ideal base for the leisure traveller while touring the North West of England, or halfway house when travelling north or south. For further details, please send for brochure. *ETB* ♛♛♛♛, *AA and RAC***.

SPRINGFIELD HOUSE HOTEL & RESTAURANT,

Wheel Lane, Pilling, Near Preston, Lancashire PR3 6HL

Tel: 01253 790301
Fax: 01253 790907

Fully licensed; 8 bedrooms, all with private bathrooms; Historic interest; Children and pets welcome; Fleetwood 7 miles; £.

This beautiful country house hotel is set within walled gardens in the heart of the Fylde countryside. Enjoy superb food and accommodation in the gracious surroundings of this lovely old Georgian house. The delightful restaurant serves lunches from Tuesday to Friday, as well as evening meals and traditional Sunday lunch. There are several excellent golf courses nearby and the hotel is well placed for visiting holiday resorts such as Blackpool and Morecambe as well as the Lake District. ♛♛♛♛ *Highly Commended, Les Routiers Casserole Award.*

NORTON GRANGE HOTEL,

Manchester Road, Rochdale, Lancashire OL11 2XZ

Tel: 01706 30788
Fax: 01706 49313

Fully licensed; 51 bedrooms, all with private bathrooms; Historic interest; Children and pets welcome; Conference facilities; Egton 8 miles; ££££.

Delightfully set in 9 acres of landscaped grounds and with an air of elegance that characterises its Victorian origins, Norton Grange is a relaxing place to visit. It has been skilfully modernised and its spacious and opulently furnished guest rooms include private bathrooms, colour television, radio, direct-dial telephone, tea and coffee-making facilities and many extras. The hotel is particularly popular with businessmen who habitually foregather in the cheerful Pickwick Bar. The bright and attractive restaurant presents an excellent cuisine ranging from traditional Lancashire fare to European and Oriental classics, all prepared by a team of talented chefs. A programme of special (and imaginative) events is organised throughout the year. *NWTB* ♛♛♛♛, *AA ***, **** for Food.*

SCAITCLIFFE HALL COUNTRY HOUSE HOTEL,
Burnley Road, Todmorden,
Lancashire OL14 7DQ

Tel: 01706 818888
Fax: 01706 818825

Fully licensed; 13 bedrooms, all with private bathrooms; Historic interest; Children and pets welcome; Leisure and conference facilities; Rochdale 8 miles; £££.

Handy for several commercial centres, Scaitcliffe Hall nestles in 16½ acres of beautiful grounds and has fine Pennine views. On the Yorkshire/Lancashire border, this is a recommended centre for exploring the Dales, Lake District and Brontë Country. The main hall was built in 1666; today, spacious public and private rooms are delightfully furnished with bedrooms all having en suite facilities, television, direct-dial telephone, tea and coffee-makers, hair dryer and trouser press. For dining reasonably and well in elegant surroundings, the restaurant proffers a classical and innovative cuisine. Good company and fare in the evenings and weekend lunchtimes may be found in the adjacent Coach House Inn with its open log fire. ♛♛♛♛♛ *Commended, RAC and AA***.*

HOLLAND HALL HOTEL,
Lafford Lane, Upholland,
Lancashire WN8 0QZ

Tel: 01695 624426
Fax: 01695 622433

Fully licensed; 34 bedrooms, all with private bathrooms; Historic interest; Children welcome; Conference facilities; Wigan 4 miles; ££/£££.

Experience luxury and quality at historic Holland Hall Hotel where the emphasis is on comfort and style. Situated in the heart of Lancashire adjacent to Dean Wood golf course, this is the perfect home from home for the business executive seeking a tranquil haven. 34 tastefully furnished bedrooms all have en suite facilities, television and direct-dial telephones. The hotel offers the choice of two restaurants: experience unique classic cuisine in the elegant Churchill's Restaurant with the emphasis on individually prepared fresh food, or taste award-winning pizza in Winston's Restaurant and Bar. There are banqueting and conference facilities for up to 200, and promotional events, sales seminars, personalised corporate golf days etc can be catered for. The hotel has a large car park and sumptuous gardens and grounds. ♛♛♛♛, *AA and RAC ***.*

NOTE

All the information in this book is given in good faith in the belief that it is correct. However, the publishers cannot guarantee the facts given in these pages, neither are they responsible for changes in policy, ownership or terms that may take place after the date of going to press. Readers should always satisfy themselves that the facilities they require are available and that the terms, if quoted, still apply.

Leicestershire

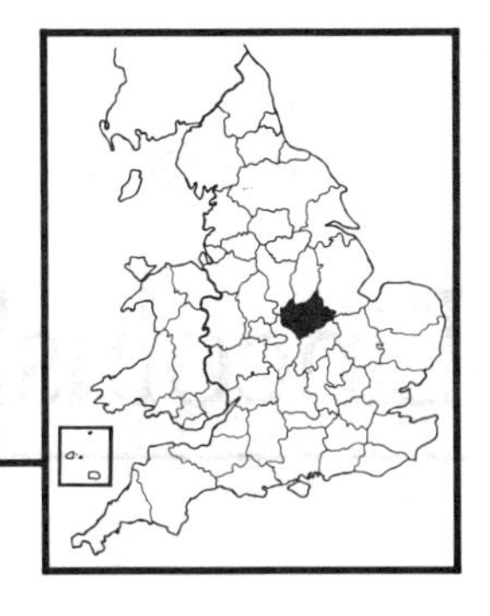

SKETCHLEY GRANGE COUNTRY HOUSE HOTEL,

Burbage, Hinckley,
Leicestershire LE10 3HU

Tel: 01455 251133
Fax: 01455 631384

Fully licensed; 38 bedrooms, all with private bathrooms; Historic interest; Children and pets welcome; Conference facilities; Leicester 12 miles; ££££.

For business or pleasure, this prestigious country house hotel on the Leicestershire/Warwickshire border is charmingly appointed throughout. In addition to the handsome en suite bedrooms, luxury four-poster suites and executive rooms are available, all with spa baths. Quietly situated yet easy of access, being close to Junction 1 of the M69, the hotel has a warm and informal atmosphere and draws tourists and businessmen to seek the traditional environment of the Grange Bar with its fine range of drinks and bar food. Serious diners could do no better than sample the delights of the award-winning Willow Restaurant overlooking the garden and fields and where the impressive à la carte menu is complemented by an interesting wine list. *EMTB* ♛♛♛♛ *Highly Commended, AA Rosette.*

QUORN GRANGE,

88 Wood Lane, Quorn,
Leicestershire LE12 8DB

Tel: 01509 412167
Fax: 01509 415621

Restaurant and residential licence; 15 bedrooms, all with private bathrooms; Children and pets welcome; Conference facilities; Loughborough 3 miles; ££££.

This charming, creeper-clad, 18th century hotel standing in its own landscaped grounds, presents a tranquil and most agreeable face to the world — just the place in which to unwind and appreciate the worthwhile things of life. Backed by friendly and efficient service, the superlative English cuisine certainly comes into this category, as does the well-planned accommodation; guest rooms are delightfully decorated and have private facilities, colour television and direct-dial telephone. Stylish arrangements exist for social functions of all sorts. Horse riding, swimming, golf, squash, angling and clay pigeon shooting are sporting amenities that can be arranged for guests. *EMTB* ♛♛♛.

Lincolnshire

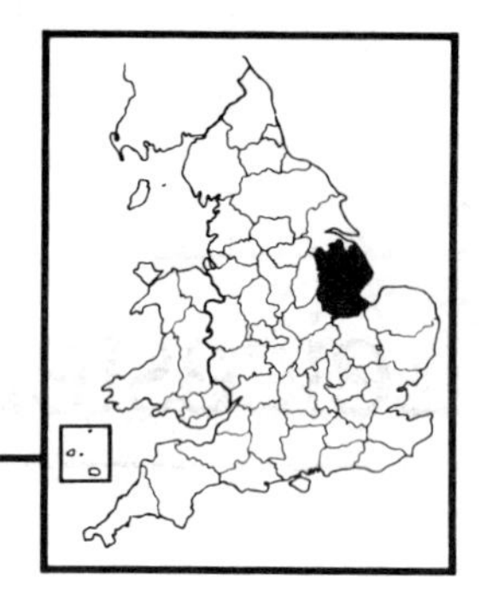

KENWICK PARK HOTEL,
Kenwick Park, Louth,
Lincolnshire LN11 8NR

Tel: 01507 608806
Fax: 01507 608027

Fully licensed; 24 bedrooms, all with private bathrooms; Children and pets welcome; Leisure and conference facilities; Grimsby 14 miles; ££££.

This is a real find where one may savour first-class food and wines and wonder at the superb standards of culinary creativity exhibited in the Fairway Restaurant. Diners may well have reached this happy state having played a round on the adjacent golf course and dallied awhile in the Keepers Bar. This magnificent Georgian country house oozes luxury both within and without. Reached via a majestic tree-lined drive, it stands in 500 imposing acres. Tourists and businessmen are offered accommodation in the most elegantly furnished suites and bedrooms, all of which feature en suite facilities, satellite television, direct-dial telephone and a host of practical extras. All residents have full use of the amenities of the exclusive Health and Leisure Complex. *EMTB* ♛♛♛♛♛ *Highly Commended, RAC****.*

Norfolk

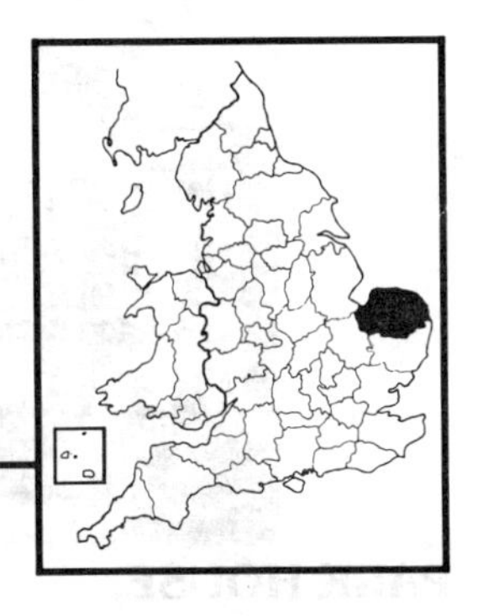

SPROWSTON MANOR HOTEL,

Wroxham Road, Norwich,
Norfolk NR7 8RP

Tel: 01603 410871
Fax: 01603 423911

Fully licensed; 87 bedrooms, all with private bathrooms; Historic interest; Children welcome; Leisure and conference facilities; Honingham 8 miles; ££££.

One approaches this grand old manor house along an avenue of equally grand oaks: on either side stretch 10 acres of parkland which, in turn, is surrounded by the 18-hole Sprowston Golf Course. Built in 1559 and considerably altered by John Gurney, banker and one-time Lord Mayor of Norwich, in late Victorian years, the house retains all the grace and unvulgar opulence of those times, creating an aura that blends happily with the unconfined luxury of recently introduced appointments to which superb leisure and conference facilities have been added. The spacious guest rooms are delightfully furnished and the stylish restaurant and lavishly draped Orangery present just the right atmosphere in which to enjoy the fine cuisine. The Leisure Club with its exotic pools and palms is a haven in which one may relax in tropical splendour and the fitness room and beauty salon prove popular; a poolside bar which dispenses light meals completes the mood of contentment. Various special breaks are organised throughout the year and offer excellent value. There are numerous places of historic, sporting and geographical interest close at hand: Norwich is a beautiful and ancient cathedral city which will reward an extended visit. *ETB ♛♛♛♛♛ Highly Commended, RAC and AA ****.*

PARK HOUSE,
Sandringham, King's Lynn,
Norfolk PE35 6EH

Tel: 01485 543000
Fax: 01485 540663

Residential licence; 16 bedrooms, all with private bathrooms; Historic interest; Guide dogs only; Leisure facilities; King's Lynn 7 miles; ££.

This delightful country hotel, presented to the Leonard Cheshire Foundation by H.M. the Queen, has been specially adapted and equipped for use by people with physical disabilities. Situated in its own picturesque grounds, it offers first-class accommodation, either Bed and Breakfast, Half or Full Board, for up to a maximum of four weeks. Single and twin-bedded rooms each have their own toilet, bath or shower, colour television, radio, telephone, tea/coffee making facilities and staff intercom. The hotel has outstanding leisure amenities including a library and games room, and entertainment is provided on some evenings. There is also a heated outdoor pool with a hoist for use in summer months, and the seaside resort of Hunstanton is near at hand. Guests are assured of an exceptional standard of care by qualified and experienced staff. ♛♛♛, *Grade 1 Accessibility Award.*

Northumberland

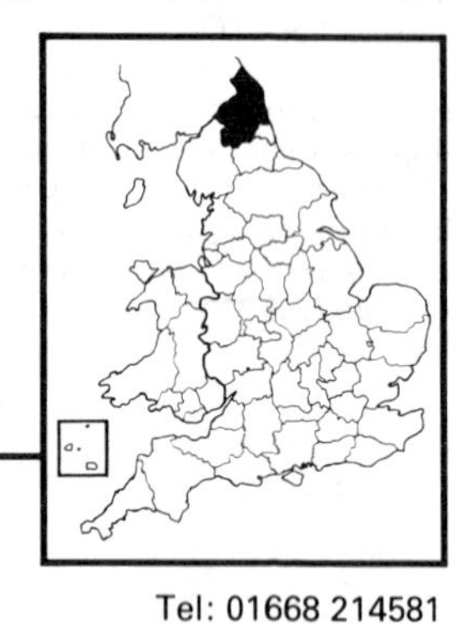

WAREN HOUSE HOTEL,
Waren Mill, Belford,
Northumberland NE70 7EE

Tel: 01668 214581
Fax: 01668 214484

Fully licensed; 7 bedrooms, all with private bathrooms; Pets by arrangement; Belford 2 miles; £££.

Set in six acres of mature wooded grounds and garden overlooking Holy Island, just two miles from majestic Bamburgh Castle, Waren House has been reborn under the talented and loving hands of owners, Anita and Peter Laverack. Anita has designed and overseen the refurbishment of the public rooms, five bedrooms and two suites. Bathrooms are superbly fitted out and generous in size. At Waren House everything is done for your comfort. Beautifully presented food is served in the elegant dining room, and the wine list, a copy of which is in every bedroom, is a most fascinating read. Smoking is restricted to the library. Probably the icing on the cake is that the beauty of this uncrowded Heritage Coast makes it much like the Lake District was 40 years ago, before it was well and truly discovered. Please do "discover" Waren House — it will be a choice you will never regret. ♛♛♛♛ *Highly Commended, AA**, RAC***.*

EMBLETON HALL, Longframlington, Morpeth, Northumberland NE65 9LR

Tel: 01665 570249/570206
Fax: 01665 570056

Fully licensed; 10 bedrooms, all with private bathrooms; Historic interest; Children and pets welcome; Leisure and conference facilities; Rothbury 5 miles; £££.

On the fringe of the Northumbrian National Park, this fine historic building lies in the heart of the Border Country in an area of awe-inspiring beauty. Also near a relatively deserted coastline and numerous places of time-honoured interest, Embleton Hall stands four-square in 5 acres of landscaped gardens, surveying the wild scenery with lofty dignity. The original house was built in 1675 and the spacious grandeur of former years is still apparent despite tasteful modernisation. Now a splendidly decorated country hotel of great character run with enthusiasm by young owners, Judy and Trevor Thorne, the old house offers en suite accommodation in elegantly furnished rooms and a worthy dinner menu featuring home produce. ♛♛♛♛ *Highly Commended.*

WARKWORTH HOUSE HOTEL, 16 Bridge Street, Warkworth, Northumberland NE65 0XB

Tel: 01665 711276
Fax: 01665 713323

Fully licensed; 14 bedrooms, all with private bathroom; Historic interest; Children and pets welcome; Alnwick 7 miles.

A salient feature of an unspoilt village famed for its imposing 12th century castle, we found this homely hotel, in the efficient hands of the Oliver family, to be a delightful place in which to stay whilst seeking out the numerous places of historic interest, uncrowded sandy beaches, and the Kielder Forest and Northumbrian National Parks. A feast of things to see and do, and always on return to one's base, the promise of an appetising selection of à la carte and table d'hôte dishes in the Eden Restaurant and rewarding repose in comfortable, well appointed bedrooms, each with bathroom en suite, colour television, central heating and tea and coffee making facilities. This is an eminently friendly place and a pre-dinner "snifter" with locals in the bar might prove entertaining. ♛♛♛♛ *Commended, RAC **.*

The **£** symbol when appearing at the end of the italic section of an entry shows the anticipated price, during 1996, for **single full Bed and Breakfast.**

Under £35	**£**	**Over £50 but under £65**	**£££**
Over £35 but under £50	**££**	**Over £65**	**££££**

This is meant as an indication only and does not show prices for Special Breaks, Weekends, etc. Guests are therefore advised to verify all prices on enquiring or booking.

Nottinghamshire

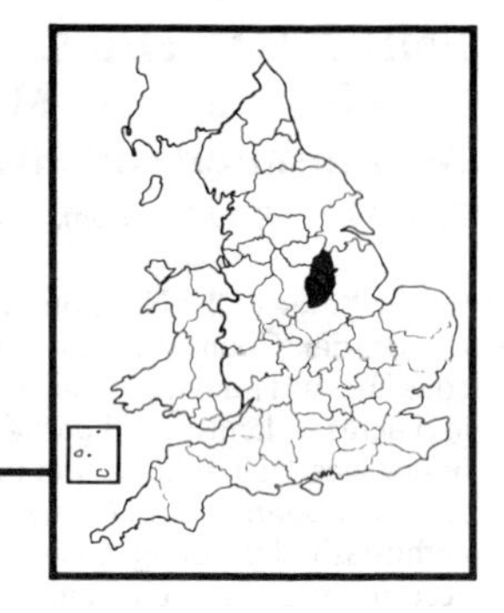

PINE LODGE HOTEL,
281-283 Nottingham Road, Mansfield,
Nottinghamshire NG18 4SE

Tel: 01623 22308
Fax: 01623 656819

Restaurant and residential licence; 20 bedrooms, all with private bathrooms; Children welcome; Leisure and conference facilities; Nottingham 14 miles; ££.

We offer quality, value, service and a warm welcome, in addition to the good food, car parking, garden and sauna/solarium room. All bedrooms are en suite and feature remote-control colour television with Fastext and satellite stations, direct-dial telephone and tea/coffee making facilities. Close to Coxmoor, Hollinwell and Sherwood Forest Golf Clubs. ♛♛♛♛, *AA and RAC**.*

WEST RETFORD HOTEL,
North Road, Retford,
Nottinghamshire DN22 7XG

Tel: 01777 706333
Fax: 01777 709951

Fully licensed; 60 bedrooms, all with private bathrooms; Historic interest; Children and pets welcome; Conference facilities; Nottingham 27 miles; £££.

An elegant Georgian manor set in beautiful grounds, the house has been lovingly restored to its former glory with the tasteful furnishings a delight to behold. Sympathetically introduced, the modern practicalities are of the finest, the handsome guest rooms having private bathrooms, colour television, radio, direct-dial telephone and many thoughtful extras. A smart cocktail bar encourages concourse with fellow residents, possibly when enjoying an aperitif prior to dining stylishly and well. An imaginative selection of international dishes is on offer in the restaurant with an extensive range of wines in support. The hotel is conveniently situated just off Junction 30 of the M1 and two minutes' drive from Retford main line railway station. ♛♛♛♛ *Commended.*

OLD ENGLAND HOTEL, High Street, Sutton-on-Trent, Near Newark, Nottinghamshire NG23 6QA

Tel: 01636 821216

Restaurant licence; 10 bedrooms, all with private facilities; Historic interest; Children and dogs welcome; London 133 miles, Nottingham 28, Newark-on-Trent 8; £££.

Appropriately named, the Old England Hotel, owned and run by the Pike family for over fifty years, epitomises traditional hospitality, charm and courtesy, together with the modern amenities we expect from a first-class establishment. All bedrooms are individually appointed, with private facilities and colour television, and the hotel is graced with a large collection of antique furniture, delightfully displayed in its old world setting. The menu too is selected from the very best of traditional fare, using locally produced meat and fresh vegetables. Extensive grounds invite the stroller, and Sherwood Forest and Southwell Minster are readily accessible.

Oxfordshire

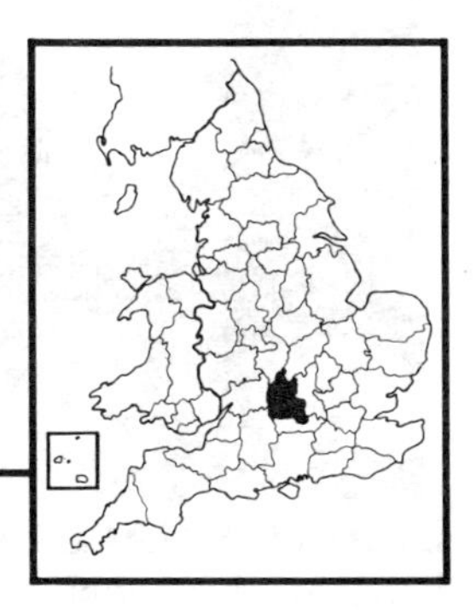

FOXCOMBE LODGE HOTEL, Fox Lane, Boars Hill, Oxford, Oxfordshire OX1 5DP

Tel: 01865 326326
Fax: 01865 730628

Fully licensed; 20 bedrooms, all with private bathrooms; Children and pets welcome; Leisure and conference facilities; Oxford 3 miles; ££.

Opened as recently as 1985, this former private residence is now a distinctive hotel in the country house style; by reason of its position on the outskirts of Oxford, it is a popular venue for conferences and private functions. It is also an excellent place to stay for exploration of the "city with her dreaming spires", the Cotswolds, Chilterns and Thames Valley. Peacefully set in lovely grounds, the hotel has well-appointed accommodation, all bedrooms having en suite facilities, colour television, radio/alarm, direct-dial telephone and tea/coffee makers; some ground floor rooms are especially suitable for disabled visitors. Residents have free use of a fine leisure centre. A high reputation has already been acquired for the imaginative table d'hôte and à la carte cuisine. *RAC***.

PLEASE ENCLOSE A STAMPED ADDRESSED ENVELOPE WHEN WRITING TO ENQUIRE ABOUT ACCOMMODATION FEATURED IN THIS GUIDE

Shropshire

BURLTON HALL COUNTRY HOTEL, Burlton, Shrewsbury, Shropshire SY4 5SX

Tel: 01939 270430
Fax: 01939 270574

Restaurant/supper licence; 4 bedrooms, all with private bathrooms; Historic interest; Children and pets welcome; Conference facilities; Wem 4 miles; ££.

This historic edifice, dating in part from the 15th century, made an immediate visual impact on our tour of Shropshire by reason of its timber-latticed facade and its setting in 3 acres of lovely mature gardens. Convenient for Shrewsbury, the Welsh Marches and an idyllic countryside, the hotel gains top marks for its comforts and cuisine. The tastefully decorated en suite bedrooms have king-size beds, remote-control colour television, direct-dial telephone and tea and coffee tray. Sporting opportunities abound in the area; golf at Hawkstone Park, riding, fishing and shooting. Guests returning from such activities may be assured of a hearty repast chosen from an à la carte menu, steaks being a speciality. ♛♛♛ *Highly Commended.*

LONGMYND HOTEL, Church Stretton, Shropshire SY6 6AG

Tel: 01694 722244
Fax: 01694 722718

Fully licensed; 50 bedrooms, all with private bathrooms; Historic interest; Children and dogs welcome; Leisure facilities; Ludlow 15 miles, Shrewsbury 13; £££.

Perched high above the pleasant town of Church Stretton in grounds of ten acres, this fine hotel enjoys sweeping views over the beautiful Welsh border country. A subtle mixture of superb modern and period rooms, the hotel possesses outstanding amenities. Luxury suites and bedrooms are equipped with every refinement demanded by the discerning guest of today, an outdoor heated swimming pool (covered in winter months), 9-hole pitch-and-putt course, trim gym, sauna and solarium. Riding, fishing, shooting and gliding may also be arranged nearby. The cuisine is noteworthy for its excellence and variety and there are superb facilities for conferences and other functions. There are also self-catering lodges in the hotel grounds. ♛♛♛♛, ***, *Johansens, Ashley Courtenay.* **See also Colour Advertisement on page 8.**

STRETTON HALL HOTEL, All Stretton, Church Stretton, Shropshire SY6 6HG

Tel: 01694 723224
Fax: 01694 724365

Fully licensed; 14 bedrooms, all with private bathrooms; Historic interest; Children welcome; Conference facilities; Shrewsbury 12 miles; ££.

This historic country house is idyllically set in its own grounds with magnificent views of the Shropshire Hills. The house has incorporated in its decor many features of a bygone age, and an atmosphere of comfort and gracious living prevails. All bedrooms are en suite, and there is a Honeymoon Four-Poster bedroom. An extensive à la carte menu is available in the Egon Ronay Recommended restaurant, with an extensive wine cellar and choice of real ales to accompany one's selection. Convenient for the motorway and rail networks, the hotel is within half an hour's drive of the historic towns of Ludlow, Shrewsbury and Telford. Local leisure activities include golf, walking, gliding, riding, shooting and cycling; attractions include the Long Mynd, Ironbridge Gorge Museum, castles and the Severn Valley Railway. ♛♛♛♛, *AA and RAC****. **See also Colour Advertisement on page 10.**

THE REDFERN HOTEL, Cleobury Mortimer, Shropshire DY14 8AA

Tel: 01299 270395
Fax: 01299 271011

Licensed; 11 bedrooms, all with private bathrooms or showers; Children and dogs welcome; Ludlow 11 miles, Bewdley 8; ££/£££.

For centuries past travellers have stayed in the old market town of Cleobury Mortimer. Now a conservation area on the edge of the 6000-acre Forest of Wyre, it forms a perfect centre for exploring the Welsh Marches, Ironbridge Industrial Museum and 2000 years of English history. The Shire horses at Acton Scott Farm Museum and the steam engines on the Severn Valley railway will conjure up nostalgia of times past. After a day's adventuring or walking in the Shropshire hills, what better place to relax than in this warm and comfortable hotel, where good fresh food, fine wines and friendly service will make your stay one to remember. All bedrooms have tea/coffee making facilities, baby-listening, hairdryer and direct-dial telephone. Bargain breaks available throughout the year *ETB* ♛♛♛♛ *Commended, AA ** and Rosette, RAC **.*

VALLEY HOTEL, Ironbridge, Telford, Shropshire TF8 7DW

Tel: 01952 432247
Fax: 01952 432308

Fully licensed; 34 bedrooms, all with private bathrooms; Historic interest; Children welcome; Conference facilities; Dawley 3 miles; £££.

With acres of gardens and parkland sweeping down to the River Severn, this beautifully modernised Georgian building is an imposing sight. No less imposing are its facilities. The old servants' quarters and stables now form part of the main building to provide luxurious mews-style accommodation, each room (some with four-poster beds) having en suite amenities, remote-control television with satellite channels, direct-dial telephone and tea and coffee-makers. In the impressive Severn Gorge and just 10 minutes' walk from the world-famous Iron Bridge and adjacent to the many Ironbridge Gorge Museum sites, this is a fascinating place to visit. The Chez Maw Restaurant presents an extensive à la carte selection and a table d'hôte menu which is changed daily. ♛♛♛♛, *AA****.

DINHAM WEIR HOTEL,
Dinham Bridge, Ludlow,
Shropshire SY8 1EH

Tel: 01584 874431

Fully licensed; 8 bedrooms, all with private bathrooms; Historic interest; Children over 5 years welcome; Shrewsbury 24 miles; ££££.

To visit lovely Ludlow is to step back into history with its imposing Norman castle, old houses and inns to fascinate and delight. By the banks of the River Teme we made acquaintance with the delectable Dinham Weir Hotel, certainly a visual attraction in its own right. It occupies the site of the 17th century Castell Myll which was worked as an iron foundry until late Victorian times. For a relaxing holiday in historic surroundings and with the peaceful Shropshire countryshire to explore, this splendidly furnished hotel is well recommended. All rooms overlook the garden and river and have en suite facilities, television, telephone, radio and tea and coffee-makers. Dining here by candlelight is a special pleasure with full à la carte and table d'hôte menus available. 👑👑👑👑 *Commended, AA**, Ashley Courtenay, Logis.*

BOURTON MANOR,
Bourton, Much Wenlock, Near Telford,
Shropshire TF13 6QE

Tel: 0174636 531
Fax: 0174636 683

Licensed; 8 bedrooms, all with private bathrooms; Historic interest; Children and dogs welcome; Conference facilities; Telford 10 miles; £££.

This 16th century country house has recently been refurbished to offer comfortable hotel facilities. Accommodation comprises eight luxury bedrooms for single, twin and double occupancy, each with radio, colour television and direct-dial telephone. Conference facilities include a room for up to forty delegates; and the hotel restaurant and bars are open to non-residents. Bourton Manor is situated in its own private landscaped grounds and is ideal for walking, riding, or driving in the beautiful Welsh Border countryside. Many places of historic and cultural interest are within easy reach. **See also Colour Advertisement on page 10.**

PARK HOUSE HOTEL,
Park Street, Shifnal, Telford,
Shropshire TF11 9BA

Tel: 01952 460128
Fax: 01952 461658

Fully licensed; 54 bedrooms, all with private bathrooms; Children welcome, pets by prior arrangement; Leisure and conference facilities; Newport 7 miles; ££££.

More and more people are discovering the special delights of Shropshire — its magnificent countryside, historic towns and many places of interest such as the Ironbridge Gorge and Museum. Within this area Park House presents an ideal base for those wishing to enjoy the surroundings, atmosphere and standards of English country house living at its very best. Transformed from two classical Georgian buildings, the hotel provides all the amenities one expects to find at the finest modern hotels, but with an interior of period elegance and beauty. Special mention must be made of the award-winning Silvermere Restaurant which is gaining a reputation that stretches far beyond the county borders. An excellent range of leisure amenities offers relaxation in most attractive surroundings, and conference facilities are first class. 👑👑👑👑👑 *Highly Commended, AA**** and Rosette.*

SHELTON HALL HOTEL,
Shelton, Shrewsbury,
Shropshire SY3 8BH

Tel: 01743 343982
Fax: 01743 241515

Fully licensed; 9 bedrooms, all with private bathrooms; Historic interest; Children welcome; Conference facilities; Crudgington 10 miles; £££.

The fine cedar and copper beech trees on the lawns surrounding this lovely old house have witnessed a long and interesting history. Today it occupies an elevated position overlooking the medieval town of Shrewsbury and is ideally placed for touring North and Mid Wales. Bedrooms are appointed to the highest standards, with en suite facilities, colour television, and direct-dial telephone, and enjoy views over the spacious grounds. The excellent restaurant enjoys an enviable reputation by virtue of its varied menus and comprehensive wine list; local delicacies such as Shropshire Smokeys or Saltone Steak are often featured. Conferences and private functions can be catered for in the elegant Blue Room. *HETB* ♛♛♛♛ *Highly Commended, **.*

TELFORD HOTEL, GOLF AND COUNTRY CLUB,
Great Hay, Sutton Hill,
Shropshire TF7 4DT

Tel: 01952 429977
Fax: 01952 586602

Licensed; 86 bedrooms, all with private bathrooms; Historic interest; Children and pets welcome; Leisure and conference facilities; Shifnal 5 miles; ££.

Overlooking the famous Ironbridge Gorge, the Telford Hotel complex presents a magnificent array of facilities for those who want to unwind, keep fit, have fun and tone up the system. The leisure amenities offer remarkable variety with golf, perhaps, the salient attraction. With a resident golf professional on hand, there are both 18-hole and 9-hole courses, the former with full fairway irrigation ensuring good grass conditions throughout the year; in addition, there is an 8-bay floodlit driving range. After a round, one may repair to the bright and spacious Captain's Bar in which to extol (or exaggerate!) one's prowess. Change of sporting emphasis is provided by a superb indoor swimming pool, squash court, gymnasium and snooker table plus the relaxing qualities of a steam room, sauna, solarium and spa bath. Physical activity will promote a hearty appetite and, in this connection, the complex is extremely well served. In the Ironbridge Restaurant, a delicious selection of traditional British and classical French dishes will enthuse the palate and then there is the Kyoto Restaurant with its Japanese menu for the more adventurous or Darby's Pantry for light lunches and coffee and where there is a children's play area. Of great appeal to businessmen and holidaymakers alike, the complex has modern sophistications of the highest standards with suites and bedrooms all having en suite facilities, colour television, trouser press, hair dryer and beverage-makers. *ETB* ♛♛♛♛♛ *Commended.*

TERRICK HALL COUNTRY HOTEL, Hill Valley, Whitchurch, Shropshire SY13 4JZ

Tel: 01948 663031
Fax: 01948 663020

Fully licensed; 22 bedrooms, all with private bathrooms; Children and pets welcome; Leisure facilities; Shrewsbury 18 miles; ££.

Adjoining the Hill Valley Championship Golf Club with its twin courses, this comfortable, family-owned hotel is set in 4 acres of secluded woodland in the midst of the undulating and tranquil countryside. The ideal place for a really relaxing holiday, the hotel has beautifully appointed bedrooms, all with private bathroom, colour television, radio, telephone and tea and coffee-making facilities. Delightful public rooms include the Oak Room Lounge with carved wooden beams, chandelier and refined decor. Also stylish and elegant is the Edwardian Bar as well as the traditional Royale Restaurant, overlooking the 10th green, where dishes may be chosen from an interesting and varied international menu. 👑👑👑👑

Somerset

LORDLEAZE HOTEL, Henderson Drive (off Forton Road) Chard, Somerset TA20 2HW

Tel: 01460 61066
Fax: 01460 66468

Licensed; 16 bedrooms, all with private bathrooms; Historic interest; Children welcome; Taunton 12 miles; ££.

Only a few minutes away from the busy A30, we found this converted 18th century farmhouse to be a veritable oasis of peace and tranquillity, the warmth of greeting epitomised in the impressive lounge bar where a glowing log fire and a drop of one's fancy induces an equally glowing feeling of well-being. Decor throughout is just as impressive and the accommodation is of high calibre. Delightfully appointed en suite bedrooms overlook a gentle countryside. Dining here in the charming restaurant is a special pleasure: top quality food and excellent service. The magic of rural Somerset, Dorset and Devon calls without having to venture too far to fall under the spell. Real countryside contentment. 👑👑👑👑 *Highly Commended.*

BROADVIEW, East Street, Crewkerne, Near Yeovil (Dorset Border), Somerset TA18 7AG

Tel: 01460 73424

Unlicensed; 3 bedrooms, all with private bathrooms; Children welcome, pets by arrangement; Yeovil 8 miles; £.

Friendly, informal atmosphere — extremely comfortable and relaxing in an unusual colonial ambience. Carefully furnished en suite rooms have easy chairs, colour television, tea/coffee making facilities and central heating. Set in "National Garden Scheme" feature gardens with many unusual plants. Enjoy award-winning traditional English home cooking; stay a while and explore varied and contrasting places, National Trust gardens, houses, moors, quaint old villages, Dorset coast and Hardy country (a list is provided of 50 places). This is a no smoking house. Open all year. *ETB* 👑👑👑 *De Luxe, AA QQQQQ Premier Selected (both top quality awards).*

LANGTRY COUNTRY HOUSE HOTEL,
Washford, Watchet,
Somerset TA23 0NT

Tel: 01984 640484*

Residential licence; 6 bedrooms, all with private bathrooms; Children over 5 years welcome; Watchet 2 miles; £.

Sheltered by Exmoor to the west, the Quantocks to the east and the Brendons to the south, in an undulating swathe of green, this verdant part of West Somerset is one of our favourite parts of England. Here, nestling in 4 acres of beautiful gardens, two miles via our own one-time village of Old Cleeve from sandy Blue Anchor Bay, the exclusively non-smoking and ultra-comfortable Langtry Country House provides elegant accommodation of the highest calibre, all rooms having a private bathroom, colour television, clock radio, tea and coffee-makers and much more besides. This is a peaceful and rewarding place in which to stay. *Highly Commended.*

BATCH FARM COUNTRY HOTEL,
Lympsham, Near Weston-super-Mare,
Somerset BS24 0EX

Tel: 01934 750371*

Restaurant and residential licence; 8 bedrooms, all with private bathrooms; Historic interest; Children welcome; Weston-super-Mare 5 miles, Burnham-on-Sea 4; £/££.

An air of old world charm pervades Batch Farm Country Hotel, lending atmosphere to the modern accommodation. The eight bedrooms, all en suite, are comfortably fitted and have colour television and tea/coffee facilities; all enjoy panoramic views of hills and countryside. For guests' relaxation there is a fully licensed lounge bar and three lounges, one with colour television. Traditional home cooking using local produce and home-reared beef when possible is offered in the à la carte restaurant. Fishing is available in the grounds, and riding, swimming, tennis and golf are to be found locally. Ideal for touring, just three miles from the coast and with Cheddar, Wells, Longleat, Bristol and Bath all within easy reach. Personal attention from the resident proprietors will ensure that your holiday is a happy one. Most credit cards accepted. *AA and RAC**, Egon Ronay and Ashley Courtenay Recommended.* **See also Colour Advertisement on page 10.**

DANESWOOD HOUSE HOTEL,
Cuck Hill, Shipham, Near Winscombe,
Somerset BS25 1RD

Tel: 0193-484 3145
Fax: 0193-484 3824

Fully licensed; 13 bedrooms, all with private bathrooms; Historic interest; Children welcome, dogs by arrangement; Conference facilities; Cheddar 3 miles; £££.

High up in the Mendips and only two miles from Cheddar Caves, this imposing Edwardian structure has been transformed into a charming country house hotel under the inspired aegis of Proprietors, David and Elise Hodges who set great store by their first-class and imaginative cuisine. Traditional English and French dishes are combined with more adventurous influences, all admirably supported by a well-chosen list of wines and liqueurs. The accommodation is delightfully modernised without detriment to its original elegance, rooms being decorated to a high standard and featuring private baths and/or showers. Of special note is the magnificent Honeymoon Suite with a 7ft bed and large bathroom with sunken bath. *WCTB Commended, AA***, 2 Red Rosettes.*

WESTERCLOSE COUNTRY HOUSE HOTEL,
Withypool,
Somerset TA24 7QR

Tel: 01643 831302
Fax: 01643 831307

Licensed; 10 bedrooms, all with private bathrooms; Children welcome; Exford 2 miles; £.

This country house hotel nestles in the heart of Exmoor, set in nine acres of its own land, complete with donkeys and chickens! Bedrooms are all en suite and charmingly furnished. Guests can relax in the conservatory bar in summer or settle in front of a log fire in comfortable chairs in winter. Endless walks and places of interest to visit will leave you spoilt for choice and ready to enjoy a meal in the excellent restaurant, which specialises in traditional English and West Country dishes, accompanied by any of the wines from the hand-picked (and tasted!) list. Vegetarian dishes are always available. *Highly Commended, AA and RAC 2 Stars, AA Rosette.* **See also Colour Advertisement on page 11.**

YEOVIL COURT HOTEL,
West Coker Road, Yeovil,
Somerset BA20 2NE

Tel: 01935 863746
Fax: 01935 863990

Fully licensed; 18 bedrooms, all with private bathrooms; Children and pets welcome; Conference facilities; Taunton 21 miles; £££.

In the gentle Somerset countryside, only minutes from the market town of Yeovil, this attractively furnished hotel exhibits expertise and efficiency in all aspects. Decorated with style and flair, suites and bedrooms are luxuriously equipped with private bathrooms incorporating shower, handbasin and WC, remote-control colour television with video, radio, direct-dial telephone, hospitality tray and several practical extras. The magnificent honeymoon suite has a half-tester bed. This is a cheerful and friendly port of call and its pub-style bar provides a variety of refreshment to suit all tastes. A delightful award-winning restaurant of Georgian decor is the perfect setting for the excellent and commendably straightforward cuisine with a comprehensive selection of wines to further titillate the palate. ♛♛♛♛ *Highly Commended, AA*** and Red Rosette, RAC*** and Awards for Hospitality and Service.*

Staffordshire

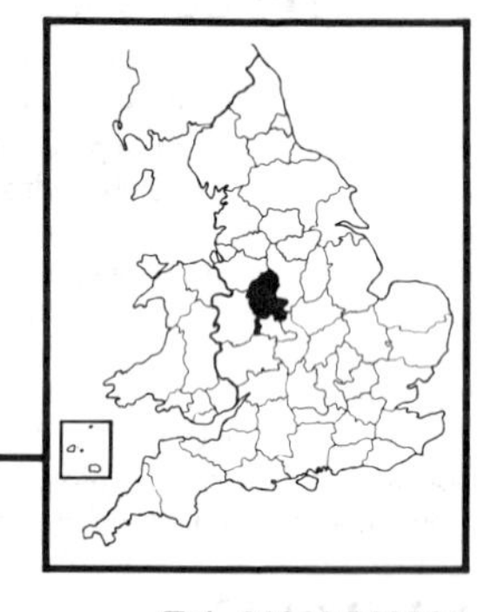

JARVIS NEWTON PARK HOTEL,
Newton Solney, Near Burton-on-Trent,
Staffordshire DE15 0SS

Tel: 01283 703568
Fax: 01283 703214

Fully licensed; 50 bedrooms, all with private bathrooms; Historic interest; Children and small dogs welcome; Conference facilities; Burton-on-Trent 3 miles; ££££.

Discerning travellers who expect that little bit more will find everything very much to their satisfaction at Jarvis Newton Park. Of great architectural interest, this fine Grade II Listed property has been sympathetically converted to provide comfortable en suite accommodation in bedrooms and suites with colour television, direct-dial telephone and a choice of hot beverages. Modern English cuisine, carefully prepared from the freshest ingredients, has made the oak-panelled restaurant a popular venue, while lighter appetites are catered for in the Derbyshire Bar. Set in carefully tended gardens just three miles from Burton-on-Trent, Jarvis Newton Park is well placed for access to the road, rail and air networks. *ETB* ♛♛♛♛ *Commended.*

SWINFEN HALL HOTEL,
Swinfen, Near Lichfield,
Staffordshire WS14 9RS

Tel: 01543 481494
Fax: 01543 480341

Fully licensed; 19 bedrooms, all with private bathrooms; Historic interest; Children welcome; Leisure and conference facilities; Birmingham 15 miles; ££££.

This attractively furnished hotel lies only 20 minutes from Birmingham's National Exhibition Centre, International Conference Centre and the East Midlands Airport. As such, it is justly popular for business as well as pleasure and has excellent conference and function facilities. With spacious public and private rooms, this 18th-century Manor House Hotel offers a combination of traditional elegance and modern comfort. All guest rooms and suites have private bathrooms, colour television, clock radio, direct-dial telephone, trouser press, hospitality tray and hairdryer. Particularly impressive is the Grand Entrance Hall with its balustraded minstrels' gallery and beautiful carved ceiling. *ETB* ♛♛♛♛♛.

HATHERTON COUNTRY HOTEL,
Pinfold Lane, Penkridge,
Staffordshire ST19 5QP

Tel: 01785 712459
Fax: 01785 715532

Fully licensed; 47 bedrooms, all with private bathrooms; Children and pets welcome; Leisure and conference facilities; Stafford 6 miles; ££££.

The live-wire Proprietors of this go-ahead hotel have compiled an interesting Diary of Events throughout the year from a Murder Mystery evening to a Sportsman's Dinner with guest personality. Furthermore, there is the profound attraction of a superb Leisure Centre with squash courts, jetstream pool, fully-equipped gymnasium, saunas and sunbeds. Additionally, a range of outdoor activities, including tennis, clay pigeon shooting, horse riding and golf can be arranged with prior notice. Quietly situated with spectacular views over the Staffordshire countryside, the hotel has splendid en suite accommodation and outstanding cuisine. Some rooms are specially designed for disabled guests. ♛♛♛♛.

STONE HOUSE HOTEL,
Stone,
Staffordshire ST15 0BQ

Tel: 01785 815531
Fax: 01785 814764

Fully licensed; 47 bedrooms, all with private bathrooms; Children welcome; Conference and leisure facilities; Stafford 7 miles; ££££.

Easily reached from the M6, this eminently comfortable and convivial hotel is popular with tourists and businessmen alike whilst refugees from the urban Midlands regularly make it a haven of escape at weekends. The elegant Garden Restaurant overlooks lovely grounds and offers a tempting selection of à la carte dishes, a prior visit to the spruce cocktail bar being an added joy. Charming furnishings betray a gifted eye for colour co-ordinates and guest rooms have private bathrooms, television with satellite channels, direct-dial telephone and beverage-makers. Many guests are attracted by the leisure and exercise facilities in the form of mini-gym, swimming pool, sauna and solarium whilst tennis and putting may be enjoyed in the grounds. *AA/RAC***.*

YE OLDE DOG AND PARTRIDGE HOTEL,
High Street, Tutbury, Burton-upon-Trent,
Staffordshire DE13 9LS

Tel: 01283 813030
Fax: 01283 813178

Fully licensed; 17 bedrooms, all with private bathrooms; Historic interest; Children and pets welcome; Derby 11 miles, Burton-upon-Trent 4; £££.

One of the most enchanting buildings in Tutbury's High Street, with flower-filled baskets and window boxes decorating its splendid oak-beamed frontage, this 500-year-old coaching inn tempts all to cross its threshold and loiter awhile. Two bars offer a choice of venue to partake of refreshment, and those seeking sustenance have the formal surroundings of the Carvery Rotisserie, where live music on the grand piano provides a background for the extensive display of wholesome hot and cold fare. Bedrooms, reached by an elegant Georgian spiral staircase, have television, fridge bar, tea and coffee facilities, hairdryer, radio alarm and luxury bathroom en suite. Some four-poster rooms are available. ♛♛♛♛, *AA***, RAC*** Merit Award, BTA Commended, Egon Ronay.*

HOAR CROSS HALL,
Hoar Cross, Near Yoxall, Staffordshire DE13 8QS

Tel: 01283 575671
Fax: 01283 575652

Fully licensed; 84 bedrooms, all with private bathrooms; Historic interest; Leisure and conference facilities; Lichfield 6 miles; ££££.

A health spa in the elegant and historic surroundings of a stately home with the facilities of a multi-starred hotel, Hoar Cross Hall is as unusual as it is unparalleled. Here, in an atmosphere of tranquillity, guests may relax in sumptuous splendour and revivify body and soul in a wide range of treatment programmes and sporting opportunities. From hydrotherapy baths and jet douches, flotation therapy, saunas, steam rooms to the superb hydrotherapy swimming pool, plus many other innovative treatments and classes, the expertise and vigilance of professional caring therapists is paramount. Outside, there are acres of woodland in which to stroll, a pitch and putt golf improvement course, tennis, croquet, trim trail, boules and badminton and the facility of taking a bicycle ride through the peaceful countryside. Pampered and perked up systems are rewarded by an exceptional and well-planned à la carte cuisine with special diets willingly catered for. The very ambience of this gracious Grade II listed building contributes to a feeling of well-being; restored to its former splendour by owners, Steve and Janet Joynes, the house is charmingly furnished with great attention given to cleverly co-ordinated colour schemes. An oak-panelled Jacobean staircase leads to the magnificently appointed en suite bedrooms, all of which have crown or half-tester beds; many also have four-poster water beds and corner whirlpool baths. The Penthouse Suites set a new standard in luxury, complete with balcony, lounge, master bedroom, dressing room, walk-in wardrobes, whirlpool bath and sauna. *AA*****.

Surrey

WARREN LODGE HOTEL,
Church Square, Shepperton-on-Thames, Surrey TW17 9JZ

Tel: 01932 242972
Fax: 01932 253883

Residential and restaurant licence; 48 bedrooms, all with private bathrooms; Children welcome; London 15 miles; £££.

Relaxation comes naturally at the Warren Lodge, strolling around the riverside lawn and gardens or enjoying a leisurely drink on the terrace watching the world float by. Situated close by the River Thames, it affords first-class facilities for the businessman, weekender or tourist, and London is easily reached by road or rail. The village of Shepperton has retained much of its old-world charm, and the historic Church Square has been designated a conservation area. The Hotel is well known for its food, featuring a wide choice of dishes which are served in the attractive panelled restaurant; tasty snacks and drinks are available in the cocktail lounge. All bedrooms are en suite, with hospitality trays, colour TV and hairdryers. ♛♛♛ *Commended.*

Suffolk

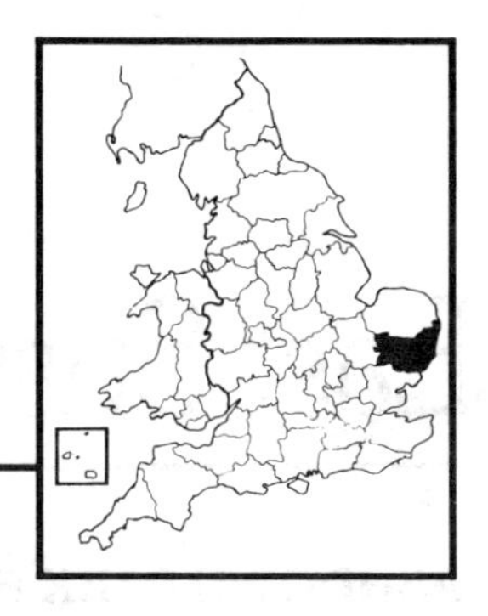

CHIPPENHALL HALL,
Fressingfield, Eye,
Suffolk IP21 5TD

Tel: 01379 586733 588180
Fax: 01379 586272

Residential licence; 4 bedrooms, all with private bathrooms; Historic interest; Children over 15 years welcome; Leisure facilities; Diss 8 miles; £.

With a fascinating history, this lovely heavily-beamed Listed Tudor house has origins dating back to Saxon times. With its mellow ambience unsullied, the house has been carefully modernised to incorporate the best of contemporary comforts. Full of character, each spacious guest room now has either an en suite shower or bathroom. A sense of timelessness is aided in no small way by relaxing before a roaring log fire in the sitting room or enjoying a satisfying candlelit dinner round the refectory table in the dining room. The house stands in seven acres in the heart of unspoiled Suffolk, and in the summer months a heated outdoor swimming pool, set in a sheltered courtyard, is a popular attraction. ♛♛♛ *Highly Commended, AA Selected QQQQ, Johansen Award for Excellence.*

East Sussex

ASHDOWN PARK HOTEL,
Forest Row,
East Sussex RH18 5JR

Tel: 01342 824988
Fax: 01342 826206

Fully licensed; 95 bedrooms, all with private bathrooms; Historic interest; Children welcome; Leisure and conference facilities; East Grinstead 3 miles; ££££.

Victorian grandeur with the finest modern appointments, such is the allure of this magnificent hotel set in 186 beautifully landscaped acres in the heart of the Ashdown Forest. Luxurious comfort is complemented to perfection by high embossed ceilings, leaded windows, rich drapes and open log fires. Suites and bedrooms have individual charisma and are exquisitely furnished, some having elegant four-posters. Overlooking a lake and immaculate lawns, the Anderida Restaurant is the setting for memorable dining, outstanding cuisine supported by fine wines and attentive service. Relaxing leisure diversions include a fine swimming pool, beauty therapy, fitness studio, croquet and snooker whilst, for the energetic there are squash courts and a 9-hole par 3 golf course. ♛♛♛♛♛ *De Luxe, RAC Blue Ribbon, AA Red Stars.*

BEAUPORT PARK HOTEL,
Battle Road, Hastings,
East Sussex TN38 8EA

Tel: 01424 851222
Fax: 01424 852465

Licensed; 16 double bedrooms, 7 single, all with bathrooms; Leisure facilities; Battle 3 miles, Hastings 3; ££.

This fine three-star country house hotel, set amidst 33 acres of woodland and picturesque formal gardens, offers old-fashioned personal service from resident directors Kenneth and Helena Melsom. All guest rooms have private bathrooms and are equipped with remote-control colour television, electric trouser press, direct-dial telephone, hairdryer and tea/coffee making facilities. There is a heated swimming pool in the grounds, country walks, tennis courts, croquet lawn, badminton, outdoor chess, French boules and putting green, with an 18-hole golf course, riding stables and squash courts adjoining. Prospective guests are invited to write or telephone for brochure and tariff, and a country house bargain breaks leaflet. "Country House Getaway Breaks" are available all year. ♛♛♛♛, *AA and RAC***.*

CLEAVERS LYNG COUNTRY HOTEL,
Church Road, Herstmonceux, East Sussex BN27 1QJ

Tel: 01323 833131
Fax: 01323 833617

Fully licensed; 8 bedrooms; Historic interest; Children and pets welcome; Eastbourne, Bexhill and Hastings all 11 miles; £.

For excellent home cooking in traditional English style, comfort and informality, this small family-run hotel in the heart of rural East Sussex is well recommended. Peacefully set in beautiful landscaped gardens extending to 1·5 acres featuring a rockpool with waterfall. Adjacent to Herstmonceux Castle West Gate, the house dates from 1577, as its oak beams and inglenook fireplace bear witness. This is an ideal retreat for a quiet sojourn away from urban clamour. The castles at Pevensey, Scotney, Bodiam and Hever are all within easy reach as are Battle Abbey, Kipling's House, Batemans, Michelham Priory and the seaside resorts of Eastbourne, Bexhill and Hastings. Bedrooms are fully ensuite, and all have central heating and tea/coffee making facilities. On the ground floor there is an oak-beamed restaurant with a fully licensed bar, cosy residents' lounge with television and an outer hall with telephone and cloakrooms. Children and pets welcome. Peace, tranquillity and a warm welcome await you. Special attraction: Badger Watch. **See also Colour Advertisement on page 11.**

THE ROSE & CROWN INN,
Mayfield, East Sussex TN20 6TE

Tel and Fax: 01435 872200

Licensed; Bedrooms with private bathrooms; Historic interest; Children over 7 years welcome; Tunbridge Wells 8 miles; ££/£££.

This famous inn sits on the village green of the historic and picturesque village of Mayfield. Dating back to 1546, its unspoilt oak-beamed bars with log fires serve excellent real ales and quality bar meals, or you may choose to dine in the informal candlelit restaurant which serves award-winning food and excellent wines. Each luxury period bedroom has en suite bathroom, central heating, colour television, radio alarm, hairdryer, tea and coffee making facilities, and trouser press. 👑👑👑👑 *Commended, AA QQQQ Selected and Food Rosette, Egon Ronay.*

LITTLE ORCHARD HOUSE,
West Street, Rye,
East Sussex TN31 7ES

Tel: 01797 223831

3 bedrooms, all with private bathrooms; Historic interest; London 67 miles, Canterbury 33, Battle 14, Tenterden 12; £/££.

Rye is the most complete small medieval hill town in Britain, and this charming Georgian townhouse is a delightful surprise right at the heart of the Ancient Town, quietly situated in the picturesque cobbled streets with a traditional walled Old English garden and its unique Smugglers Watch Tower. Each bedroom, one with traditional four-poster, has a bathroom en-suite, colour television and hot drinks making facilities. The house is stylishly decorated and furnished with antiques throughout, lots of books, paintings and an open fire in winter. Guests will enjoy a generous country breakfast which features as much local, organic produce as possible, and a good choice of outstanding restaurants are within easy walking distance.

SPINDLEWOOD COUNTRY HOUSE HOTEL,
Wallcrouch, Wadhurst,
East Sussex TN5 7JG

Tel: 01580 200430
Fax: 01580 201132

Restaurant and residential licence; 5 bedrooms, all with private bathrooms; Children welcome; Conference facilities; Ticehurst 1 mile; ££.

Amidst the quiet lanes of verdant East Sussex, Spindlewood is a late-Victorian country house with an informal air of well-being. For some years in the care of the Fitzsimmons family, the house adheres to the highest standards of modern comfort. Central heating is installed throughout and handsomely decorated bedrooms have en suite facilities, colour television, radio/alarm, direct-dial telephone and tea and coffee-makers. The house stands proudly in 5 acres of gardens, bright with colour in summer months whilst winter chill is rebuffed by log fires in public rooms. The spacious restaurant with its high patterned ceiling and large windows has a fine reputation for its gourmet food and select wines.

West Sussex

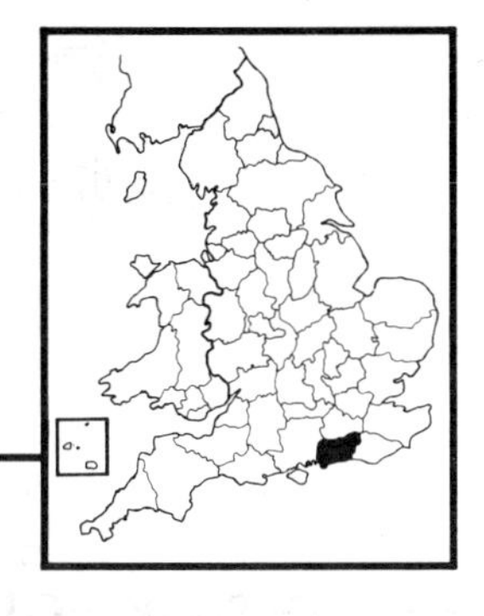

BURPHAM COUNTRY HOTEL,
Old Down, Burpham, Near Arundel,
West Sussex BN18 9RJ

Tel and Fax: 01903 882160

Residential and restaurant licence; 10 bedrooms, all with private bathrooms; Historic interest; Children over 10 welcome; Conference facilities; Little Hampton 4 miles; £.

In a picturesque, unspoilt English village complete with historic church, inn and green with cricket pitch, this lovely country house stands in an old-world garden enjoying superb views over the South Downs. It is reputed to have been a hunting lodge for the Duke of Norfolk. Certainly, its warm ambience remains but to its gracious style modern touches have been added without spoiling its elegance. The spacious en suite bedrooms are delightfully appointed, each having colour television, tea-maker, and direct-dial telephone. The charming licensed restaurant with its splendid table d'hôte menu and excellent wine list is open to non-residents and vegetarian dishes are available. Facilities exist for small functions, business meetings and seminars for about 20 people. *ETB* ♛♛♛, *AA**, AA Rosette for Culinary Excellence, Ashley Courtenay Recommended.*

OCKENDEN MANOR HOTEL,
Ockenden Lane, Cuckfield,
West Sussex RH17 5LD

Tel: 01444 416111
Fax: 01444 415549

Residential licence; 22 bedrooms, all with private bathrooms; Historic interest; Children welcome; Conference facilities; Haywards Heath 2 miles; ££££.

Spacious and elegantly furnished, Ockenden Manor has its origins in Tudor times, since when it has been considerably extended, the exterior presenting an intriguing blend of old and new architectural styles. Within, the decor is skilfully planned to bring out the best features of time-honoured grace and modern convenience. The beautiful restaurant, with its painted ceiling, oak panelling and stained glass windows, provides a perfect setting in which to enjoy the excellent food. Each bedroom, deliciously draped, has fine appointments that include a private bathroom, telephone and tea and coffee making facilities. Standing in nine acres of gardens, the Ockenden Suite welcomes private lunch and dinner parties. *SEETB* ♛♛♛♛, *AA 3 Rosettes.*

HILTON PARK HOTEL,
Cuckfield, Haywards Heath,
West Sussex RH17 5EG

Tel: 01444 454555
Fax: 01444 457222

Restaurant and residential licence; 15 bedrooms, all with private bathrooms; Children welcome; Conference facilities; Brighton 12 miles; ££.

With magnificent views of the South Downs, this is a spacious and gracious Victorian country house beautifully set in park-like grounds of 3 acres. Conveniently placed for a variety of rural, historic, cultural, sporting and seaside pleasures, the hotel is furnished to a high degree of comfort; terms for a room with private bathroom, colour television, direct-dial telephone, radio and tea and coffee-makers are reasonable indeed. Children under 16, sharing a family room with two adults, are accommodated free of charge, only paying for meals taken. The licensed restaurant and Vinery Bar are justly popular, the cuisine having an international influence backed by an excellent cellar. First-rate facilities exist for small meetings and private functions. *SEETB* ♛♛♛♛.

GHYLL MANOR,
Rusper, Near Horsham,
West Sussex RH12 4PX

Tel: 01293 871571
Fax: 01293 871419

Fully licensed; 24 bedrooms, all with private bathrooms; Historic interest; Children and pets welcome; Leisure and conference facilities; Crawley 4 miles; £££/££££.

A superb base from which to explore the verdant South Downs, Sussex coast or the myriad attractions of London, Ghyll Manor combines the elegance of the past with the exacting requirements of the modern age. The building dates from the Tudor period and the oak beams of the restaurant are those of the original tithe barn. The aura associated with a classical English country house pervades the atmosphere, blending harmoniously with the contemporary refinements that have been skilfully introduced. The accommodation may be termed fairly as luxurious. Suites have been individually furnished and decorated, and there is a four-poster apartment which has an inglenook fireplace and magnificent views and which is a favourite with honeymoon couples. Each guest room is equipped to the highest standard with private bathroom, colour television, radio, direct-dial telephone; a number of pleasant and practical extras can be arranged on request. The restaurant has an enviable reputation for its fine cuisine, table d'hôte and à la carte menus being available for luncheon and dinner. One may sample an aperitif in the cocktail bar and round off the meal with coffee in the lounge or on the patio. The Manor has first-class facilities for conferences, business meetings and private functions. *ETB* ♛♛♛♛♛, *AA****, Rosette for restaurant.*

CHEQUERS HOTEL,
Pulborough,
West Sussex RH20 1AD

Tel: 01798 872486
Fax: 01798 872715

Residential and restaurant licence; 11 bedrooms, all with private bathrooms; Historic interest; Children and dogs welcome; London 49 miles, Brighton 19, Arundel 9; DB&B ££.

Tastefully extended over the years, the original Queen Anne house huddles on the edge of Pulborough village, gazing peacefully out over the Arun Valley to the South Downs beyond. Excellent home-cooked dishes using local produce and fresh vegetables have given Chequers its reputation for fine cuisine, enhanced now by the award of an AA Rosette for the restaurant. Accommodation is luxurious and well appointed with private bathrooms, and also includes colour television, direct-dial telephone, trouser press, hairdryer and tea/coffee facilities. Four-poster bedrooms and ground floor bedrooms also available. Open fires make this as pleasant a holiday venue in winter as it is in summer. Places to visit include Parham, Petworth, Goodwood, Arundel, Chichester and the Weald & Downland Open Air Museum. New garden conservatory. BARGAIN BREAKS are available throughout the year. *ETB ♛♛♛♛ Highly Commended, RAC and AA **, Ashley Courtenay, Egon Ronay and Johansens Recommended.*

Warwickshire

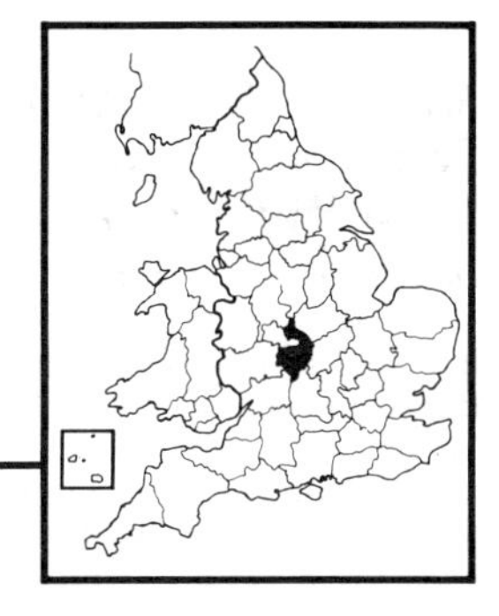

AYLESBURY HOUSE HOTEL,
Aylesbury Road, Packwood, Near Hockley Heath,
Warwickshire B94 6PL

Tel: 01564 779207; Fax: 01564 770917

Residential licence; 34 bedrooms, all with private bathrooms; Historic interest; Children and pets welcome; Leisure and conference facilities; Coventry 4 miles; £££.

Built in the time of the Stuarts and with several features added in subsequent centuries, Aylesbury House is not only architecturally fascinating; today, it is a supremely comfortable hotel conveniently located for many places of cultural, sporting and historic interest. In addition, it is of considerable attraction to businessmen. Set in 12 acres of grounds, the hotel has 6 spacious guest rooms in the main house and 28 cottage bedrooms across the courtyard. Each has an en suite bath or shower room, satellite television, radio, telephone, hair dryer, trouser press and tea and coffee-making facilities. Taking its name from the ancient tree on the croquet lawn, the elegant Mulberry Restaurant is a popular venue for discerning diners. *♛♛♛♛, AA***.*

ALVESTON MANOR,
Clopton Bridge, Stratford-upon-Avon,
Warwickshire CV37 7HP

Tel: 01789 204581
Fax: 01789 414095

Fully licensed; 106 bedrooms, all with private bathrooms; Historic interest; Children welcome, pets by arrangement; Conference facilities; Warwick 8 miles; ££££.

Rich in history, as epitomised by carved oak doors, panelled walls and draped leaded windows, this is the ideal base for a host of active and passive pleasures that the area provides. Just 5 minutes' stroll away from the Royal Shakespeare Theatre and Shakespeare's birthplace, the lovely house and modern annexe stand in beautifully landscaped gardens. The AA Rosette-awarded restaurant is renowned for its splendid English and international cuisine. In winter, log fires add to the natural warmth of public rooms whilst guest rooms are handsomely appointed with bathrooms en suite, television with satellite channels, direct-dial telephone, tea and coffee making facilities and 24-hour room service. *Heart of England Tourist Board* 👑👑👑👑👑 *Highly Commended, AA****.*

West Midlands

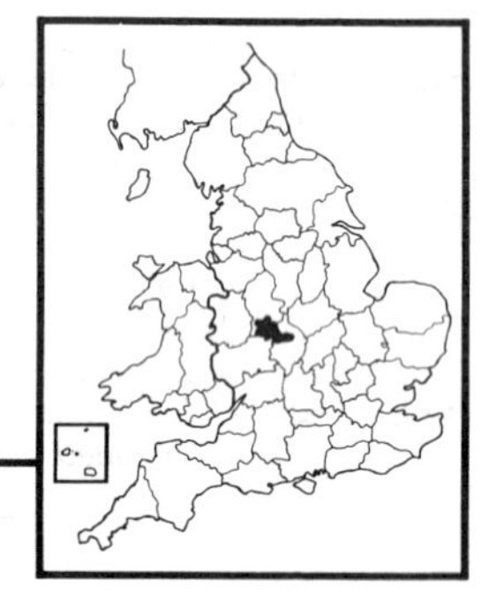

MOOR HALL HOTEL,
Four Oaks, Sutton Coldfield,
West Midlands B75 6LN

Tel: 0121 308 3751
Fax: 0121 308 8974

Fully licensed; 75 bedrooms, all with private bathrooms; Historic interest; Children welcome, pets by arrangement; Leisure and conference facilities; Birmingham 7 miles; ££££.

It is hard to believe that this spacious country house hotel is just fifteen minutes from Birmingham city centre, with excellent road, air and rail links to all parts of the country. Secluded in carefully tended gardens and parkland, it offers luxury and comfort, blending the most up-to-date amenities with the traditional character of the English country house. Each of the 75 bedrooms has en suite facilities and is equipped to the highest standards; for an extra touch of luxury superior rooms are available, including one with its own whirlpool spa bath. Diners can choose between the elegant French Restaurant or the Country Kitchen Carvery. For relaxation, there is a superbly equipped fitness centre and indoor pool. *RAC***.*

Please mention
Recommended COUNTRY HOTELS
when seeking refreshment or
accommodation at a Hotel
mentioned in these pages

JARVIS PENNS HALL HOTEL & COUNTRY CLUB,

Penns Lane, Walmley, Sutton Coldfield, West Midlands B76 1LH

Tel: 0121-351 3111
Fax: 0121-313 1297

Fully licensed; 136 bedrooms, all with private bathrooms; Children and pets welcome; Leisure and conference facilities; Birmingham 7 miles; ££££.

A happy amalgam of old and new, set in 10 acres of rolling grounds and overlooking a beautiful tree-lined lake, elegant Penns Hall is not only a magnificent conference and leisure centre, but also an intimate venue for those who appreciate comfort, personal service and international cuisine of the highest standard. Developed from a simple 17th century house, the hotel offers major reception suites and delightfully appointed bedrooms all of which incorporate a private bathroom, colour television, and tea and coffee making facilities. Many of those in the new extension have balconies dominating views of lake or garden. Being only 6½ miles from the city centre and 10 miles from the National Exhibition Centre, with easy access to motorway link and M6, M40, M42 and M5, this conveniently placed hotel is justly popular for private or business functions for which it is superbly appointed. One of the finest leisure centres in the Midlands has been built in the grounds, reached by means of a glass-covered corridor from the hotel. The amenities here will delight all ages. Relax in the sauna or solarium, or work out in the squash court or gym, and then visit the swimming area where a spa bath bubbles its way into a large rippling pool that curves beneath palm trees. Snooker is also available, and for the children there is a special pool and supervised playroom and playground. The poolside bar is an attraction in itself. 👑👑👑👑👑, *AA and RAC****.*

Wiltshire

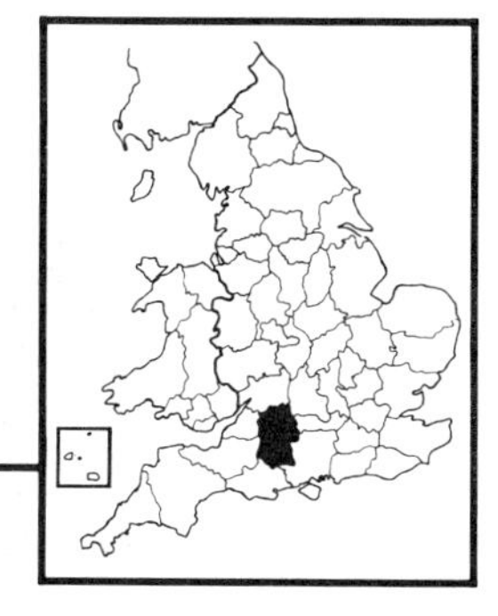

ANTROBUS ARMS HOTEL,

Church Street, Amesbury, Near Salisbury, Wiltshire SP4 7EY

Tel: 01980 623163
Fax: 01980 622112

Fully licensed; 20 bedrooms, 16 with private bathrooms; Children and pets welcome; Salisbury 6 miles; ££.

This attractive town hotel, with a magnificent walled garden at the rear, is situated six miles from Salisbury and half a mile off the A303. All bedrooms have central heating, colour television, tea/coffee making facilities and direct-dial telephone; most are en suite. Our highly acclaimed Fountain Restaurant serves table d'hôte and à la carte menus; bar meals are also available. This is an ideal base for touring many local places of interest, including Stonehenge, Woodhenge, Salisbury Cathedral, Wilton House and the New Forest. Fishing, tennis, golf courses, motor racing (Thruxton) are all close by. 👑👑👑 *Approved, Les Routiers.* **See also Colour Advertisement on p12.**

LEIGH PARK HOTEL,
Bradford-on-Avon,
Wiltshire BA15 2RA

Tel: 01225 864885
Fax: 01225 862315

Fully licensed; 22 bedrooms, all with private bathrooms; Historic interest; Children and pets welcome; Leisure and conference facilities; Trowbridge 3 miles; £££.

A charming Georgian country house standing within 5 acres of grounds with a walled garden and commercial vineyard, Leigh Park presents spacious and well-furnished accommodation, each tastefully appointed guest room having a private bathroom and/or shower, colour television, radio, direct-dial telephone and tea and coffee-making facilities. The popular Wiltshire Restaurant, open to non-residents, has the benefit of a chef-inspired traditional English and French cuisine with imaginative dishes cooked to order. Most of the fruit and vegetables are home grown. Bradford-on-Avon is a picturesque Saxon stone-built town with old houses and steep alleys whilst the historic attractions of Bath may be reached within 20 minutes. *WETB* ♛♛♛♛ *Commended, RAC****.

STANTON MANOR HOTEL,
Stanton Saint Quintin, Near Chippenham,
Wiltshire SN14 6DQ

Tel: 01666 837552
Fax: 01666 837022

Restaurant and residential licence; 10 bedrooms, all with private bathrooms; Children welcome; Chippenham 4 miles; ££££.

Set in 5 acres of delightful gardens and woodland, Stanton Manor's sense of history lives on. The original house was listed in the Domesday Book and was later held by Lord Burghley, Elizabeth I's Chief Minister. All that remains of those far-off times is the dovecote although the large stone fireplaces that adorn the present 19th century building were probably salvaged from the old manor. Sympathetically converted into a first-class country hotel of style and elegance, the house offers spacious and individually furnished bedrooms all with en suite facilities, colour television, hair dryer, trouser press, tea and coffee-makers and lovely countryside views. Genteel in every respect, the hotel places emphasis on its fine English cuisine and courteous service. *AA***, Rosette for Restaurant.*

KNOLL HOUSE HOTEL,
Swindon Road, Malmesbury,
Wiltshire SN16 9LU

Tel: 01666 823114
Fax: 01666 823897

Fully licensed; 22 bedrooms, all with private bathrooms; Historic interest; Children and pets welcome; Leisure and conference facilities; Swindon 14 miles; ££.

On the southern edge of the Cotswolds, historic Malmesbury is the oldest borough in England. Almost surrounded by the River Avon, it boasts an imposing Norman abbey whilst its thoroughfares are lined with picturesque stone cottages. In such a charming setting, the solidly-built Knoll House has recently been extensively refurbished to a high standard, at the same time preserving its period features. Bedrooms all have en suite facilities, remote-control colour television, direct-dial telephone and tea and coffee-makers. Culinary flair and style is evident in the award-winning Cedar Room Restaurant and Brasserie and special dietary requirements are willingly catered for. The hotel has a large garden with a heated swimming pool. ♛♛♛♛ *Commended, RAC***, AA*** and Rosette.*

Key to Tourist Board Ratings

The Crown Scheme

(England, Scotland & Wales)

Covering hotels, motels, private hotels, guesthouses, inns, bed & breakfast, farmhouses. Every Crown classified place to stay is inspected annually. *The classification:* Listed then 1-5 Crown indicates the range of facilities and services. Higher quality standards are indicated by the terms APPROVED, COMMENDED, HIGHLY COMMENDED and DELUXE.

The Key Scheme

(also operates in Scotland using a Crown symbol)

Covering self-catering in cottages, bungalows, flats, houseboats, houses, chalets, etc. Every Key classified holiday home is inspected annually. *The classification:* 1-5 Key indicates the range of facilities and equipment. Higher quality standards are indicated by the terms APPROVED, COMMENDED, HIGHLY COMMENDED and DELUXE.

The Q Scheme

(England, Scotland & Wales)

Covering holiday, caravan, chalet and camping parks. Every Q rated park is inspected annually for its quality standards. The more ✓ in the Q – up to 5 – the higher the standard of what is provided.

Worcestershire

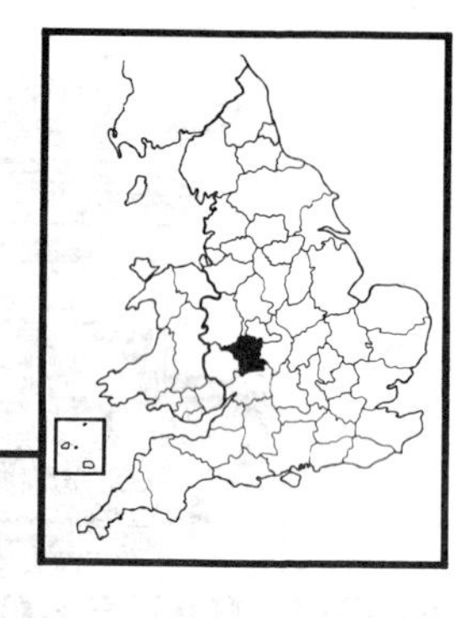

DORMY HOUSE HOTEL,
Willersey Hill, Broadway,
Worcestershire WR12 7LF

Tel: 01386 852711*
Fax: 01386 858636

Fully licensed; 49 bedrooms, all with private bathrooms; Children and pets welcome; Leisure and conference facilities; Evesham 5 miles; £££.

Golfers will recognise the term "dormy" as meaning "unbeatable" — and few who have had the pleasure of visiting this first-rate establishment would argue with that description of its facilities. Polished wood, pretty fabrics and fresh flowers combine with attentive service and first-class amenities to make a stay in this seventeenth-century converted farmhouse a truly memorable experience. Set in the heart of the rolling Cotswold countryside, the hotel is ideally placed for exploring the many places of interest in the area, including Cheltenham and Stratford-upon-Avon. To sample the delights of this charming spot why not try a temptingly named "Champagne Weekend" or "Carefree Midweek Break" — details will gladly be sent on request. *ETB ♛♛♛♛ Highly Commended, AA***, RAC*** Merit Award Highly Commended and Recommended.*

---

* The appearance of an asterisk after the telephone number indicates that the hotel in question is closed for a period during the winter months. Exact dates should be ascertained from the hotel itself.

SALFORD HALL HOTEL, Abbots Salford, Evesham, Worcestershire WR11 5UT

Tel: 01386 871300
Fax: 01386 871301

Fully licensed; 33 bedrooms, all with private bathrooms; Historic interest; Children welcome; Leisure and conference facilities; Worcester 13 miles; ££££.

A beautiful Grade I listed building, Salford Hall is some 500 years old. Rescued from near dilapidation by a team of craftsmen who worked for over a year to restore its original features, it now performs sterling duty as a country house hotel of high distinction. Residents may now view the magnificent display of stained glass and oak panelling whilst taking full advantage of newly-introduced luxury appointments. The reception hall exudes the warmth and splendour of bygone days with an open log fire and massive oak beams. Along one side runs the medieval screens passage leading to the oldest part of the building — and the cosy bar. Originally built as a guest residence for the monks of nearby Evesham Abbey, it has been noted over the years for good living and extravagant entertaining. How appropriate, therefore, that the Hall is following in the same tradition. Each bedroom, named after personages connected with the Hall in its eventful past, is lavishly equipped with its own bathroom en suite, colour television, in-house video, mini-bar, direct-dial telephone and tea and coffee-makers amongst its many amenities. In an area steeped in history and nestling in the Avon Valley between Stratford, the Cotswolds and the fertile Vale of Evesham, this noble and romantic Tudor manor, with its gracious appointments, cheerful service and gourmet cuisine, extends warm hospitality of which the good-living monks of old would have been proud. *HEETB ♛♛♛♛ Highly Commended.*

FOLEY ARMS HOTEL,
14 Worcester Road, Malvern,
Worcestershire WR14 4QS

Tel: 01684 573397
Fax: 01684 569665

Fully licensed; 28 bedrooms, all with private bathrooms; Children and pets welcome; £££.

A Regency Coaching Inn with the style and ambience of a Country House Hotel, the Foley Arms was built in 1810 and has 28 bedrooms, some with spectacular views over the Severn Valley. It is situated in the centre of Great Malvern with its own gardens and car parking. This family-run hotel has been awarded AA***RAC with Merit Awards for hospitality and its restaurant. The elegant Elgar's Restaurant serves fine English cuisine and the Foley Tavern adjoining the hotel offers a pub-style bar with real ales and an interesting choice of bar meals. Malvern is conveniently located for touring the Cotswolds, Wales, Hereford and Cheshire; M5 and M50 motorways are only 15 minutes away. *ETB* 👑👑👑👑.

North Yorkshire

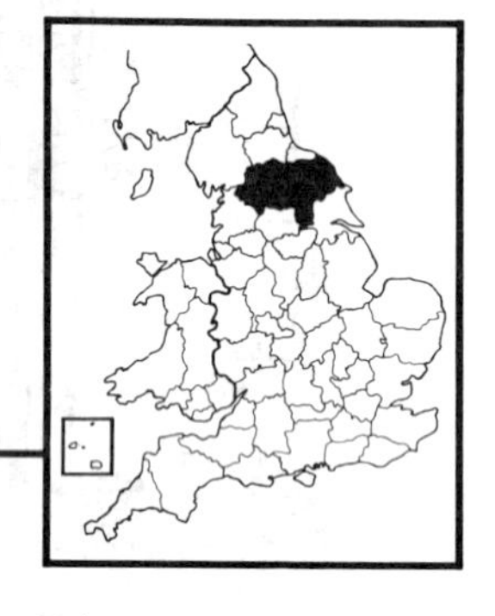

THE SHIP INN,
Acaster Malbis, York,
North Yorkshire YO2 1VH

Tel: 01904 705609/703888
Fax: 01904 705971

Licensed; 8 bedrooms, all with private bathrooms; Historic interest; Children welcome; Leeds 17 miles, York 4; ££.

This friendly and attractive hostelry on the banks of the Ouse is only a short distance from the magnificence of York, the United Kingdom's second most popular tourist attraction. Offering first-class fare and spruce accommodation which includes a four-poster bedroom and a family room, the inn makes a superb holiday headquarters and is equally popular with boating enthusiasts and businessmen. Excellent evening dinners are served in the relaxed olde worlde atmosphere of the restaurant, whilst a wide range of lunches and evening snacks may be enjoyed in the friendly Riverside Bar.Those with a penchant for fishing may be well accommodated, and the inn has its own moorings. Further afield, the Yorkshire Dales beckon, and the coast may be reached in less than an hour. *Tourist Board Listed Commended, AA Listed.*

LIME TREE FARM,
Hutts Lane, Grewelthorpe, Near Ripon,
North Yorkshire HG4 3DA

Tel: 01765 658450

Unlicensed; 3 bedrooms, all with private bathrooms; Historic interest; Children and well-behaved pets welcome; Masham 3 miles; £.

The farmhouse is almost 200 years old, with exposed beams, oak panelling, open fires, clipped rugs, grandfather clocks, etc, and is situated on a secluded Dales farm near Ripon, ideal for touring and visiting Yorkshire's many attractions. All bedrooms are en suite and have colour television and tea/coffee making facilities; the dining room has separate tables; guests have their own lounge with access to books and games. There is central heating throughout. A full English breakfast is served, and good traditional home cooking is a feature of the four-course evening meals (optional). Open all year. 👑👑👑.

VALLEY VIEW FARM,
Old Byland, Helmsley, York,
North Yorkshire YO6 5LG

Tel: 01439 798221

Licensed; 4 bedrooms, all with private bathrooms; Children and pets welcome; Thirsk 12 miles; £.

A well appointed farmhouse situated on the edge of a small village within the North York Moors National Park, with outstanding views across beautiful countryside. Relax in rural peace and tranquillity; excellent walking country. The warm, spacious, en suite rooms all have central heating, colour television and tea/coffee making facilities, and there is a traditionally furnished residents' lounge with open fires. Leisurely farmhouse dinners and substantial breakfasts are served in the dining room (vegetarian meals and packed lunches available on request). Three super self catering cottages sleeping two/four/six also available. Please phone for brochure. ♛♛♛ *Highly Commended.*

MOORGARTH HALL COUNTRY GUEST HOUSE HOTEL,
New Road, Ingleton,
North Yorkshire LA6 3DN

Tel: 015242 41946
Fax: 015242 42252

Licensed; 8 bedrooms, all with private bathrooms; Children welcome, dogs by arrangement; Car park (14); Settle 9 miles, Kirkby Lonsdale 8; £.

Built in 1891 and set well back from the road in wooded gardens, Moorgarth Hall is within easy travelling distance of the Lake District and North Lancashire's Trough of Bowland. The spacious, centrally heated bedrooms afford superb views, and have colour television and tea and coffee trays. On chillier evenings a log fire burns in the cosy sitting room. An evening meal can be provided most days if required. Children are very welcome — toys and children's meals are available, and reduced rates apply when sharing with parents. Places of interest in the surrounding area include Ingleborough Cave, Kirkby Lonsdale and the Three Peaks.

THE DOWER HOUSE,
Bond End, Knaresborough,
North Yorkshire HG5 9AL

Tel: 01423 863302
Fax: 01423 867665

Restaurant and residential licence; 32 bedrooms, all with private bathrooms; Historic interest; Children and pets welcome; Leisure and conference facilities; Harrogate 3 miles; £££.

With a reputation for hospitality that goes back to Jacobean times, this fine English country house today reveals amenities that exceed normal standards. Assured of outstanding accommodation with innovative cuisine in the best British tradition, guests return again and again to the warmest of welcomes from the Davies family. Guest rooms are delightfully appointed, each having en suite facilities, direct-dial telephone and hospitality tray. Residents are invited to make full use of the luxurious Corniche Health and Leisure Club where amenities include a gymnasium, swimming pool and jacuzzi, plus the relaxing properties of a sauna or steam cabin; followed, perhaps, by a drink with friends in the bar or on the terrace. *YHTB ♛♛♛♛ Commended, AA and RAC ***.*

MONK FRYSTON HALL,
Monk Fryston, Leeds,
North Yorkshire LS25 5DU

Tel: 01977 682369
Fax: 01977 683544

Fully licensed; 28 bedrooms, all with private bathrooms; Historic interest; Children and pets welcome; Selby 7 miles; ££££.

This lovely old manor house exudes the warmest of welcomes through its mullioned windows, rich oak-panelled lounges and bars, log fires and willing service. Peacefully ensconced in wooded grounds where a wide terrace leads to the Italian gardens and an ornamental lake, the hotel is an historic attraction in its own right. Serving holidaymakers and businessmen with equal facility, it is only a short distance from the A1, and conveniently placed for the county's tourist and commercial centres. Guest rooms are beautifully appointed; all have a private bathroom, colour television, radio and direct-dial telephone. Just as excellent is the catering for which a deserved reputation has been achieved for the extensive choice of its à la carte and table d'hôte dishes. 👑👑👑👑, *AA***, RAC*** and Merit Awards, Egon Ronay, Johansens.*

GREENACRES COUNTRY GUEST HOUSE,
Amotherby, Malton,
North Yorkshire YO17 0TG

Tel and Fax: 01653 693623*

Restaurant and residential licence; 9 bedrooms, all with private bathrooms; Children welcome; Leisure facilities; Malton 3 miles; £.

A beautiful country house in the heart of Rydedale with 2½ acres of landscaped gardens, Greenacres has amenities that would shame many a vaunted country hotel. A special feature is a superb indoor swimming pool. Spacious public rooms are supremely comfortable and betray a fine eye for colour co-ordinates. The traditional home cooking is a prime attraction; a full English breakfast is served and packed lunches supplied with the promise of a four-course dinner in the evening. Vegetarian and special diets are catered for by arrangement. Rooms of varying sizes all have an en suite bath or shower, colour television, tea and coffee-making facilities and hair dryer: four of them are on the ground floor with french windows opening on to a patio. *YHTB* 👑👑 *Highly Commended, RAC Highly Acclaimed.*

MILLERS HOUSE HOTEL, Middleham, Wensleydale, North Yorkshire DL8 4NR

Tel: 01969 622630*
Fax: 01969 623570

Fully licensed; 7 bedrooms, all en suite; Leyburn 2 miles; ££.

Standing just off the cobbled market square in the historic village of Middleham, a major racehorse training centre, this peaceful Georgian country house commands splendid views from its elevated position. Nestled in the heart of the Yorkshire Dales, this is the perfect base from which to explore Herriot Country, with its pretty villages, ancient market towns, castles and abbeys. Everything is designed for your comfort and convenience, all bedrooms having en suite facilities and a full range of amenities. A candlelit dinner in the elegant dining room is a special pleasure, the imaginative menus featuring a variety of fresh local produce, including vegetables and herbs from the hotel's own garden. A variety of Special Breaks are available, including Wine Tasting and Racing Weekends — details on request. ♛♛♛♛ *Highly Commended, AA Red Rosette, RAC Triple Merit Award.*

OLD FARMHOUSE COUNTRY HOTEL & RESTAURANT, Raskelf, York, North Yorkshire YO6 3LF

Tel: 01347 821971*

Residential and restaurant licence; 10 bedrooms, all with private bathrooms; Children welcome, pets by prior arrangement; Easingwold 2 miles; £.

The Old Farmhouse is an award-winning friendly Country Hotel which has retained its original farmhouse character while offering every modern comfort. The ten en-suite bedrooms are centrally heated and have colour television, direct-dial telephones and tea and coffee facilities. The food is something special and offers a good choice of dishes, complemented by an extensive wine list and a choice of malts. The area is a haven for many historic houses, magnificent ruined abbeys and castles. For the sporting enthusiast — riding, golf, fishing and swimming are available locally, and several famous racecourses are within driving distance. ♛♛♛ *Highly Commended, AA QQQQ.*

RIPON SPA HOTEL, Park Street, Ripon, North Yorkshire HG4 2BU

Tel: 01765 602172
Fax: 01765 690770

Fully licensed; 40 bedrooms, all with private bathrooms; Children and pets welcome; Conference facilities; Harrogate 10 miles; £££.

Only five minutes' walk from the town centre, this splendid Edwardian building basks peacefully in attractive gardens. Its traditional values of hospitality soon make an impact which, perhaps, is not surprising as the flourishing hotel has been in the same family ownership for 80 years. The delightful guest rooms all have en suite facilities, satellite television, direct-dial telephone, tea and coffee-makers and hair dryer. Four rooms are on the ground floor and there is a lift. The main restaurant features traditional English dishes on its à la carte and table d'hôte menus and it is easy to understand its popularity with local diners. Equally popular is the Turf Tavern where bar food is available every lunchtime and evening. ♛♛♛♛, *RAC/AA***.*

---

* The appearance of an asterisk after the telephone number indicates that the hotel in question is closed for a period during the winter months. Exact dates should be ascertained from the hotel itself.

EAST AYTON LODGE COUNTRY HOTEL,
Moor Lane, East Ayton, Scarborough,
North Yorkshire YO13 9EW

Tel: 01723 864227
Fax: 01723 862680

Fully licensed; 31 bedrooms, all with private bath and shower; Children and pets welcome; Scarborough 4 miles; ££.

Perfectly situated between the North Yorkshire Moors and the popular resort of Scarborough, this small but beautifully appointed "Restaurant with Rooms" is ideal for exploring either. The hotel is situated in three acres of lovely, tranquil gardens beside the River Derwent. The Cecilia Garden Restaurant provides the wherewithal to dine in elegant surroundings and enjoy the extensive English, French and Vegetarian cuisine by the Chef-Patron. The dining room has a dance floor making it an ideal and popular location for Dinner Dances and private functions. Guest rooms are furnished and thoughtfully equipped to high standards: all are en suite with Colour TV, Clock Radios, Trouser Presses, Hairdryers, Direct Dial Telephones, Courtesy Trays, etc. The hotel is fully centrally heated. There are 4 Honeymoon Suites with traditional 4 poster beds. *AA/RAC***, ETB* ♛♛♛♛, *Les Routiers, Johansens, Ashley Courtenay.*

STAKESBY MANOR HOTEL,
Manor Close, High Stakesby, Whitby,
North Yorkshire YO21 1HL

Tel: 01947 602773
Fax: 01947 602140

Fully licensed; 8 bedrooms, all with private bathrooms; Children welcome; Conference facilities; Scarborough 17 miles; ££.

In its own well-tended gardens and just a mile or so from the beach, golf course and town centre, Stakesby Manor is an attractively converted Georgian manor which enjoys extensive sea and country views. Public and private rooms have been furnished and decorated with a perceptive eye to form and colour and the centrally heated guest rooms are appointed with en suite facilities, colour television and tea-making equipment. This is very much a family hotel offering the combined attractions of a sea and country holiday with children of all ages welcomed. The popular Manor Bar features a rare Italian marble fireplace and the panelled Oak Room Restaurant provides an intimate setting in which to savour good food. *YHTB* ♛♛♛♛ *Commended, AA**.*

WELLGARTH HOUSE,
Wetherby Road, Rufforth,
York YO2 3QB

Tel: 01904 738592 and 738595

Unlicensed; 7 bedrooms, all with private bathrooms; Children welcome, pets by arrangement; Harrogate 18 miles, York 4; £.

Quietly situated in the village of Rufforth, just five minutes from York, Wellgarth House is ideally situated for exploring this historic city, the breathtaking landscape of the Moors and Dales, and the Heritage Coast with its splendid resorts at Scarborough, Whitby and Filey. Accommodation is spacious, comfortable and well furnished, and all rooms have been decorated to the highest standard. Colour television and tea/coffee making facilities are provided, and thermostatically controlled central heating ensures complete comfort and warmth; ironing facilities and hairdryers are available on request. There is a ground floor bedroom which is ideal for the elderly or for anyone wishing to avoid stairs. On summer days guests can relax and unwind in the colourful gardens which overlook lovely rolling countryside. ♛♛, *AA QQ, FHG Diploma.*

South Yorkshire

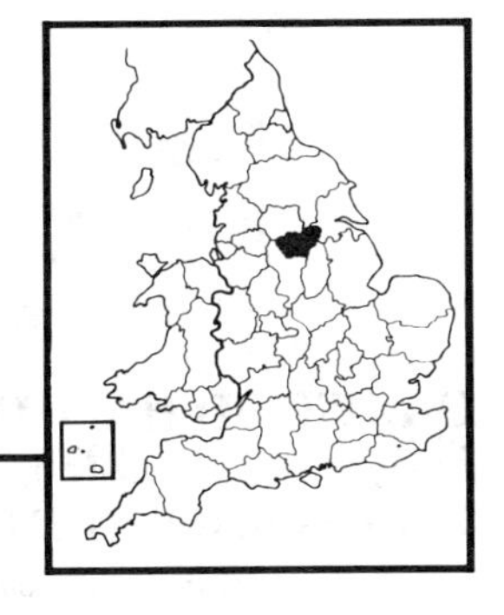

MOSBOROUGH HALL HOTEL,
High Street, Mosborough, Near Sheffield,
South Yorkshire S19 5AE

Tel: 0114 2484353
Fax: 0114 2477042

Fully licensed; 23 bedrooms, all with private bathrooms; Historic interest; Children and pets welcome; Conference facilities; Killamarsh 3 miles; £££.

Basking in the aura of 800 years of stirring history, this fascinating old manor house stands in an elevated position on the Yorkshire/Derbyshire border. Lovingly brought into line with modern requirements and with no expense spared, the house retains its time-honoured ambience through architecture and legend. Pass through an ancient doorway to the Oak Bar, with its minstrels' gallery and stone-mullioned windows, to relax with an aperitif before sampling the superb cuisine for which the John d'Arcy Restaurant has a well-established reputation. Historic tittle-tattle has it that Henry VIII, having tired of his pregnant mistress, Mary Boleyn and desirous of marrying Anne Boleyn, arranged Mary's marriage to William Carey of Mosborough Hall where his son, Henry, was born. Elizabeth I later conferred a baronetcy upon him and he became Baron Hunsden. The White Lady of Mosborough, the hall's friendly ghost, has been seen regularly in both the restaurant and the country lane adjoining. Legend has it that she lived here as a governess and after an illicit affair with her master, was murdered and her body was hidden within the walls of the Hall. Today, however, all is sweetness and light. All bedrooms have en suite facilities and individual decor and some have four-poster beds to complement the room's authentic wall-panelling — behind which — maybe . . .! Social functions are superbly catered for. *AA, RAC ***.*

West Yorkshire

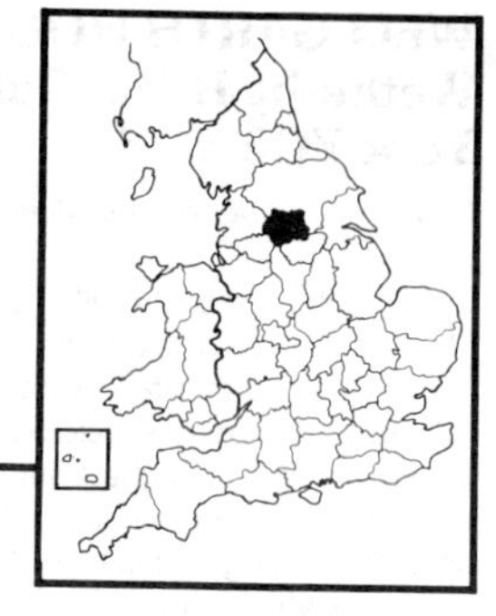

OAKWOOD HALL HOTEL,
Lady Lane, Bingley,
West Yorkshire BD16 4AW

Tel: 01274 564123
Fax: 01274 561477

Fully licensed; 20 bedrooms, all with private bathrooms; Historic interest; Children and pets welcome; Conference facilities; Bradford 5 miles; £££.

A feature of the picturesque Aire Valley and wonderfully placed for exploration of the Yorkshire dales and moors and Bronte Country, this distinctive hotel is built in Gothic style with an imposing Victorian facade. Spacious guest rooms, some with four-poster beds and jacuzzi, are beautifully equipped complete with private facilities, remote-control colour television, direct-dial telephone and tea and coffee-makers. Ground floor rooms available. The hotel has a high reputation for its excellent à la carte menus, the restaurant being open to non-residents. Despite its rural aspect and proximity to the Leeds and Liverpool Canal, urban conveniences at Bingley and Bradford are within easy reach. *YHTB* ♛♛♛♛ *Commended, AA***, Les Routiers.*

NOTE

All the information in this book is given in good faith in the belief that it is correct. However, the publishers cannot guarantee the facts given in these pages, neither are they responsible for changes in policy, ownership or terms that may take place after the date of going to press. Readers should always satisfy themselves that the facilities they require are available and that the terms, if quoted, still apply.

BAGDEN HALL HOTEL,
Wakefield Road, Scissett, Near
Huddersfield, West Yorkshire HD8 9LE

Tel: 01484 865330
Fax: 01484 861001

Fully licensed; 17 bedrooms, all with private bathrooms; Historic interest; Children welcome; Leisure and conference facilities; Denby Dale 2 miles; £££/££££.

15 minutes' driving time from Barnsley, Huddersfield and Wakefield and 30 minutes from Leeds and Sheffield, this captivating and conveniently situated country hotel is a veritable oasis for the urban dweller and businessman, hence its popularity as a venue for conferences and social occasions; moreover, this lovely hotel is a superb holiday retreat in its own right. Retaining all the character of a bygone age, the hall has recently been completely renovated and is now amongst the finest hotels in the country for accommodation, comfort, surroundings, and traditional English and classical French cuisine. The gracious house stands in 40 acres of parkland, only minutes away from Junctions 38 and 39 of the M1. ♛♛♛♛ *Highly Commended, AA Rosette, RAC ***.*

WATERTON PARK HOTEL,
Walton Hall, Walton, Wakefield,
West Yorkshire WF2 6PW

Tel: 01924 257911
Fax: 01924 240082

Fully licensed; 42 bedrooms, all with private bathrooms; Historic interest; Children welcome; Leisure and conference facilities; Wakefield 4 miles; ££££.

A beautiful Georgian mansion, otherwise known as Walton Hall, this superb hotel, leisure and business centre enjoys a most unusual situation. Accessible only via a picturesque iron bridge, it stands on an island in the middle of a 26-acre lake which, itself, is surrounded by a wildlife sanctuary. With a tradition for good food and service which makes the grand old mansion a popular venue for functions of all kinds, Walton Hall has been lovingly restored to its former glory; all is elegance in an aura of good living. Under the supervision of a talented chef and his team, the cuisine comprises an extensive selection of traditional and classical English dishes and carefully chosen wines. The accommodation is of a notably high standard, guest rooms (some with four-poster beds) being attractively decorated and possessed of en suite facilities, colour television, direct-dial telephone, tea and coffee-makers and numerous thoughtful extras. The leisure facilities here are second to none and will appeal to both keep-fit fanatics and those seeking gentle relaxation. Overlooking the lake is a magnificent indoor heated swimming pool with spa bath, sauna, steam room and solarium as well as a full-size snooker table. Others may be drawn to the possibilities of the lake, well stocked with trout and where other water-based activities may be undertaken. 👑👑👑👑 *Highly Commended.*

WALES

Clwyd

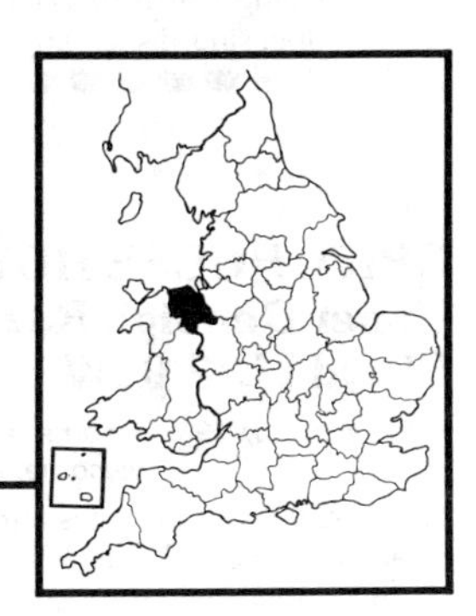

KINMEL MANOR HOTEL,
St. George's Road, Abergele,
Clwyd LL22 9AS

Tel and Fax: 01745 832014

Fully licensed; 42 bedrooms, all with private bathrooms; Children and pets welcome; Leisure and conference facilities; Rhyl 5 miles; ££.

Looking at the splendid modern hotel that it is today, it is hard to believe that part of the present building dates from 1570. Many changes have taken place since its elevation to one of the most outstanding hotels in North Wales but despite its contemporary outward appearance, imposing links with the past are still in evidence, notably the magnificent 'Coat of Arms' fireplace in the restaurant and the oak fireplace (circa 1600) in the reception area. Excellent à la carte and table d'hôte luncheons and dinners are only part of the reward of a sojourn here. Sprucely decorated guest rooms are all en suite and equipped with colour television, radio, in-house films, direct-dial telephone, tea and coffee-making facilities and numerous thoughtful extras. Children under 10 are accommodated free with only meals charged for. A superbly-equipped leisure complex proves a great attraction for businessmen and tourists alike. The gymnasium is appointed with a variety of keep-fit apparatus and there is also an indoor heated swimming pool, sauna, spa bath, steam room and solarium. Also in great demand are two purpose-built conference suites and a spacious ballroom, ideal for social functions. Apart from scenic beauty and an abundance of historic treasures, there are several excellent golf courses in the area. Special Mini-Weekend Breaks and 2-day Golfing and Fishing Breaks offer exceptional value. *WTB ♛♛♛♛ Highly Commended, RAC Merit Award for Hospitality and Service.*

LLYNDIR HALL HOTEL,
Llyndir Lane, Rossett,
Clwyd LL12 0AY

Tel: 01244 571648
Fax: 01244 571258

Licensed; 38 bedrooms, all with private bathrooms; Historic interest; Children welcome; Leisure and conference facilities; Wrexham 5 miles; ££££.

A splendidly refurbished country house hotel, Llyndir Hall has all the traditional qualities of British hospitality and a Leisure Club that boasts such excellent facilities as an indoor pool, trimnasium, steam room and spa bath — all free to residents. The graceful house stands in extensive parkland and is the perfect venue from which to explore Snowdonia whilst the historic city of Chester is within 10 minutes' drive. Gracious reception rooms and individually furnished bedrooms, replete with antique furniture and fine chintzes beguile the eye. Country house cooking at its very best may be appreciated in a delightful restaurant that overlooks the lawns, appetising dishes augmented by a well-chosen wine list and friendly and efficient service. *WTB ♛♛♛♛♛, AA***.*

ORIEL HOUSE HOTEL,
Upper Denbigh Road, St. Asaph,
Clwyd LL17 0LW

Tel: 01745 582716
Fax: 01745 585208

Fully licensed; 19 bedrooms, all with private bathrooms; Historic interest; Children and pets welcome; Conference facilities; Rhyl 5 miles; ££/£££.

This family-owned hotel is attractively furnished and is a fine base from which to enjoy the adjacent scenic and seaside beauties of North Wales. Chester and Anglesey must come high on any touring itinerary as should St. Asaph's famous cathedral, literally only yards away. The impressive Fountain Restaurant presents a tempting and reasonably-priced selection of imaginative à la carte dishes and a comprehensive range of light meals is on offer in the spruce lounge bar. Guest rooms all have en suite facilities, hairdryers, colour television, radio, direct-dial telephone and baby-listening device. Within easy reach of this splendid hotel are such sporting diversions as golf, tennis, riding and fishing. The hotel also has a snooker room with full-sized tables. *WTB ♛♛♛ Highly Commended, AA and RAC ***.*

LLWYN ONN HALL HOTEL,
Cefn Road, Wrexham,
Clwyd LL13 0NY

Tel: 01978 261225
Fax: 01978 363233

Fully licensed; 13 bedrooms, all with private bathrooms; Historic interest; Children welcome; Conference facilities; Chester 11 miles; £££.

Open parkland and rolling countryside surround this handsome 17th century converted manor house. All the en suite bedrooms have been individually designed and are appointed with such fine modern amenities as colour television, direct-dial telephone, tea and coffee-makers and trouser press. The impeccably furnished public rooms are warmly welcoming with open fireplaces and oak-beamed ceilings contributing to the relaxed air. Extensive table d'hôte and à la carte menus more than satisfy sharpened appetites with snacks available in the cosy bar. There are beautiful woodland walks close at hand and horse riding may easily be arranged. The Snowdonia National Park and the seaside resorts of Llandudno, Colwyn Bay and Rhyl may be reached in 45 minutes. *WTB ♛♛♛♛ Highly Commended, AA/RAC***.*

Dyfed

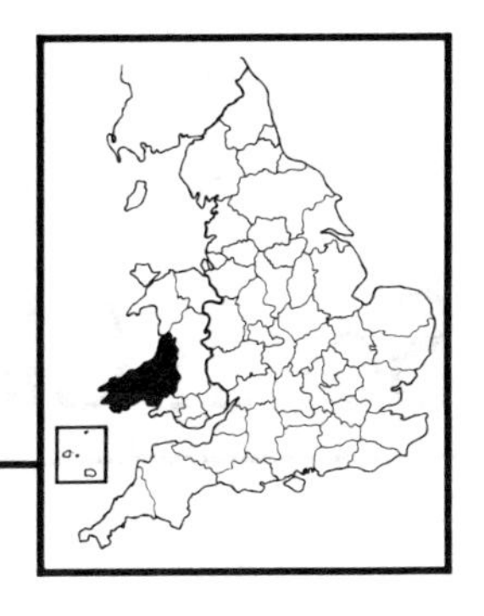

HOTEL PENRALLT,
Aberporth, Cardigan,
Dyfed SA43 2BS

Tel: 01239 810227
Fax: 01239 811375

Fully licensed; 16 bedrooms, all with private bathrooms; Children welcome, pets by arrangement; Leisure and conference facilities; Cardigan 6 miles; £££.

Aberporth, with its two sandy beaches and low sheltering cliffs, is an ideal little resort for family holidays, and children are especially welcome at this comfortable Edwardian hotel. Set in delightful grounds, it commands lovely views over Cardigan Bay and its splendid leisure amenities will appeal to guests of all ages; these include an open-air heated swimming pool with poolside bar and cafeteria, gymnasium, hard tennis court, children's play area, sauna and solarium. Food is a high priority, being varied and generous. Accommodation is exceptionally well appointed, with family rooms available. Business guests are well catered for too, with a small conference room and secretarial services at their disposal. Self catering apartments are also available. 👑👑👑👑 *Highly Commended, AA/RAC***.*

MILTON MANOR HOTEL,
Milton, Near Tenby,
Dyfed SA70 8PG

Tel: 01646 651398
Fax: 01646 651897

Restaurant and residential licence; 19 bedrooms, all with private bathrooms; Children and pets welcome; Pembroke 4 miles; ££.

An imposing tree-lined drive leads to this fine example of Georgian architecture with 6 acres of grounds ensuring seclusion. For a quiet vacation with secret coastal gems and the beauties of the Pembrokeshire National Park to discover, the facilities offered by the Manor merit serious consideration. Friends are easily made in the convivial bar and lounge and the excellent restaurant presents first-rate à la carte and table d'hôte menus. Vegetarian and special diets are catered for. The en suite accommodation includes six spacious bed-sitting rooms and all rooms have colour television, direct-dial telephone and beverage makers. Ground-floor rooms are available. *WTB* 👑👑👑.

South Glamorgan

EGERTON GREY COUNTRY HOUSE HOTEL,
Porthkerry, Near Cardiff,
South Glamorgan CF6 9BZ

Tel: 01446 711666
Fax: 01446 711690

Restaurant licence; 10 bedrooms, all with private bathrooms; Historic interest; Leisure and conference facilities; Cardiff 10 miles; ££££.

A recommended centre from which to explore the lovely and uncrowded Gower Peninsula and the Brecon Beacons, this stylish and distinguished country house was opened as a small and luxurious hotel as recently as 1988. Only 10 miles from Cardiff, it is set in a secluded, wooded valley in seven acres of gardens, with views down to Porthkerry Park and the sea. The excellent facilities accorded guests include exquisitely furnished bedrooms (all with private bathrooms), two dining rooms, library and magnificent Edwardian drawing room. Within the grounds is an all-weather tennis court and also a croquet lawn. Only a short stroll away is a well-maintained country park with an 18-hole pitch and putt course. The cuisine is outstanding and dining here by candlelight is a memorable experience. Recommended by all hotel and restaurant guides. *WTB* ♛♛♛♛ *Highly Commended, "Taste of Wales" Cuisine Award.*

The **£** symbol when appearing at the end of the italic section of an entry shows the anticipated price, during 1996, for **single full Bed and Breakfast.**

Under £35	**£**	**Over £50 but under £65**	**£££**
Over £35 but under £50	**££**	**Over £65**	**££££**

This is meant as an indication only and does not show prices for Special Breaks, Weekends, etc. Guests are therefore advised to verify all prices on enquiring or booking.

Gwent

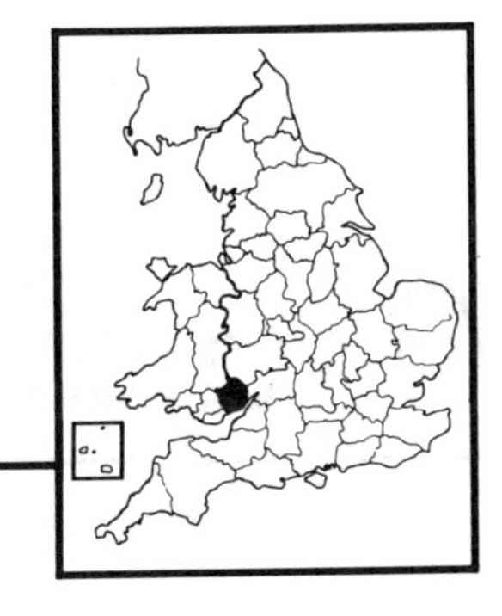

LLANWENARTH HOUSE,
Govilon, Abergavenny,
Gwent NP7 9SF

Tel: 01873 830289*
Fax: 01873 832199

Residential and restaurant licence; 5 bedrooms, all with private bathrooms; Historic interest; Children over 10 years and pets welcome; Abergavenny 2 miles; ££.

The subject of painstaking renovation and restoration, this lovely old Welsh manor house dates from the 16th century. Set within the Brecon Beacons National Park and in its own peaceful and picturesque grounds, the house offers the highest standards of comfort and cuisine. Guests are personally cared for by Bruce and Amanda Weatherill and their family, Amanda being a Cordon Bleu cook, and dining by candlelight is a most pleasurable experience. The spacious guest rooms have private bath or shower facilities, colour television and tea and coffee makers, and enjoy lovely views. The grounds border a beautiful canal, and boats may be hired locally. A three-day inclusive package is offered for Christmas 1995 (extra days optional); ideally suited to small groups but equally attractive to couples wanting to get away from it all. ♛♛♛, *AA Commended QQQQ, Johansens Award Nominated.*

ST. MELLONS COUNTRY HOTEL,
Castleton,
Gwent CF3 8XR

Tel: 01633 680355
Fax: 01633 680399

Fully licensed; 30 bedrooms, all with private bathrooms; Historic interest; Children welcome; Leisure and conference facilities; Newport 5 miles; £££/££££.

The luxury St. Mellons complex is elegance itself, yet boasts the finest modern appointments; a warm and welcoming place for a rewarding holiday in the peaceful Gwent countryside, surprisingly only a few minutes' drive from Cardiff and Newport. Stylishly furnished, the hotel stands in 7 acres of well-tended grounds and, apart from the sumptuous comfort of its en suite guest rooms and lounges, it has much to offer both tourist and businessman. The meals served in the charming Byrons Restaurant adhere to the highest standards of traditional cuisine and its popular Country Club leisure facilities comprise five squash courts, heated swimming pool, fully-equipped gymnasium and tennis courts as well as a steam room, saunas and solarium. ♛♛♛♛ *Commended, RAC***.*

Gwynedd

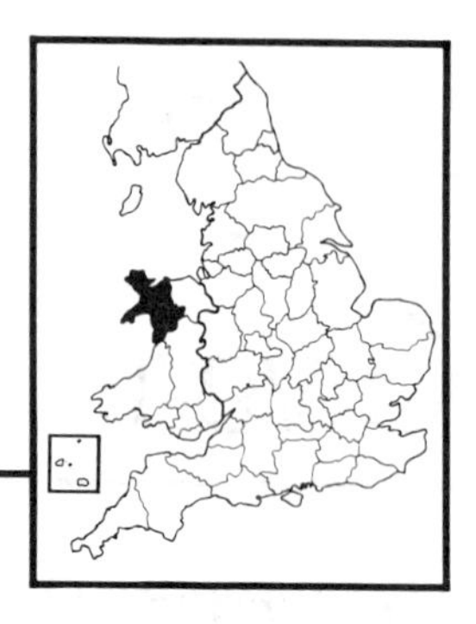

PLAS PENHELIG COUNTRY HOUSE HOTEL,

Aberdovey,
Gwynedd LL35 0NA

Tel: 01654 767676*
Fax: 01654 767783

Residential and restaurant licence; 11 bedrooms, all with private bathrooms; Historic interest; Children and pets welcome; Conference facilities; Machynlleth 9 miles; ££.

A fine country house conveniently placed near sandy beaches, the Dovey estuary and the majesty of Cader Idris, Plas Penhelig is a holiday venue with a variety of diversions near at hand; there are numerous beauty spots in the area as well as opportunities for golf, pony trekking and climbing. A visit to the charming and quaint Talyllyn Railway is also recommended. The house stands in 7 acres of lovely grounds which encompass a putting green and croquet lawn. On entering the oak-panelled entrance hall and lounge of this welcoming hotel, one is immediately aware of the tasteful furnishings and colour schemes that grace public and private rooms, the majority of which are spacious and well-appointed. Guest rooms all have en suite facilities, colour television, radio, direct-dial telephone and tea and coffee-tray. With their comfort assured, guests may relax and enjoy to the full the excellent cuisine for which the hotel has a growing reputation; local produce figures prominently on the menus and is accompanied by an interesting selection of wines. The Terrace Bar is open for snack luncheons. 'Bargain Break' holidays are organised throughout the year with special concessions available to golfers. A full range of massage and aromatherapy treatments by a fully qualified therapist are available (advance bookings recommended). ♛♛♛ *Highly Commended.*

DEUCOCH HOTEL,
Abersoch, Pwllheli,
Gwynedd LL53 7LD

Tel: 01758 712680
Fax: 01758 712670

Fully licensed; 10 bedrooms, 9 with private bathrooms; Children and pets welcome; Pwllheli 6 miles; £.

A gem of an hotel in a gem of a resort overlooking Cardigan Bay, Deucoch offers the warmest of welcomes to family parties; children under 12 are offered free accommodation if sharing a room with two adults, with discounts for teenagers also available. In this homely, one-time farmhouse, rooms are well-appointed with television, radio, baby-listening intercom and tea and coffee-makers. Sub-tropical plants abound as do seaside pleasures on and off a wide sandy beach and the attractive little harbour is overlooked by former fishermen's cottages. Golfing holidays are organised on several courses and opportunities also exist locally for sailing, surfing, fishing and riding. The table d'hôte and bar meal menus will more than satisfy sharpened appetites. ♛♛♛ *Commended, AA and RAC**, Welcome Host, Ashley Courtenay Highly Recommended.*

CASTELL CIDWM HOTEL,
Betws Garmon, Caernarvon,
Gwynedd LL54 7YT

Tel: 01286 650243

Licensed; 8 bedrooms, all with private bathrooms; Children welcome; Caernarvon 5 miles; £.

In one of the most beautiful settings in Wales on the west side of Snowdon, this delightfully tranquil lakeside hotel offers magnificent views of mountain, forest and water. Private trout fishing, boating and water sports are available from the hotel, with walking, climbing and pony trekking nearby. The hotel offers warm friendly hospitality, eight bedrooms (all en suite), a cosy bar, a bistro snack bar and an à la carte restaurant with a subtly different cuisine. Two and three day breaks available. *WTB* ♛♛♛ *Highly Commended, AA**.* **See also Colour Advertisement on page 15.**

BERTHLWYD HALL, Llechwedd, Near Conwy, Gwynedd LL32 8DQ

Tel: 01492 592409
Fax: 01492 572290

Fully licensed; 8 bedrooms, all with private bathrooms; Historic interest; Children and pets welcome; Car park (50); Conwy 2 miles; £££.

A magnificent Victorian manor house hotel situated on the edge of Snowdonia National Park with wonderful views over the Conwy Valley. The splendid oak panelling, carved fireplaces, stained glass windows and superb galleried landing exert their influence on the relaxed atmosphere. The luxurious accommodation, personal service and the delights of the award-winning Truffles Restaurant will ensure a truly memorable holiday. *WTB* ♛♛♛♛ *Highly Commended, Johansens, Ashley Courtenay, Logis, Regional Hotel of the Year 1995.*

PARCIAU MAWR HOTEL, Criccieth, Gwynedd LL52 0RP

Tel: 01766 522368*

Residential and restaurant licence; 12 bedrooms, all with private bathrooms; Children and pets welcome; Caernarvon 15 miles; £.

Offering first-rate country house facilities by the sea, Parciau Mawr is small, bright, comfortable and tastefully furnished. The house stands in secluded grounds of 3 acres yet is near all the attractions and sandy beaches of the little resort. Snowdonia with its attendant pleasures lies immediately inland. Beautifully decorated throughout, the hotel has stylish bedrooms, all of which are centrally heated and have colour television and tea and coffee-making facilities. An annexe houses six rooms, all of which have private showers. A spacious lounge, sun lounge and bar each contribute their appeal whilst the excellent and varied cuisine served in a delightfully converted, 300-year-old barn, will ensure happy memories. *WTB* ♛♛♛ *Highly Commended.*

WOODLAND HALL HOTEL, Edern, Pwllheli, Gwynedd LL53 6JB

Tel: 01758 720425

Residential licence; 13 bedrooms, 7 with private bathrooms; Conference facilities; Children and pets welcome; Morfa Nefyn 1 mile; £.

Approached through an impressive tree-lined drive, this cheerful and sunny hotel stands in 7 acres of beautiful grounds with the safe, sandy beaches of the Lleyn Peninsula close at hand and Nefyn's famous 27-hole golf course only a mile away. A fine place for restful and relaxing family holidays, the hotel sets great store by its ample and varied cuisine whilst the smart cocktail and lounge bars encourage conviviality with new-found friends. Dances are held from time to time and all members of the party will enjoy the facilities provided by a delightful games room. ***, Restaurant ***.*

BRYN BRAS CASTLE,
Llanrug, Near Caernarvon,
Gwynedd LL55 4RE

Tel and Fax: 01286 870210

Self catering accommodation (some serviced apartments with breakfast); Historic interest; Not suitable for young children; Caernarvon 4 miles.

This romantic Neo-Romanesque castle is set in gentle Snowdonian foothills near North Wales mountains, beaches, resorts and places of historic interest. Built in 1830, on the site of an earlier structure, the Regency castle reflects peace, not war. It stands in 32 acres of tranquil gardens, with delightful views. Bryn Bras offers distinctive and individual apartments for two to four persons within the Castle, each having a suite of spacious rooms radiating comfort, warmth and tranquillity, and providing freedom and independence. There are many inns and restaurants nearby. The welcoming Castle (still a family home) particularly appeals to romantic couples. Short breaks – two nights for two persons, from £95 (s/c). Open all year. Brochure sent with pleasure. *WTB Grade 5.*

PLAS HALL HOTEL,
Pont-y-Pant, Near Betws-y-Coed,
Gwynedd LL25 0PJ

Tel: 01690 750 206/306
Fax: 01690 750 526

Residential licence; 20 bedrooms, all with private bathrooms; Children and pets welcome; Betws-y-Coed 3 miles; ££.

Offering peace and seclusion in an area of outstanding natural beauty in Snowdonia National Park, Plas Hall stands in its own grounds of about 3 acres on the banks of the turbulent River Ledr where fishing is available. The hotel offers excellent facilities with all rooms being centrally heated and having private bathrooms, colour television, telephone and tea and coffee-makers. Four ground floor rooms with easy access to the car park are especially suitable for disabled guests. A traditional and international cuisine of high standing is presented in the restaurant with local delicacies such as Conwy salmon, pheasant and wild duck complemented by a worthy wine list. The attractive beaches of North and West Wales are within short driving distance. ♛♛♛♛, *AA***.*

MINFFORDD HOTEL,
Talyllyn, Tywyn,
Gwynedd LL36 9AJ

Tel: 01654 761665*
Fax: 01654 761517

Residential and restaurant licence; 6 bedrooms, all with private bathrooms; Historic interest; Car park (12); Machynlleth 10 miles; £..

At last — an opportunity to escape and rediscover lost values set to flight by modern living. At the head of the remote and beautiful Dysynni Valley, this former coaching inn is a scenic gem in itself. Homely, warm and comfortable, the hotel is full of character. Guest rooms are tastefully furnished and each is centrally heated and has private bath and toilet facilities. Beauty spots and places of interest abound in the area, part of the dramatic patterns woven by mountains and streams, Talyllyn Lake, the famous Talyllyn Railway, Cader Idris, Dolgoch Falls amongst them. Always on one's return is the prospect of a sumptuous dinner and the recounting of the day's adventures before a log fire. ♛♛♛♛ *Highly Commended, AA Red Rosette, RAC Merit Awards for Hospitality and Comfort.*

HOTEL MAES-Y-NEUADD,
Talsarnau, Near Harlech,
Gwynedd LL47 6YA

Tel: 01766 780200
Fax: 01766 78211

Restaurant and residential licence; 16 bedrooms, all with private bathrooms; Historic interest; Children and pets welcome; Conference facilities; Harlech 4 miles; £££.

Over the years, this has become one of the best known country hotels in Wales, winning numerous awards for its all-round excellence. Nestling in a wooded mountainside and amidst some of the most beautiful scenery in Britain, this gracious and historic manor has benefited from additions and extensions made in the 16th, 18th and 20th centuries. Comfort and luxury walk hand in hand in its delightfully furnished rooms and the views on all sides are spectacular. After a day's exploration of the Snowdonia National Park or seaside, evening brings the promise of good company and first-class fare. An aperitif in the oak-beamed bar, or on warm summer nights on the terrace, is the prelude to dining in style and good humour in the elegant dining room. This is some experience for the cuisine is exceptional and the subject of high recommendation. Delicious dishes created by talented chefs feature fresh local produce and an interesting selection of Welsh farmhouse cheeses. Surrounded by 8 acres of landscaped grounds and with a wealth of fascinating places to visit in the vicinity and sports to enjoy, Maes-y-Neuadd has all the ingredients for a memorable and relaxing holiday. Bedrooms and suites, both in the main house and Coach House annexe, are sumptuously appointed, ensuring sound and restful repose. ♛♛♛♛ *De Luxe, AA Red Stars and Three Rosettes, RAC Blue Ribbon, Johansen's "Excellent Service" Award.*

Powys

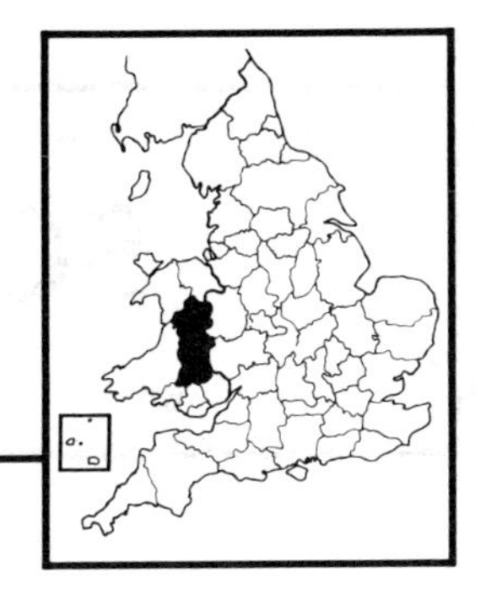

PENCERRIG GARDENS HOTEL,
Llandrindod Road, Builth Wells,
Powys LD2 3TF

Tel: 01982 553226
Fax: 01982 552347

Fully licensed; 20 bedrooms, all with private bathrooms; Historic interest; Children and pets welcome; Conference facilities; Brecon 14 miles; ££.

Surrounded by beautiful gardens and with glorious views of the verdant, undulating countryside, Pencerrig has been developed from a farmhouse reputedly dating back to the 15th century. This is a warm and friendly place a short distance from the market town of Builth Wells with much of interest to see and do in the area. A delicious table d'hôte menu is offered in the restaurant, whilst bar meals are also available at lunchtime and in the evening. En suite bedrooms are well appointed and have colour televisions, radio/alarm clocks, self-dial telephones and tea and coffee-making facilities; five rooms are on the ground-floor which means that disabled guests may be catered for. *WTB ♛♛♛♛, AA/RAC**.*

BODFACH HALL,
Llanfyllin,
Powys SY22 5HS

Tel and Fax: 01691 648272*

Fully licensed; 9 bedrooms, all with private bathrooms; Historic interest; Children and pets welcome; Welshpool 12 miles; £.

Set in beautiful and varied scenery, this small family-run hotel stands just off the main Oswestry to Lake Vyrnwy road, offering a haven of peace in today's strident world. The alterations and additions which have been made to the 300-year-old building only serve to enhance its dignity and charm, and some fine oak panelling and ornamental ceilings have been preserved. All bedrooms have colour television, direct-dial telephone, hot beverage making facilities, hairdryers and clock radios, and either en suite bath or shower. There is a residents' lounge, a spacious bar, sun room and terrace. Lunches and supper meals are available each day, and dinner, which is served in the Oak Room, features classic country fare, plus a vegetarian selection. *♛♛♛ Highly Commended, AA and RAC **, Ashley Courtenay, Johansens.*

---

* The appearance of an asterisk after the telephone number indicates that the hotel in question is closed for a period during the winter months. Exact dates should be ascertained from the hotel itself.

SCOTLAND

Aberdeenshire

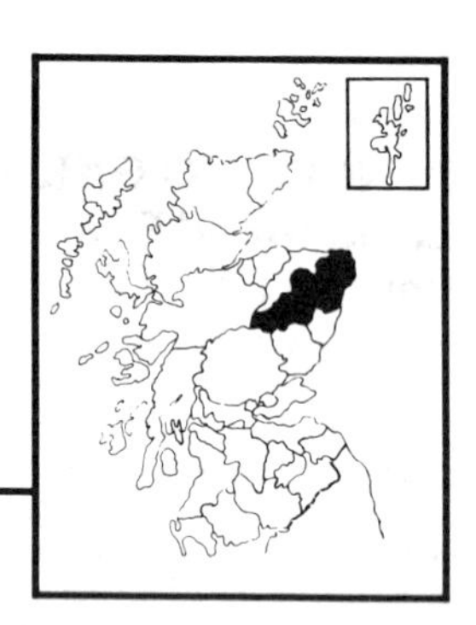

KILDRUMMY CASTLE HOTEL,
Kildrummy, By Alford,
Aberdeenshire AB33 8RA

Tel: 019755 71288*
Fax: 019755 71345

Hotel licence; 16 bedrooms, all with private bathrooms; Historic interest; Aberdeen 23 miles; £££.

The ideal base from which to explore a countryside rich in history, natural beauty and sporting opportunity, this warm and welcoming hotel is set in the heart of Donside overlooking the ruins of the 13th century castle from which it takes its name. Elegantly furnished, it has an enviable reputation for its food and service, both table d'hôte and à la carte menus specialising in local prime beef, game and fish. Guest rooms are delightfully appointed with private bathroom, television, radio, telephone, tea-maker, trouser press and hair-dryer. This is just the place for an action-packed outdoor holiday, with a three and a half mile stretch of private trout and salmon fishing, twenty golf courses within an hour's drive, and pony trekking nearby. ♛♛♛♛ *De Luxe, AA 3 Red Stars and Food Rosette, RAC*** and 3 Commendations, Taste of Scotland.*

MARYCULTER HOUSE HOTEL,

South Deeside Road, Maryculter,
Aberdeenshire AB1 0BB

Tel: 01224 732124
Fax: 01224 733510

Licensed; 23 bedrooms, all with private bathrooms; Historic interest; Children welcome; Peterculter 1 mile; ££££.

With spectacular views of the River Dee and Royal Deeside, this first-class country hotel stands in five acres of secluded gardens with a wide range of sporting and social activities within easy reach. Steeped in tradition with its origins in the 13th century, the house has recently been refurbished to the highest standards and now offers 23 spacious en suite bedrooms. The Cocktail Bar built above cellars dating from 1225 and with an open hearth fireplace is a favourite venue for an aperitif, prior to sampling the delights of traditional Scottish cuisine. In the summer months dine informally in the Poachers Bar or on the patio overlooking the River Dee. ♛♛♛♛, *Egon Ronay, Taste of Scotland.*

Angus

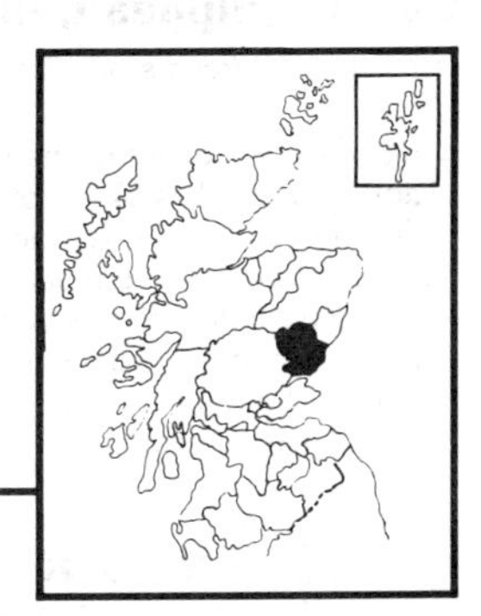

CASTLETON HOUSE HOTEL,

By Glamis, Forfar,
Angus DD8 1SJ

Tel: 01307 840340
Fax: 01307 840506

Fully licensed; 6 bedrooms, all with private bathrooms; Children welcome; Dundee 10 miles; £££.

Earlier visitors to Castleton House tended to receive a somewhat chilly welcome; so much so, in fact, that the owners constructed the fort and moat on which the house now stands. Today, the door stands open wide, extending the warmest of welcomes. Now a distinctive country hotel set in extensive grounds, the house is beautifully appointed throughout. Each of the double bedrooms has been tastefully furnished to the highest standard and all have private bathrooms, colour television, telephone and refreshment facilities. After a day spent touring through splendid scenery or enjoying exhilarating sport, one may look forward to dining well in convivial surroundings; the menus are interesting and the cuisine outstanding. ♛♛♛♛ *De Luxe, AA Food Rosette, RAC Merit Awards.*

Argyll

BRIDGE HOUSE HOTEL,
St Clair Road, Ardrishaig,
By Lochgilphead, Argyll PA30 8HB Tel: 01546 606379

Licensed; 6 bedrooms, all with private bathrooms; Children and pets welcome; Lochgilphead 2 miles; ££.

Situated on the banks of the Crinan Canal with superb views down Loch Fyne, this large Victorian house has been totally renovated and refurbished to a very high standard. All bedrooms are spacious and well-proportioned, with en suite facilities, radio alarms, remote-control television, tea/coffee making facilities and direct-dial telephone. Guests can relax in the comfortable residents' lounge or in the well-stocked lounge bar, while the pleasant dining room is the setting for excellent Scottish cuisine, using local produce wherever possible. There are several good golf courses within easy reach; other attractions include beautiful gardens, walks and sites of historic interest. *STB* ♛♛♛♛ *Highly Commended.*

PUTECHAN LODGE MOTEL AND RESTAURANT,
Bellochantuy, Kintyre, Tel: 01583 421323
Argyll PA28 6QE Fax: 01583 421343

Fully licensed; 12 bedrooms, all with private bathrooms; Dogs welcome; Campbeltown 9 miles; DB&B £££.

At Putechan Lodge our reputation for good food stretches near and far; experience our extensive and exciting menus, including creative vegetarian options, which utilise the very best of local produce. Succulent lobsters are caught in season and our food is complemented by an international range of fine wines and excellent malts, including the unique Springbank of Campbeltown. Local crafts are very much in evidence in Kintyre, and we have a permanent display of seascape water colours by the internationally renowned artist Bill Wright. There are numerous places of interest to visit, and the outdoor sportsman is well catered for, with four golf courses including world-famous Machrihanish, clay shooting, sea angling and loch fishing, pony trekking and numerous scenic walks. Special Break terms are available from November to April and in July. ♛♛♛.

KNIPOCH HOTEL,
Knipoch, By Oban,
Argyll PA34 4QT

Tel: 01852 316251*
Fax: 01852 316249

Fully licensed; 17 bedrooms, all with private bathrooms; Historic interest; Children welcome; Oban 6 miles; ££££.

Just six miles south of the ferry terminal at Oban and offering advanced standards of comfort and cuisine, this is an ideal base from which to explore the Western Highlands and Islands as well as the many historic buildings and gardens lying amidst beautiful mountain and loch scenery. Guest rooms are luxuriously appointed with private bath and shower, television, radio, direct-dial telephone and hairdryer; all have countryside or loch views. The food here is renowned for its excellence and the hotel produces its own smoked salmon. Good cheer reigns in the bar where a selection of old malt whiskies may be contemplated whilst the cellar has a staggering(!) range of over 350 wines from around the world. ♛♛♛♛ *Highly Commended.*

LOCH ETIVE HOUSE HOTEL,
Connel Village, Near Oban,
Argyll PA37 1PH

Tel: 01631 710400*
Fax: 01631 710680

Restricted hotel licence; 6 bedrooms, 4 with private bathrooms; Children and pets welcome; Oban 5 miles; £.

Set in its own grounds just five miles from Oban, close to Loch Etive and bordered by a small river, this family-run hotel offers personal service by the owners. Bob and Francoise are here to help you enjoy your stay, providing home cooking, good wine, comfortable rooms which have private facilities, central heating, colour television, tea-making, radio alarm, etc. Car park. ♛♛♛ *Commended, AA QQQQ, RAC Acclaimed, Les Routiers.*

---

* The appearance of an asterisk after the telephone number indicates that the hotel in question is closed for a period during the winter months. Exact dates should be ascertained from the hotel itself.

KILCAMB LODGE HOTEL,
Strontian,
Argyll PH36 4HY

Tel: 01967 402257*
Fax: 01967 402041

Restricted hotel licence; 10 bedrooms, all with private bathrooms; Historic interest; Children welcome, pets by prior arrangement; Salen 11 miles.

The remote and wild grandeur and beautiful beaches of the Ardnamurchan Peninsula offer the ultimate escape from the trammels of the workaday world. Offering the very best of Highland hospitality, this first-class hotel stands in 30 acres of grounds with its own private beach on Loch Sunart, a haven of peace and plenty. Central heating is installed throughout, and public and private rooms are bright, cheerful and well equipped. The cuisine is excellent and there is a convivial bar with a fine selection of malt whiskies. Boats, fishing rods and picnic hampers are available from the hotel and a good road leads to Lochaline where the ferry departs for its 15-minute journey to the Isle of Mull — a recommended day trip. *Highly Commended, AA Courtesy and Care Award, Two Rosettes for Food, Finalist Restaurant of the Year for Scotland.*

Dumfriesshire

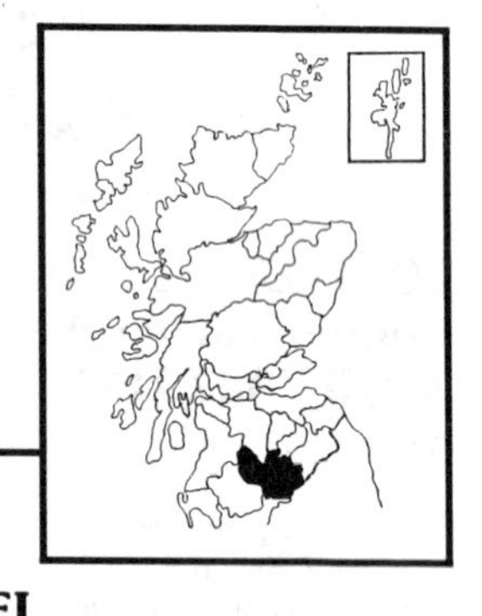

LOCKERBIE MANOR COUNTRY HOTEL,
Boreland Road, Lockerbie,
Dumfriesshire DG11 2RG

Tel: 01576 202610/203939
Fax: 01576 203046

Fully licensed; 30 bedrooms, all with private bathrooms; Historic interest; Children and pets welcome; Conference facilities; Dumfries 10 miles; ££/£££.

A Georgian manor with connections with the Marquis of Queensberry, this splendidly furnished house became an hotel in 1920. Change of rules maybe, but its traditional charm remains, epitomised by period features and oil paintings. Modern comforts and conveniences have been skilfully introduced and today, guests have a choice of regular, de luxe and four-poster rooms. Accommodation is arranged on two floors, each individually designed room having a private bathroom, colour television, direct-dial telephone and coffee-making facilities. Dining well from a selective menu is a pleasure to treasure, meals being enhanced by the ambience of the Queensberry Dining Room with its fine wood panelling, ornate chandeliers and superb views over 78 acres of tranquil park and woodland. *Dumfries & Galloway Tourist Board*, *RAC ***.*

Dunbartonshire

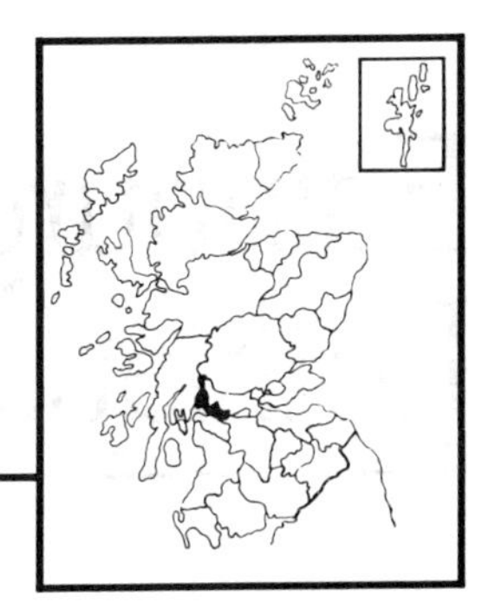

CAMERON HOUSE HOTEL AND COUNTRY ESTATE,

Loch Lomond, Alexandria,
Dunbartonshire G83 8QZ

Tel: 01389 755565
Fax: 01389 759522

Fully licensed; 68 bedrooms, all with private bathrooms; Historic interest; Children welcome; Leisure and conference facilities; Glasgow 20 miles; ££££.

Green lawns, glades of ancient oaks and gardens extending in all to 108 acres sweep down to the banks of Loch Lomond from the seasoned walls of Cameron House. With a long tradition of warm hospitality, the house exudes an air of imposing elegance, giving promise of the quiet luxury and innate charm of the rooms within. Rich panelling, marble fireplaces and decorated ceilings complement the exquisite furnishings and stylish modern comforts and, all the while, one is aware of a precise attention to detail which renders a sojourn here one to be forever remembered. Tastefully decorated guest rooms incorporate every contemporary requirement and several specially designed family rooms have separate sleeping alcoves for children. For the ultimate in cossetting, there are five magnificent suites, all with a jacuzzi, and three with four-poster beds. For superlative dining, one may choose from the gracious Georgian Room or the easy informality of the Brasserie. Hand in hand with all these outstanding virtues are leisure facilities including a private watersports marina with clubhouse, two swimming pools, gymnasium, squash, badminton, tennis, croquet, archery, and a challenging 9-hole golf course, as well as a games room and beauty salon — the complete holiday complex. Alas, one would need a vacation of at least six months to do full justice to all these magnificent amenities. No need to say "Happy Holiday". ♛♛♛♛♛ *De Luxe, AA/RAC****, Taste of Scotland "Hotel of the Year", Egon Ronay De Luxe Rating.*

Edinburgh & Lothians

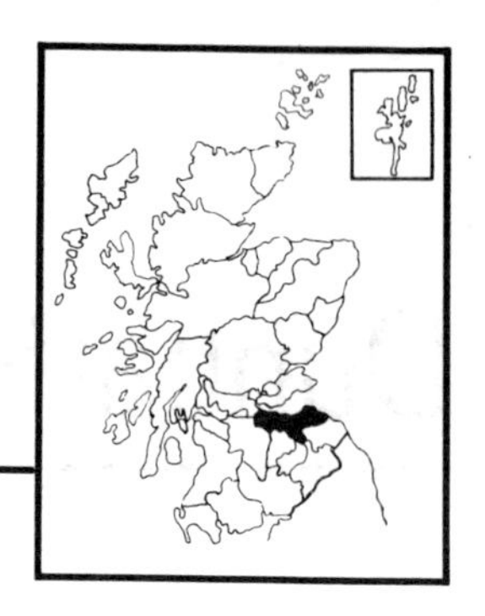

JOHNSTOUNBURN HOUSE HOTEL, Humbie, Near Edinburgh, East Lothian EH36 5PL

Tel: 01875 833696
Fax: 01875 833626

Fully licensed; 20 bedrooms, all with private bathrooms; Historic interest; Children and pets welcome; Leisure and conference facilities; Haddington 8 miles; ££££.

In a beautiful spot on the edge of the Lammermuir Hills and just 15 miles south of Edinburgh, Johnstounburn has a tradition of hospitality that goes back over 350 years. Today, this historic country house provides all the facilities and comforts one could wish for in a modern hotel with the guest rooms all having private bathrooms, colour television, radio and telephone. The finest local meats and poultry feature regularly on the à la carte and table d'hôte menus whilst delicious bar meals are served at lunchtime. The area offers walking, fishing, shooting, golf (including the Championship courses at Gullane and Muirfield) with many places of historic interest within easy distance. *STB* 👑👑👑👑 *Commended, Taste of Scotland.*

NORTON HOUSE HOTEL, Ingliston, Edinburgh EH28 8LX

Tel: 0131 333 1275
Fax: 0131 333 5305

Fully licensed; 47 bedrooms, all with private bathrooms; Historic interest; Children and pets welcome; Conference facilities; Edinburgh 7 miles; ££££.

When planning to visit the sights that make Edinburgh such a popular international attraction, one is recommended to consider the delights of this country house which nestles in 55 acres of parkland just outside Scotland's capital city. You will be treated to a warm and friendly welcome, comfortable period surroundings and first-class cuisine throughout your stay. The romantic Conservatory Restaurant, with countryside views, offers a wide-ranging menu based on Scottish and French traditions. For a more informal meal, the Tavern pub in the hotel grounds serves an excellent range of snacks and main meals at reasonable prices. The adjacent walled garden is a safe place for children to play whilst parents relax. Virgin Hotels. *STB* 👑👑👑👑👑 *De Luxe, RAC and AA ***.*

NOTE

All the information in this book is given in good faith in the belief that it is correct. However, the publishers cannot guarantee the facts given in these pages, neither are they responsible for changes in policy, ownership or terms that may take place after the date of going to press. Readers should always satisfy themselves that the facilities they require are available and that the terms, if quoted, still apply.

Fife

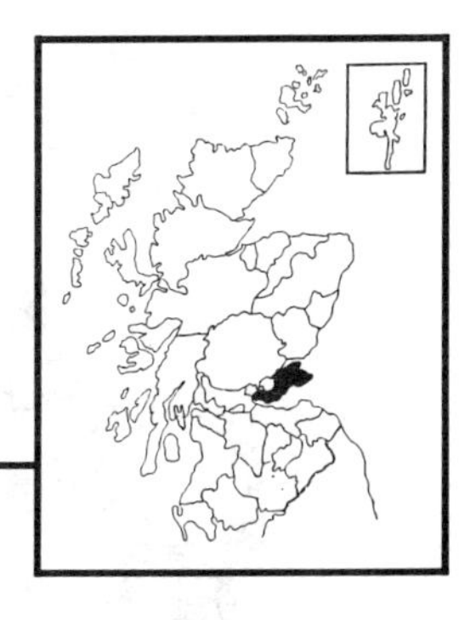

BALBIRNIE HOUSE HOTEL,
Balbirnie Park, Markinch,
Fife KY7 6NE

Tel: 01592 610066
Fax: 01592 610529

Fully licensed; 30 bedrooms, all with private bathrooms; Historic interest; Children welcome, pets in bedrooms only; Leisure and conference facilities; Kirkcaldy 8 miles; ££££.

Balbirnie is a delightful Grade 'A' Listed mansion house, the centrepiece of a 400 acre estate, which includes an 18-hole golf course. Located in the heart of Fife, only half an hour between both Edinburgh and St Andrews, the hotel comprises memorable and delightful public rooms, 30 individually designed bedrooms and suites, private dining rooms, together with a range of traditional or hi-tech special event, banqueting and conference areas. Balbirnie is many things to many people and several things to individuals – feature breaks, corporate gatherings, tailor-made special events, just call for details. Alan C. Russell is Managing Director and Co-Proprietor. ♛♛♛♛♛ *De Luxe, Four Red Stars, 1995 Regional Hotel of the Year.* **See Colour Advertisement on page 12.**

Inverness-shire

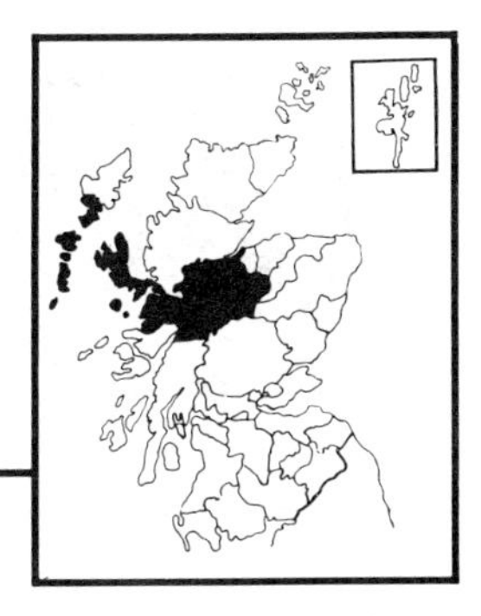

GLENGARRY CASTLE,
Invergarry,
Inverness-shire PH35 4HW

Tel: 01809 501254*
Fax: 01809 501207

Residential licence; 26 bedrooms, all with private bathrooms; Historic interest; Children and pets welcome; Inverness 41 miles, Fort William 25; ££.

A country house hotel, privately owned and personally managed by the MacCallum family for over 35 years, the Glengarry Castle is a Victorian baronial mansion situated in 50 acres of woodland by the shores of Loch Oich. The building was designed by David Bryce, the noted Victorian architect, for the Ellices of Glengarry. Located in the heart of the Great Glen, this is a perfect centre for touring. To the west lies Fort William, Ben Nevis (Britain's highest mountain), and Glen Finnan, where the Jacobites started their ill-fated rebellion; to the east is Loch Ness, home of the infamous "Nessie"; Inverness, the capital of the Highlands; and the Whisky Trail of Speyside. Farther north-west is picturesque Eilean Donan Castle, the romantic Isle of Skye and the Outer Isles. ♛♛♛♛ *Commended, AA and RAC***. **See also Colour Advertisement on page 13.**

BUNCHREW HOUSE HOTEL,
Bunchrew, Inverness,
Inverness-shire IV3 6TA

Tel: 01463 234917
Fax: 01463 710620

Fully licensed; 11 bedrooms, all with private bathrooms; Historic interest; Children and pets welcome; Conference facilities; Inverness 3 miles; ££/£££.

Dating back to 1621 and built by the eighth Lord Lovat, this charming country house presents accommodation that is definitely in the luxury class, comprising sumptuously appointed suites, each with its own distinctive feature such as a four-poster or half-tester bed. The traditional Scottish hospitality is much in evidence. Guests may relax in the panelled dining room, warmed by a roaring log fire in winter and dine splendidly in the candlelit restaurant to the sight of waves breaking on the shore. Fishing on the beautiful 20 acre estate for salmon, sea trout, etc. is provided free of charge to guests and cruises may be arranged. *STB* ♛♛♛♛ *Commended, AA and RAC ***, Taste of Scotland.*

THE LODGE ON THE LOCH,
Creag Dhu, Onich, By Fort William,
Inverness-shire PH33 6RY

Tel: 0185 582 1237
Fax: 0185 582 1463

Licensed; 20 bedrooms, 18 with private bathrooms; Children and dogs welcome; Edinburgh 120 miles, Glasgow 93, Oban 39, Fort William 10, Ballachulish 3; ££.

The Lodge On The Loch enjoys one of the most romantic and spectacular lochside settings, in a land famed for its splendid scenery. Visitors to this lovely spot will enjoy a really warm Highland welcome, where old world standards of hospitality unite with modern comforts to ensure a restful, peaceful stay. All bedrooms are individually designed and furnished, and feature fine woven fabrics from the Islands, while the public rooms are cheered by log fires. The hotel is justly proud of its fine Highland cuisine, with local seafood, salmon, trout and venison; or you may care to try the wholefood vegetarian menu and irresistible home baking. *Recommmended by leading food and accommodation guides; STB* ♛♛♛♛ *Highly Commended.*

Isle of Mull

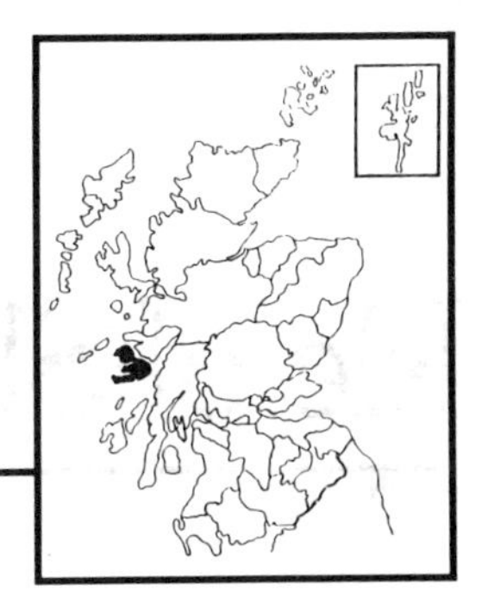

ULVA HOUSE HOTEL, Tobermory, Isle of Mull PA75 6PR

Tel: 01688 302044*

Table licence; 6 bedrooms, 4 with private bathrooms; Craignure ferry terminal 20 miles; £.

One constantly hears of the romance of the islands. Visiting Mull, one understands why. Magnificent scenery, the sigh of the surf, the cry of the kittiwake — home of the golden eagle, sea eagle and sea otter — in a landscape that seems untouched by time. Romance indeed! The mid-Victorian Ulva House makes the most of its idyllic position overlooking horseshoe-shaped Tobermory Bay from its terraced garden. This same bay has its own touch of romance in the form of a sunken Spanish galleon. Stylishly furnished with log fires crackling a welcome in the lounge and bar, the hotel has lots of character. It is known for its exceptional food, including an exciting range of home-made sweets. Wildlife expeditions by Landrover are organised. Non-smokers please. *Highly Commended.*

The **£** symbol when appearing at the end of the italic section of an entry shows the anticipated price, during 1996, for **single full Bed and Breakfast.**

Under £35	**£**	**Over £50 but under £65**	**£££**
Over £35 but under £50	**££**	**Over £65**	**££££**

This is meant as an indication only and does not show prices for Special Breaks, Weekends, etc. Guests are therefore advised to verify all prices on enquiring or booking.

Isle of Skye

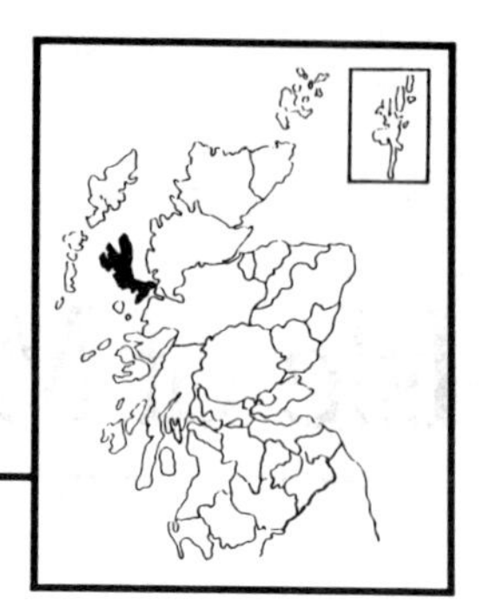

UIG HOTEL,
Uig, Portree,
Isle of Skye IV51 9YE

Tel: 01470 542205*
Fax: 01470 542308

Fully licensed; 17 bedrooms, all with private bathrooms; Historic interest; Children and pets welcome; Portree 15 miles; ££.

'Over the sea to Skye' — speed bonny boat to a land of spectacular scenery, the golden eagle, white coral beaches, wild flowers, the curvaceous Cuillins — and the Talisker distillery! An unspoilt heaven on earth that becomes ever nearer through easier access by road, rail and air. And where to stay on this magic island? We suggest this fine hotel almost at its most northerly point, the ferry departure point for the Outer Hebrides. Comfortable in the extreme, with coal and wood fires exuding a warm welcome, the hotel has a full licence, and guest rooms which have private facilities and are appointed with direct-dial telephone, television and tea and coffee-makers. Accommodation of equally high standing is also available in the attractive Sobhraig House annexe in the grounds from where there are far-reaching views. For a holiday that is definitely different and with the spice of gentle adventure about it, Uig Hotel is well worth considering. Pony trekking on the hotel's own quiet Highland ponies is a popular diversion; rides are organised each morning and afternoon and are supervised by an experienced leader. There is plenty to do on the island with a heated indoor pool and facilities for squash and tennis at Portree and a 9-hole golf course at Sconser as well as local craft enterprises to see. ♛♛♛♛ *Commended.*

Kincardineshire

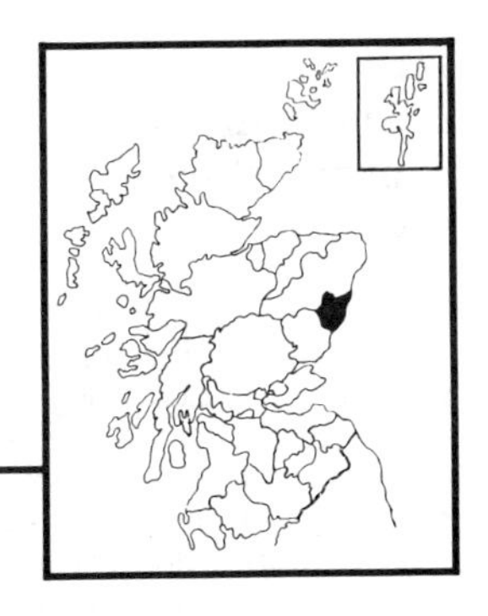

TOR-NA-COILLE HOTEL,
Inchmarlo Road, Banchory,
Kincardineshire AB31 4AB

Tel: 01330 822242*
Fax: 01330 824012

Licensed; 23 bedrooms, all with private bathrooms; Children and pets welcome; Leisure and conference facilities; Stonehaven 11 miles; £££.

An imposing Victorian mansion of great character, Tor-na-Coille is set in lovely wooded surroundings. Bedrooms, furnished in Victorian and Edwardian style, are very well appointed with en suite facilities, colour television, clock radio, direct-dial telephone and tea and coffee-makers. This is a homely and relaxed place in which to stay and the cuisine gains full marks for its variety and all-round excellence. There is much to see and do in the delightful area of Royal Deeside: Balmoral Castle is only a short drive away and there are numerous other places of historic interest and ample opportunities for hill walking, golf, ski-ing, pony trekking and fishing. The hotel has squash courts and a croquet lawn at the disposal of guests. ♛♛♛♛ *Commended, AA and RAC***, Egon Ronay.*

Kinross-shire

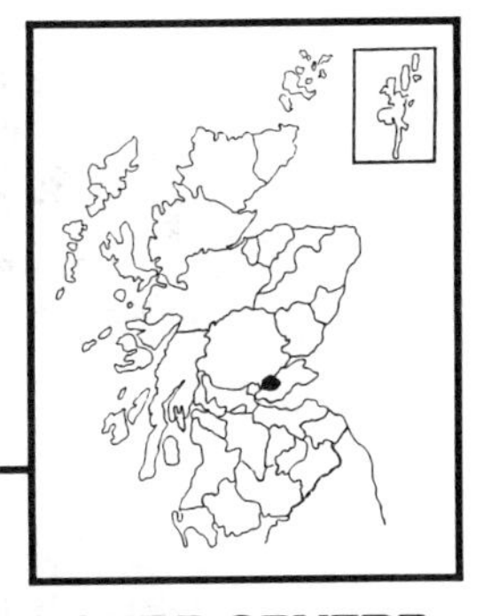

WINDLESTRAE HOTEL, BUSINESS & LEISURE CENTRE,
Kinross,
Kinross-shire KY13 7AS

Tel: 01577 863217
Fax: 01577 864733

Hotel licence; 45 bedrooms, all with private bathrooms; Historic interest; Children and pets welcome; Leisure and conference facilities; Dunfermline 9 miles; £££.

All the advantages of country living at the highest level may be found at this enchanting hotel. Nestling in secluded and landscaped gardens, yet with the convenience of an unobtrusive and charming small town, Windlestrae fulfils a trinity of functions; it is a mecca for those seeking a tranquil and relaxing holiday break, the site of an exciting and superbly-equipped leisure centre which occupies a self-contained wing and a popular venue for a wide range of business events and social functions. The hotel has a peerless reputation for its luxurious accommodation, imaginative cuisine and attentive service. The mainly spacious guest rooms have private amenities of a high order and some are specially adapted for disabled guests. ♛♛♛♛♛ *Highly Commended, RAC Merit Award.*

THE GREEN HOTEL,
2 The Muirs, Kinross,
Kinross-shire KY13 7AS

Tel: 01577 863467
Fax: 01577 863180

Fully licensed; 47 bedrooms, all with private bathrooms; Children and pets welcome; Leisure and conference facilities; Dunfermline 9 miles; ££££.

Once a coaching inn, The Green Hotel is now better known as an hotel with an impressive range of leisure activities and a wealth of modern facilities. Families are welcome, suites with baby listening devices being available. Bedrooms all have a bath or shower en suite as well as satellite television, radio and telephone. Energy may be expended in a variety of ways, such as swimming in the indoor pool, squash, table tennis or, more sedately, putting, croquet and pool. After such diversions the Defiance Bar proves a popular meeting place and offers a wide range of meals, including a special children's menu. The Douglas Restaurant is the venue for superb à la carte and table d'hôte dinners with Continental dishes vying for attention with traditional fare. ♛♛♛♛♛ *Highly Commended.* **See also Colour Advertisement on page 13.**

Lanarkshire

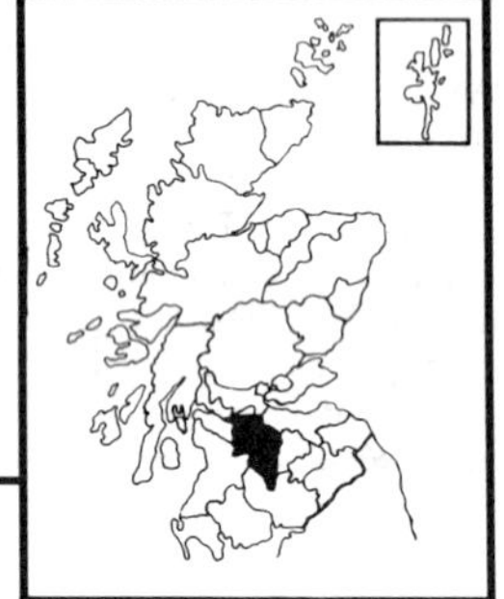

WYNDALES HOUSE HOTEL,
Symington, Near Biggar,
Lanarkshire ML12 6JU

Tel: 01899 308207
Fax: 01899 308555

Fully licensed; 14 bedrooms, all with private bathrooms; Historic interest; Children and pets welcome; Conference facilities; Biggar 3 miles; ££.

Nestling in the rural heart of an 18-acre estate in the tranquil and lovely valley of the River Clyde, all is well and at peace with the world; yet, whisper it soft, Edinburgh and Glasgow are only 40 minutes away. But tranquillity reigns supreme here, the ideal place for a revivifying break with a round or two of golf, a nibble or two on the line and, certainly, a dram or two in the cheerful bar. Add more than a memorable meal or two in either of the restaurants and the assurance of restful repose in a sumptuously comfortable bedroom and one has the ingredients of a holiday long to be remembered and sighed over. ♛♛♛♛ *Commended, RAC***.*

Orkney Isles

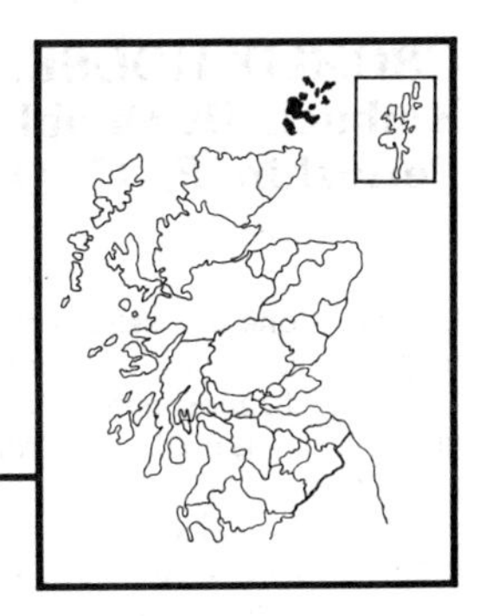

MERKISTER HOTEL,
Loch Harray, Dounby,
Orkney Islands KW17 2LF

Tel: 0185 677 1366*
Fax: 0185 677 1515

Fully licensed; 18 bedrooms, all with private bathrooms; Historic interest; Children and pets welcome; Finstown 6 miles; £.

Away from it all in the truest sense, this fine hotel provides a wonderful opportunity to commune with nature in picturesque and peaceful surroundings and enjoy some of the best loch fishing in Britain and, what is more, the cuisine is really out of this world. Guest rooms are delightfully furnished; most have en suite facilities and all have colour television, direct-dial telephone, tea-makers and appointments that would shame many a 5-star establishment. Standing on the shores of Harray Loch, the emphasis here, naturally enough, is on fishing and many major events are held. Novices are welcomed and boats, outboards and ghillies may be arranged. The views from the hotel are breathtaking and other activities available include golf, squash and rock climbing. ♛♛♛ *Commended, Egon Ronay, Good Food Guide, Vegetarian Food Guide.*

Perthshire

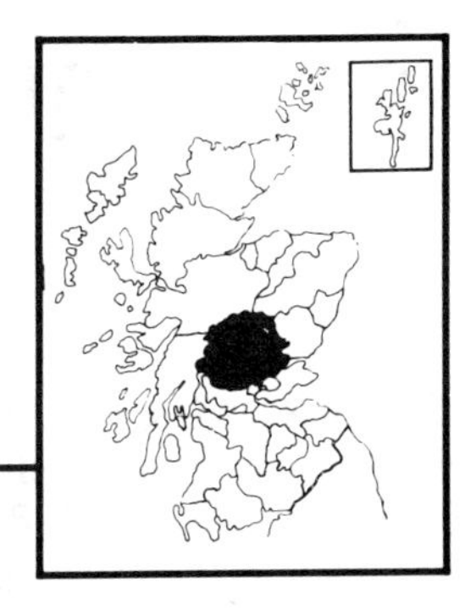

LUBNAIG HOTEL,
Leny Feus, Callander,
Perthshire FK17 8AS

Tel: 01877 330376*
Fax: 01877 330376

Residential licence; 10 bedrooms, all with private bathrooms; Historic interest; Children over 7 years welcome, pets by arrangement; Stirling 14 miles; £.

Small it may be but this lovely and supremely comfortable hotel has won several awards for its cuisine and all-round excellence. It stands in a picturesque garden just five minutes' walk from the town centre; a peaceful retreat ideally placed in Rob Roy country for touring the magnificent Highlands and historic Lowlands. The fine Scottish home-cooking featured on the table d'hôte menu is much appreciated; salmon, sea trout, grouse, pheasant, venison and Scottish beef all appearing in turn. An imaginative wine list contributes to enjoyment as do the over 20 malt whiskies available in the well-stocked bar. Guest rooms, some on the ground-floor, all have private facilities, central heating, television, radio, hairdryer and tea and coffee-makers. ♛♛♛ *Highly Commended.*

CROMLIX HOUSE,
Kinbuck, By Dunblane,
Perthshire FK15 9JT

Tel: 01786 822125*

Fax: 01786 825450

Residential and restaurant licence; 6 bedrooms and 8 large suites, all with private bathrooms; Pets in bedrooms only; Dunblane 3 miles; ££££.

Cromlix is one of a select handful of Scotland's top-rated luxury hotels. "Enchanting", "A magical experience", "Memorable", "Unique", "So hospitable", "Incredible value", "Wonderful atmosphere", "Superb staff" are a few of the many superlatives written by our guests. There is no doubt, Cromlix is very special. Within its own 3000 acre estate, the calm serenity of this "time capsule" is a different world. Above all Cromlix is for relaxation within surroundings and in a style of times past. Built in 1874 as a country mansion, the imposing exterior belies a comfortable and homely interior, each room individual in style. The atmosphere is relaxed, welcoming and unpretentious, while the ambience, antiques, authentic period decor, award-winning cuisine and genuine hospitality recall the luxurious splendour and feeling of a real Edwardian home. Situated north of Dunblane just five minutes off the A9; an enviable location for golf and for touring much of Scotland. ♛♛♛♛ *De Luxe, AA Three Red Stars and Two Rosettes, Good Hotel Guide, Good Food Guide, Egon Ronay.* **See also Colour Advertisement on page 14.**

Ross-shire

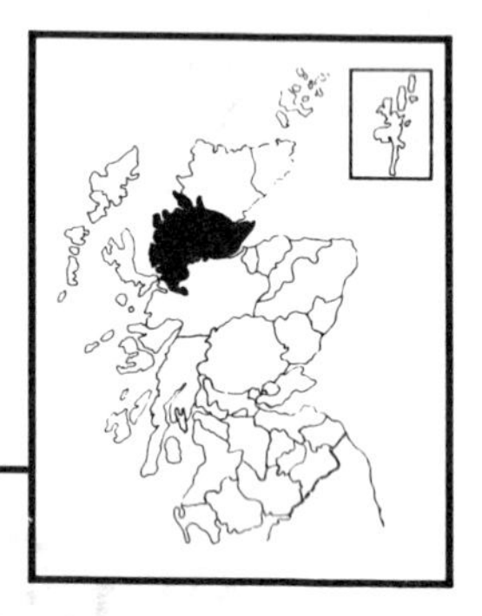

BALMACARA HOTEL,
By Kyle of Lochalsh,
Wester Ross IV40 8DH

Tel: 01599 566283

Fax: 01599 566329

Fully licensed; 30 bedrooms, all with private bathrooms; Historic interest; Children and pets welcome; Broadford 8 miles; £/££.

On the shores of Loch Alsh with the hills of Skye rising across the water, this comfortable hotel lies amidst some of the most spectacular scenery in Scotland and the picture windows make the most of the views. A feature of the hotel is its impressive timberwork and the guest rooms are sprucely appointed in Scandinavian style. Guests may mix with new-found friends in the intimate cocktail bar or enjoy lively conversation with local yachtsmen, fishermen and climbers in the cheerful 'back' bar — the range of malt whiskies is well worth investigating! The worthy à la carte and table d'hôte cuisine reflects the abundance and variety of the local produce and service throughout is unobtrusively helpful. *STB* ♛♛♛ *Commended, RAC***.*

POOL HOUSE HOTEL,
Poolewe, By Achnasheen
Ross-shire IV22 2LE

Tel: 01445 781272

Fully licensed; 13 bedrooms, 11 with private bathrooms; Historic interest; Children welcome, pets by arrangement; Car park (40); Gairloch 4 miles; ££.

With a commanding position at the head of Loch Ewe, Pool House Hotel enjoys beautiful views across the bay to the famous Inverewe Gardens and the hills, coastline and islands that typify the grandeur of Wester Ross. There is a very cosy lounge where bar meals are served and a pleasant restaurant overlooking the bay. Here, visitors will soon feel relaxed and a favourite diversion is watching for salmon, seals and otters. In this area of outstanding natural beauty, one may walk, climb, swim in the lochs or in the indoor pool in the village, golf and go boating at nearby Gairloch. The hotel is centrally heated and the attractive bedrooms are all equipped with colour TV, radio and tea/coffee facilities; most have private amenities. 👑👑👑👑 *Commended, RAC**.* **See also Colour Advertisement on page 15.**

MORANGIE HOUSE HOTEL,
Tain,
Ross-shire IV19 1PY

Tel: 01862 892281
Fax: 01862 892872

Fully licensed; 26 bedrooms, all with private bathrooms; Historic interest; Children welcome, pets by arrangement; Invergordon 10 miles; ££/£££.

A beautifully modernised and sumptuously decorated Victorian mansion close to the shores of the Dornoch Firth, this is an ideal base from which to explore the Northern Highlands, with peerless opportunities for fishing, hill walking and golf at Royal Dornoch Golf Club and Tain Golf Course (discounted green fees can be arranged). Diversions close at hand include a bowling green, tennis courts and a fine beach. Guest rooms have en suite bathrooms, television, direct-dial telephone and coffee-makers, and the master bedroom has a large four-poster and a bathroom with a whirlpool corner bath. The best of Highland cuisine served in our award-winning restaurant features salmon, venison and game in season, and there is a comprehensive selection of malt whiskies to savour. Quality Weekend Breaks available — details on request. 👑👑👑👑, *AA and RAC ***, Ashley Courtenay, Les Routiers.*

---

* The appearance of an asterisk after the telephone number indicates that the hotel in question is closed for a period during the winter months. Exact dates should be ascertained from the hotel itself.

Roxburghshire

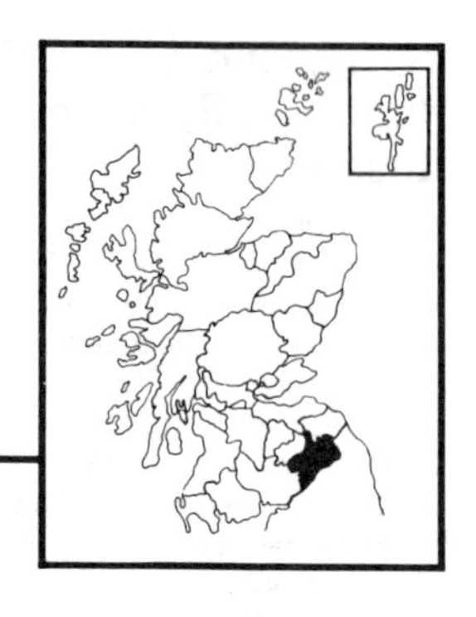

SUNLAWS HOUSE HOTEL,
Kelso,
Roxburghshire TD5 8JZ

Tel: 01573 450331
Fax: 01573 450611

Fully licensed; 22 bedrooms, all with private bathrooms; Historic interest; Children and pets welcome; Leisure and conference facilities; Hawick 18 miles; ££££.

This lovely old house is steeped in history and it is reputed that Bonnie Prince Charlie stayed here in 1745. Now a delectable country hotel, skilfully converted by the present owner, the Duke of Roxburghe, the rewards of a sojourn here are excellent modern facilities, a true Scottish welcome and superb fare in the most idyllic surroundings. The gardens and parkland alongside the River Teviot extend to 200 acres; indeed, flowers from the gardens bedeck the public rooms whilst, in cool weather, log fires add to the relaxing atmosphere. Bedrooms in the main house and stable courtyard annexe are furnished to a very high standard and all have a private bath or shower, remote-control colour television, satellite channels and C.N.N., radio and direct-dial telephone, and trouser presses. Some rooms with four-poster beds are available. Under the supervision of a skilled chef, the cuisine is memorable with hearty breakfasts and a variety of tempting dishes that include prime Scottish beef, salmon, pheasant, venison and many local specialities. The Library Bar with its fine selection of malt whiskies is a popular meeting place and it is said that after a late night, a friendly ghost walks the ground floor, the result of overcommunion with the spirits, no doubt! Numerous country pursuits may be indulged in the area, including fishing, golf, clay pigeon and game shooting. Residents are offered a 25% discount on any treatment at the Sunlaws Elixir Health and Beauty Clinique if booked in advance. ♛♛♛♛♛ *Highly Commended, Welcome Host Award.*

Sutherland

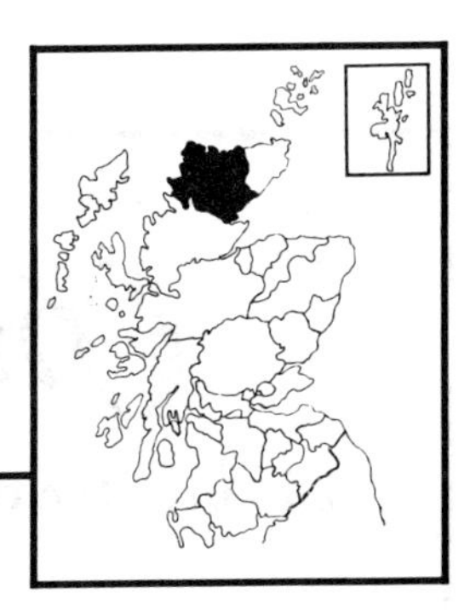

INVER LODGE HOTEL,
Lochinver,
Sutherland IV27 4LU

Tel: 01571 844496*
Fax: 01571 844395

Hotel licence; 20 bedrooms, all with private bathrooms; Pets welcome; Leisure facilities; Ullapool 18 miles; £££.

On the far north-western shores of Scotland lies the small village of Lochinver. Fishing boats glide in and out of the harbour, often attended by Atlantic grey seals; crofters' cottages dot the hillsides on which sheep graze; and stretching inland is the untamed landscape of Sutherland, teeming with wildlife and a paradise for anglers, walkers, bird-watchers and nature lovers. In such a beautiful setting Inver Lodge Hotel stands high above the village, looking out across the calm waters of the loch to the distant outline of the Isle of Lewis. Sprucely furnished throughout in modern style, the hotel offers a true Highland welcome. Food is excellent and varied and includes several specialities, meals being taken in a most attractive dining room with picture windows affording far-reaching views over the loch and countryside. Guests are accommodated in splendidly appointed rooms, each named after a nearby mountain or loch and all generously proportioned and tastefully decorated. Comfort is assured with six-foot wide double beds or extra-large twin beds, superb bathrooms en suite, colour television, direct-dial telephone, and tea and coffee making facilities. Two spacious suites are also available. Relaxation may be sought in the snooker room, sauna or solarium. ♛♛♛♛ *Highly Commended, RAC*** and Merit Awards, AA*** 79%.*

ORDER NOW! ***See Overleaf***

ONE FOR YOUR FRIEND 1996

FHG Publications have a large range of attractive holiday accommodation guides for all kinds of holiday opportunities throughout Britain. They also make useful gifts at any time of year. Our guides are available in most bookshops and larger newsagents but we will be happy to post you a copy direct if you have any difficulty. We will also post abroad but have to charge separately for post or freight.
The inclusive cost of posting and packing the guides to you or your friends in the UK is as follows:

Farm Holiday Guide ENGLAND, WALES and IRELAND
Board, Self-catering, Caravans/Camping, Activity Holidays. **£4.80**

Farm Holiday Guide SCOTLAND
All kinds of holiday accommodation. **£3.60**

SELF-CATERING HOLIDAYS IN BRITAIN
Over 1000 addresses throughout for Self-catering and caravans in Britain. **£4.60**

BRITAIN'S BEST HOLIDAYS
A quick-reference general guide for all kinds of holidays. **£3.60**

The FHG Guide to CARAVAN & CAMPING HOLIDAYS
Caravans for hire, sites and holiday parks and centres. **£3.60**

BED AND BREAKFAST STOPS
Over 1000 friendly and comfortable overnight stops. Non-smoking, The Disabled and Special Diets Supplements. **£4.80**

CHILDREN WELCOME! FAMILY HOLIDAY & ATTRACTIONS GUIDE
Family holidays with details of amenities for children and babies. **£4.60**

SCOTTISH WELCOME
Introduced by Katie Wood. A new guide to holiday accommodation and attractions in Scotland. **£4.50**

Recommended SHORT BREAK HOLIDAYS IN BRITAIN
'Approved' accommodation for quality bargain breaks. Introduced by John Carter. **£4.50**

Recommended COUNTRY HOTELS OF BRITAIN
Including Country Houses, for the discriminating. **£4.50**

Recommended WAYSIDE & COUNTRY INNS OF BRITAIN
Pubs, Inns and small hotels. **£4.50**

PGA GOLF GUIDE
Where to play. Where to stay
Over 2000 golf courses in Britain with convenient accommodation. Endorsed by the PGA. Holiday Golf in France, Portugal, Spain and USA. **£9.80**

PETS WELCOME!
The unique guide for holidays for pet owners and their pets. **£5.20**

BED AND BREAKFAST IN BRITAIN
Over 1000 choices for touring and holidays throughout Britain. Airports and Ferries Supplement. **£3.60**

THE FRENCH FARM AND VILLAGE HOLIDAY GUIDE
The official guide to self-catering holidays in the 'Gîtes de France'. **£9.80**

Tick your choice and send your order and payment to FHG PUBLICATIONS, ABBEY MILL BUSINESS CENTRE, SEEDHILL, PAISLEY PA1 1TJ (TEL: 0141-887 0428. FAX: 0141-889 7204). **Deduct** 10% for 2/3 titles or copies; 20% for 4 or more.

Send to: NAME ....

ADDRESS ....

....

.... POST CODE ....

I enclose Cheque/Postal Order for £ ....

SIGNATURE .... DATE ....

Please complete the following to help us improve the service we provide. How did you find out about our guides:

☐ Press ☐ Magazines ☐ TV ☐ Radio ☐ Family/Friend ☐ Other.

MAP SECTION

The following seven pages of maps indicate the main cities, towns and holiday centres of Britain. Space obviously does not permit every location featured in this book to be included but the approximate position may be ascertained by using the distance indications quoted and the scale bars on the maps.

Map 1

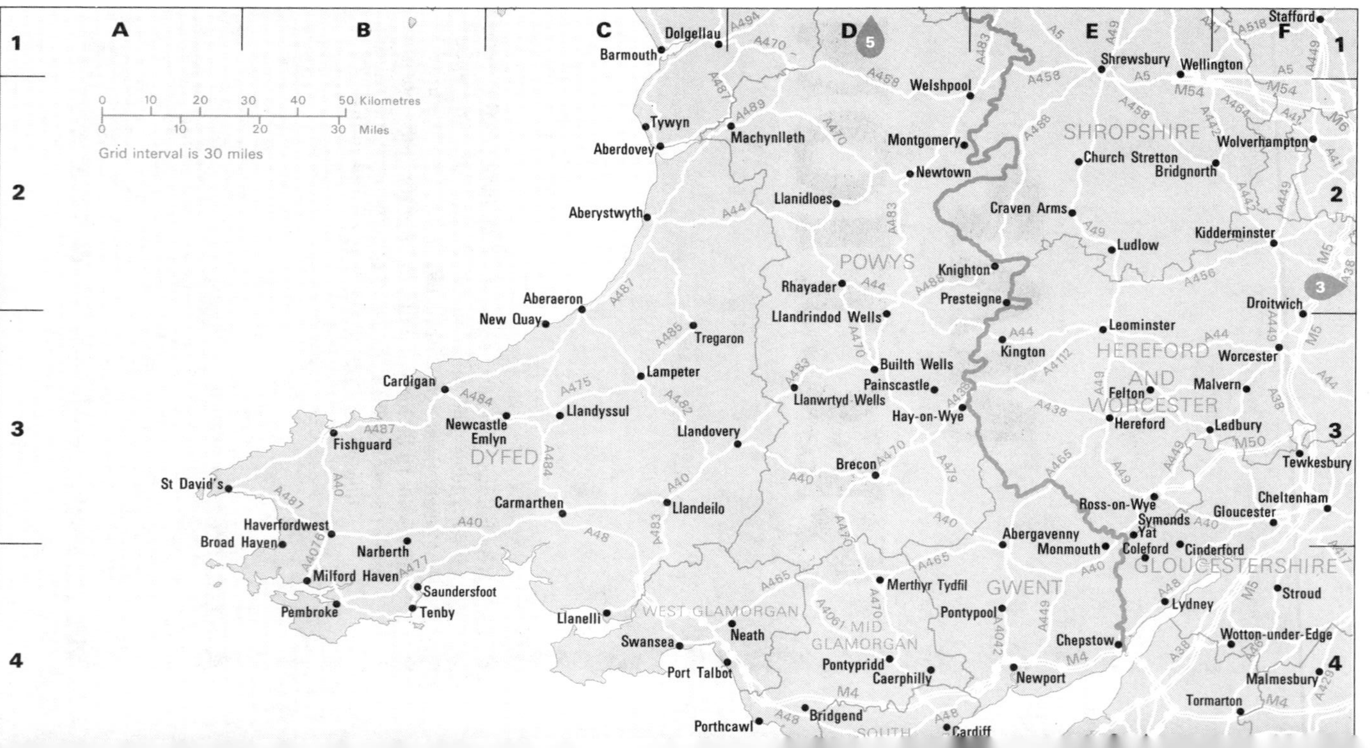

A
B
C
D
E
F
1
2
3
4
0 10 20 30 40 50 Kilometres
0 10 20 30 Miles
Grid interval is 30 miles
5
3
SHROPSHIRE
POWYS
HEREFORD AND WORCESTER
DYFED
GWENT
GLOUCESTERSHIRE
WEST GLAMORGAN
MID GLAMORGAN
Stafford
Shrewsbury
Wellington
Wolverhampton
Church Stretton
Bridgnorth
Craven Arms
Kidderminster
Ludlow
Droitwich
Leominster
Worcester
Malvern
Felton
Hereford
Ledbury
Tewkesbury
Cheltenham
Gloucester
Ross-on-Wye
Symonds Yat
Coleford
Cinderford
Monmouth
Abergavenny
Stroud
Lydney
Chepstow
Wotton-under-Edge
Malmesbury
Tormarton
Newport
Cardiff
Dolgellau
Barmouth
Welshpool
Montgomery
Newtown
Tywyn
Machynlleth
Aberdovey
Llanidloes
Aberystwyth
Knighton
Presteigne
Rhayader
Llandrindod Wells
Kington
Builth Wells
Painscastle
Llanwrtyd Wells
Hay-on-Wye
Aberaeron
New Quay
Tregaron
Lampeter
Cardigan
Llandyssul
Newcastle Emlyn
Llandovery
Fishguard
Brecon
St David's
Carmarthen
Llandeilo
Haverfordwest
Broad Haven
Narberth
Milford Haven
Saundersfoot
Pembroke
Tenby
Llanelli
Merthyr Tydfil
Pontypool
Neath
Swansea
Port Talbot
Pontypridd
Caerphilly
Bridgend
Porthcawl

Map 2

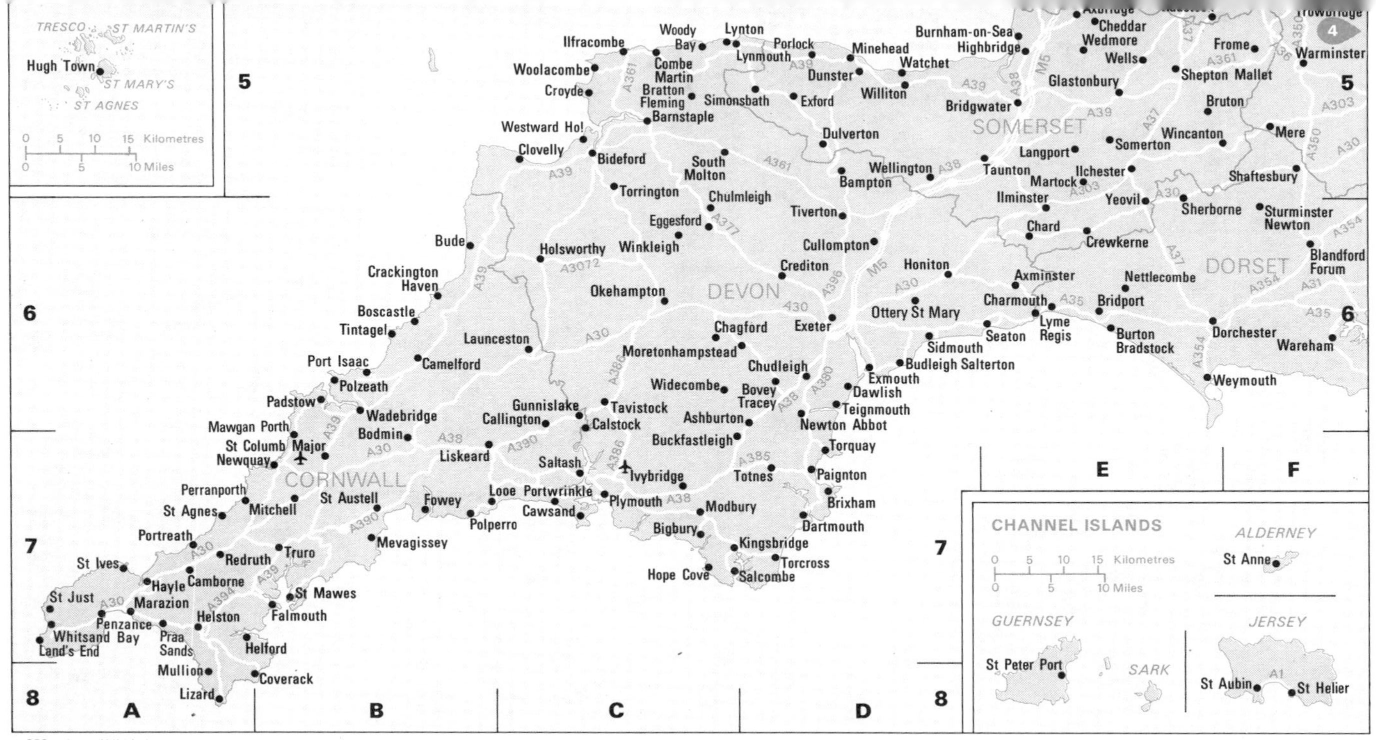

TRESCO
ST MARTIN'S
Hugh Town
ST MARY'S
ST AGNES
0 5 10 15 Kilometres
0 5 10 Miles
Ilfracombe
Woody Bay
Lynton
Lynmouth
Porlock
Minehead
Watchet
Burnham-on-Sea
Highbridge
Cheddar
Wedmore
Wells
Frome
Warminster
Woolacombe
Croyde
Combe Martin
Bratton Fleming
Barnstaple
Simonsbath
Exford
Dunster
Williton
Glastonbury
Shepton Mallet
Bruton
Bridgwater
SOMERSET
Westward Ho!
Clovelly
Bideford
Dulverton
Somerton
Wincanton
Mere
South Molton
Wellington
Bampton
Taunton
Langport
Ilchester
Martock
Shaftesbury
Torrington
Chulmleigh
Ilminster
Yeovil
Sherborne
Sturminster Newton
Eggesford
Tiverton
Chard
Crewkerne
Bude
Holsworthy
Winkleigh
Cullompton
Blandford Forum
DORSET
Crackington Haven
Crediton
Honiton
Axminster
Nettlecombe
Okehampton
DEVON
Charmouth
Bridport
Boscastle
Tintagel
Chagford
Exeter
Ottery St Mary
Lyme Regis
Seaton
Sidmouth
Burton Bradstock
Dorchester
Wareham
Launceston
Moretonhampstead
Camelford
Port Isaac
Polzeath
Chudleigh
Budleigh Salterton
Exmouth
Weymouth
Widecombe
Bovey Tracey
Dawlish
Padstow
Wadebridge
Gunnislake
Tavistock
Callington
Calstock
Ashburton
Teignmouth
Newton Abbot
Mawgan Porth
St Columb Major
Newquay
Bodmin
Buckfastleigh
Torquay
Liskeard
Saltash
Ivybridge
Totnes
Paignton
CORNWALL
Perranporth
St Austell
Fowey
Looe
Portwrinkle
Plymouth
Modbury
Brixham
St Agnes
Mitchell
Polperro
Cawsand
Dartmouth
Bigbury
Portreath
Redruth
Truro
Mevagissey
Kingsbridge
Torcross
St Ives
Hayle
Camborne
Hope Cove
Salcombe
St Just
Marazion
St Mawes
Penzance
Helston
Falmouth
Whitsand Bay
Land's End
Praa Sands
Helford
Mullion
Coverack
Lizard
A30
A39
A38
A361
A377
A3072
A386
A390
A385
A380
A396
A394
A303
A37
A35
A354
A350
A36
A31
M5
4
5
6
7
8
A
B
C
D
E
F
CHANNEL ISLANDS
0 5 10 15 Kilometres
0 5 10 Miles
ALDERNEY
St Anne
GUERNSEY
St Peter Port
SARK
JERSEY
St Aubin
A1
St Helier

Map 3

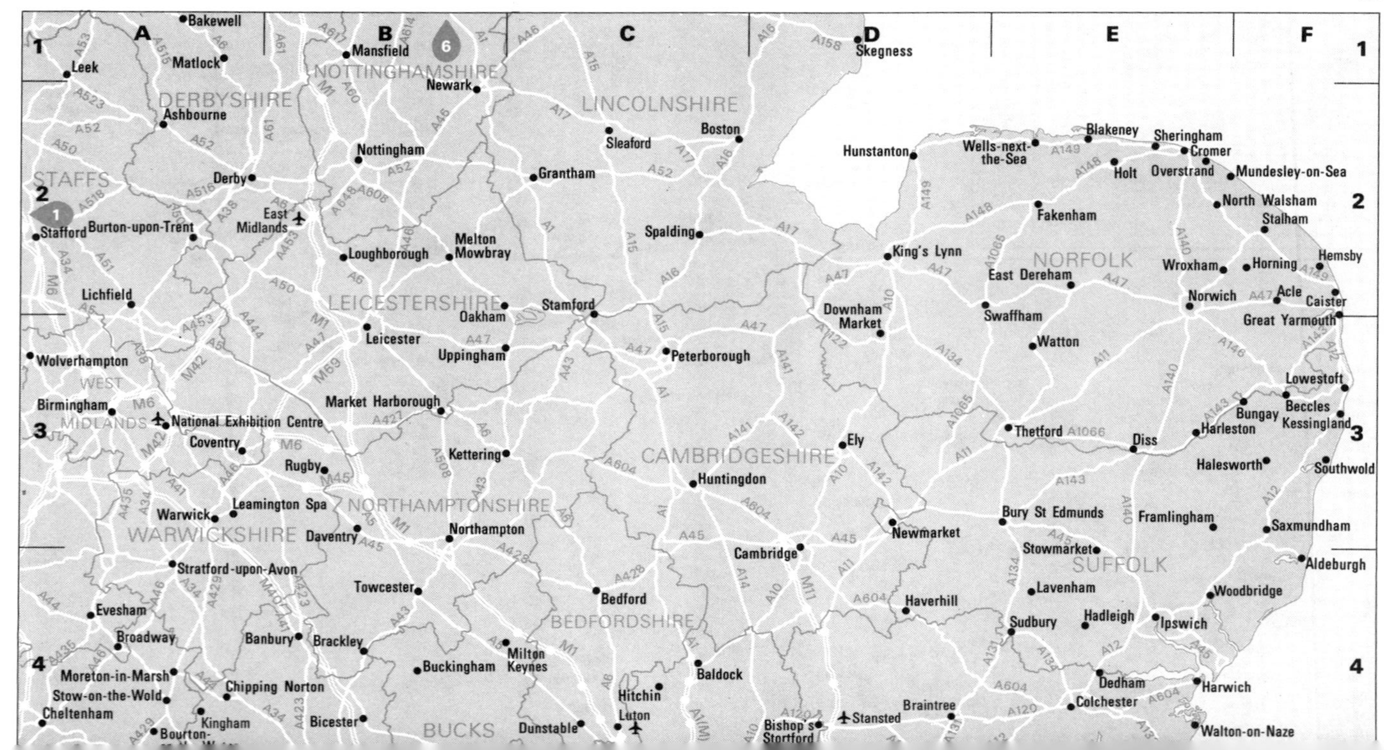
A
B
C
D
E
F
1
2
3
4
DERBYSHIRE
STAFFS
NOTTINGHAMSHIRE
LINCOLNSHIRE
LEICESTERSHIRE
WEST MIDLANDS
WARWICKSHIRE
NORTHAMPTONSHIRE
CAMBRIDGESHIRE
BEDFORDSHIRE
BUCKS
NORFOLK
SUFFOLK
Bakewell
Leek
Matlock
Mansfield
Newark
Skegness
Ashbourne
Sleaford
Boston
Nottingham
Derby
Grantham
Hunstanton
Wells-next-the-Sea
Blakeney
Holt
Sheringham
Cromer
Overstrand
Mundesley-on-Sea
North Walsham
Stalham
Hemsby
Fakenham
Stafford
Burton-upon-Trent
East Midlands
Spalding
King's Lynn
Loughborough
Melton Mowbray
East Dereham
Wroxham
Horning
Acle
Caister
Norwich
Great Yarmouth
Lichfield
Oakham
Stamford
Downham Market
Swaffham
Leicester
Uppingham
Peterborough
Watton
Wolverhampton
Birmingham
National Exhibition Centre
Market Harborough
Lowestoft
Beccles
Bungay
Kessingland
Harleston
Thetford
Diss
Coventry
Rugby
Kettering
Ely
Huntingdon
Halesworth
Southwold
Leamington Spa
Warwick
Daventry
Northampton
Bury St Edmunds
Framlingham
Saxmundham
Newmarket
Cambridge
Stowmarket
Aldeburgh
Stratford-upon-Avon
Towcester
Bedford
Lavenham
Haverhill
Woodbridge
Evesham
Broadway
Banbury
Brackley
Milton Keynes
Sudbury
Hadleigh
Ipswich
Buckingham
Baldock
Moreton-in-Marsh
Chipping Norton
Hitchin
Dedham
Harwich
Stow-on-the-Wold
Cheltenham
Kingham
Bourton-
Bicester
Dunstable
Luton
Bishop's Stortford
Stansted
Braintree
Colchester
Walton-on-Naze

Map 4

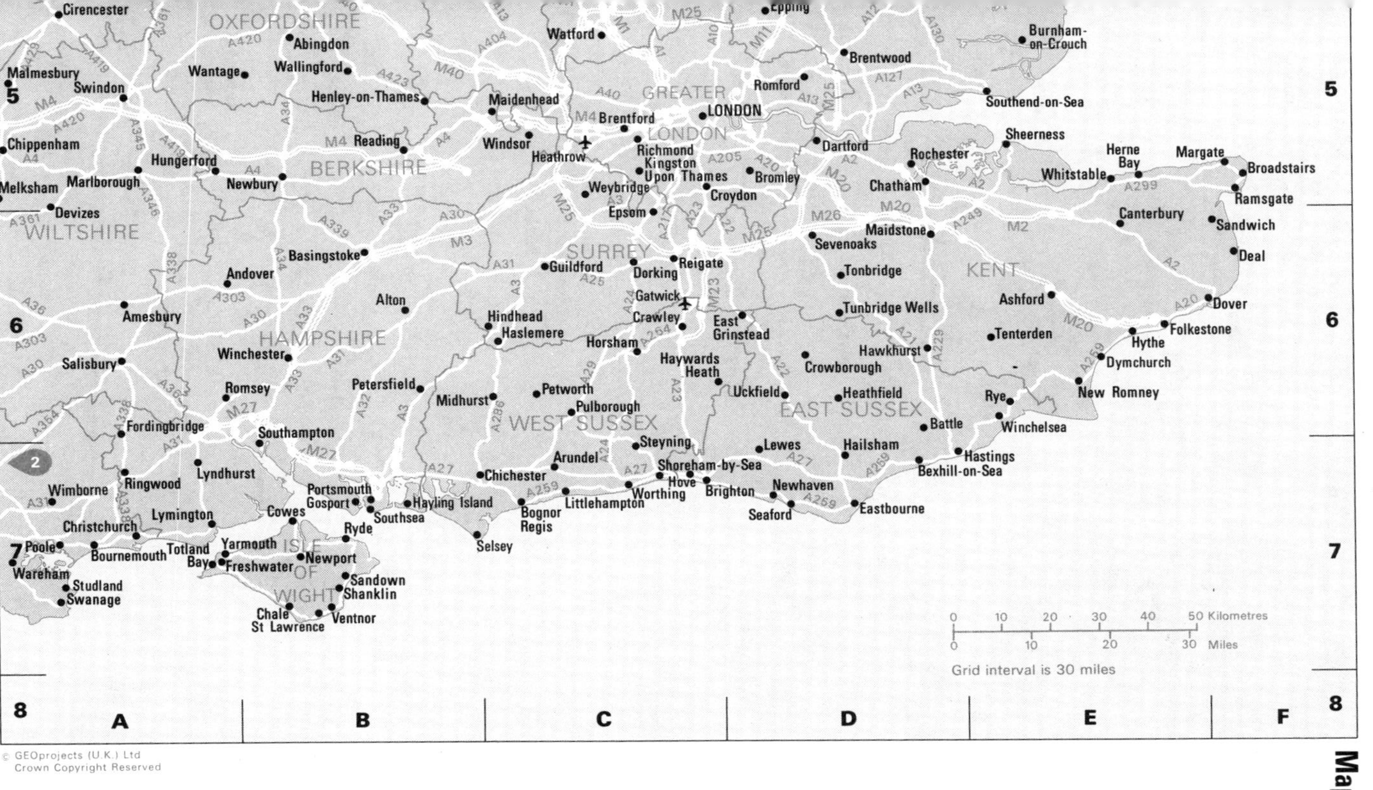

OXFORDSHIRE
BERKSHIRE
WILTSHIRE
HAMPSHIRE
GREATER LONDON
SURREY
KENT
WEST SUSSEX
EAST SUSSEX
ISLE OF WIGHT
Cirencester
Abingdon
Watford
Epping
Burnham-on-Crouch
Malmesbury
Swindon
Wantage
Wallingford
Brentwood
Romford
Southend-on-Sea
Henley-on-Thames
Maidenhead
Brentford
LONDON
Chippenham
Reading
Windsor
Heathrow
Richmond
Kingston Upon Thames
Bromley
Dartford
Rochester
Sheerness
Herne Bay
Margate
Broadstairs
Hungerford
Newbury
Weybridge
Croydon
Chatham
Whitstable
Ramsgate
Melksham
Marlborough
Devizes
Epsom
Canterbury
Sandwich
Maidstone
Sevenoaks
Deal
Basingstoke
Guildford
Dorking
Reigate
Tonbridge
Andover
Alton
Gatwick
Ashford
Dover
Amesbury
Hindhead
Haslemere
Crawley
East Grinstead
Tunbridge Wells
Folkestone
Tenterden
Hythe
Winchester
Horsham
Haywards Heath
Crowborough
Hawkhurst
Dymchurch
Salisbury
Romsey
Petersfield
Petworth
Midhurst
Pulborough
Uckfield
Heathfield
Rye
New Romney
Fordingbridge
Southampton
Steyning
Lewes
Hailsham
Battle
Winchelsea
Lyndhurst
Arundel
Chichester
Shoreham-by-Sea
Hove
Brighton
Hastings
Bexhill-on-Sea
Wimborne
Ringwood
Portsmouth
Gosport
Hayling Island
Worthing
Newhaven
Littlehampton
Bognor Regis
Seaford
Eastbourne
Christchurch
Lymington
Cowes
Southsea
Ryde
Selsey
Poole
Bournemouth
Totland Bay
Yarmouth
Freshwater
Newport
Wareham
Studland
Swanage
Sandown
Shanklin
Chale
St Lawrence
Ventnor
5
6
7
8
A
B
C
D
E
F
2
0 10 20 30 40 50 Kilometres
0 10 20 30 Miles
Grid interval is 30 miles

Map 5

DUMFRIES AND GALLOWAY
Girvan
Langholm
New Galloway
Dumfries
Newton Stewart
Annan
Gretna
Longtown
Brampton
Greenhead
Castle Douglas
Gatehouse of Fleet
Wigtown
Carlisle
Silloth
Kirkcudbright
Wigton
Port William
Alston
Maryport
Cockermouth
Bassenthwaite
Workington
Penrith
Keswick
Whitehaven
Ennerdale Bridge
Ullswater
Appleby
CUMBRIA
Shap
Kirkby Stephen
Gosforth
Little Langdale
Ambleside
Hawkshead
Seascale
Coniston
Windermere
Kendal
Ramsey
Newby Bridge
Sedbergh
Broughton-in-Furness
Peel
ISLE OF MAN
Kirkby Lonsdale
Millom
Ulverston
Port Erin
Douglas
Grange-over-Sands
Castletown
Barrow-in-Furness
Port St Mary
Morecambe
Lancaster
Fleetwood
Clitheroe
LANCASHIRE
Blackpool
Lytham St Annes
Preston
Southport
Chorley
Formby
Wigan
GREATER MANCHESTER
MERSEYSIDE
Amlwch
ANGLESEY
Hoylake
Liverpool
Birkenhead
Holyhead
Llanerchymedd
Llandudno
Colwyn Bay
Prestatyn
Rhyl
Menai Bridge
Beaumaris
Llangefni
Conwy
Abergele
Knutsford
Northwich
Bangor
Chester
CHESHIRE
Denbigh
Caernarvon
Llanrwst
Llanberis
Ruthin
Betws-y-Coed
CLWYD
Nantwich
Wrexham
GWYNEDD
Corwen
Newcastle-under-Lyme
Nefyn
Portmadoc
Ffestiniog
Criccieth
Penrhyndeudraeth
Bala
Llangollen
Pwllheli
Llanbedrog
Harlech
Wem
Market Drayton
Abersoch
Oswestry
Aberdaron
Dolgellau
SHROPSHIRE
Barmouth
Wellington
Welshpool
Shrewsbury
POWYS
Tywyn
Machynlleth

Map 6

E F G H
1 2 3 4 5 6 7

0 10 20 30 40 50 Kilometres
0 10 20 30 Miles
Grid interval is 30 miles

Morpeth
UMBERLAND
Whitley Bay
Tynemouth
Corbridge
Newcastle-upon-Tyne
Hexham
TYNE AND WEAR
South Shields
Sunderland
Durham
DURHAM
Bishop Auckland
Middleton-in-Teesdale
Middlesbrough
Redcar
Saltburn-by-the-Sea
CLEVELAND
Barnard Castle
Darlington
Guisborough
Whitby
Stokesley
Richmond
Northallerton
Leyburn
Middleham
Thirsk
Helmsley
Pickering
Scarborough
Cayton Bay
Filey
NORTH YORKSHIRE
Ripon
Castle Howard
Malton
Flamborough
Sledmere
Bridlington
Grassington
Huby
Driffield
Skipton
Harrogate
York
Hornsea
Keighley
Ilkley
Bingley
Beverley
Selby
HUMBERSIDE
Bradford
Leeds
Heptonstall
WEST YORKSHIRE
Hull
Withernsea
Halifax
Goole
Huddersfield
Scunthorpe
Grimsby
Cleethorpes
Barnsley
Doncaster
SOUTH YORKSHIRE
Glossop
Gainsborough
Louth
Mablethorpe
Sheffield
Worksop
Alford
Buxton
Macclesfield
Chesterfield
Lincoln
Horncastle
Bakewell
Skegness
Mansfield
Matlock
Congleton
Leek
DERBYSHIRE
NOTTINGHAMSHIRE
LINCOLNSHIRE
Newark
Ashbourne
Stoke-on-Trent
Sleaford
Boston
Nottingham
Grantham
Derby
STAFFORDSHIRE
East Midlands
Stafford
Burton-upon-Trent
Loughborough
Melton Mowbray
Spalding
LEICESTERSHIRE
Lichfield
Stamford
Oakham
Leicester
Uppingham
Peterborough

Map 7
0 10 20 30 40 50 Kilometres
0 10 20 30 Miles
Grid interval is 30 miles
A
B
C
D
E
F
G
1
2
3
4
5
6
7
8
9
10
11
SHETLAND ISLANDS
MAINLAND
Lerwick
Sumburgh
ORKNEY
MAINLAND
Kirkwall
Stromness
HOY
John o'Groats
Thurso
Durness
Bettyhill
Tongue
Wick
Scourie
LEWIS
WESTERN ISLES
Lochinver
Lairg
Helmsdale
Golspie
Ullapool
Bonar Bridge
Dornoch
Gairloch
Poolewe
Tain
Cullen
Banff
Fraserburgh
Dingwall
Rosemarkie
Elgin
Fochabers
Keith
HIGHLAND
Fortrose
Nairn
Forres
Turriff
Peterhead
Croy
Kilravock Castle
Beauly
Inverness
Huntly
Portree
RAASAY
SKYE
Daviot
Kyle of Lochalsh
Grantown-on-Spey
Dornie
Broadford
Kyleakin
Carrbridge
Tomintoul
GRAMPIAN
Inverurie
Aviemore
Fort Augustus
Kingussie
Aberdeen
Mallaig
Braemar
Banchory
Stonehaven
INNER HEBRIDES
Fort William
Kinlochleven
Kinloch Rannoch
Brechin
Ballachulish
Glencoe
Pitlochry
Montrose
Tobermory
Aberfeldy
TAYSIDE
Forfar
Dunkeld
Blairgowrie
Arbroath
MULL
Oban
Taynuilt
Killin
Dundee
Carnoustie
Dalmally
Lochearnhead
Perth
Monifieth
Crianlarich
Crieff
Cupar
St Andrews
Inveraray
Callander
Auchterarder
FIFE
Arrochar
Tarbet
Aberfoyle
CENTRAL
Kinross
Stirling
Lochgilphead
Luss
Drymen
Dunfermline
Kirkcaldy
JURA
Ardrishaig
North Berwick
Dunoon
Gourock
Balloch
Dumbarton
EDINBURGH
Dunbar
Tarbert
Greenock
Glasgow
Dalkeith
Haddington
Rothesay
Paisley
LOTHIAN
Eyemouth
ISLAY
Largs
Beith
Hamilton
Chirnside
Berwick upon Tweed
STRATHCLYDE
Lauder
Duns
Ardrossan
Kilmarnock
Lanark
Peebles
Coldstream
Cornhill-on-Tweed
KINTYRE
Brodick
Irvine
Biggar
Galashiels
Lamlash
Troon
Selkirk
Kelso
Wooler
Prestwick
Abington
BORDERS
Jedburgh
Campbeltown
ARRAN
Ayr
New Cumnock
Hawick
Maybole
Alnwick
Moffat
Beattock
Girvan
NORTHUMBERLAND
Langholm
Bellingham
DUMFRIES & GALLOWAY
New Galloway
Dumfries
Gretna
Longtown
Newton Stewart
Castle Douglas
Annan
Greenhead
Newcastle-upon-Tyne
Stranraer
Hexham
Corbridge
Gatehouse of Fleet
Carlisle
Wigtown
Portpatrick
Kirkcudbright
Silloth
Port William
CUMBRIA
Alston
Durham
Bassenthwaite
Penrith
5
6
A9
A836
A838
A894
A837
A835
A832
A890
A87
A82
A830
A86
A96
A98
A92
A93
A939
A94
A85
A816
A83
A8
A73
A74
A71
A77
A75
A76
A713
A701
A7
A68
A1
A69
A689
A697
A696
M8
M9
M90
M74
M6
A91
A915
A702
A703